RETHINKING GLOBAL LABO

RETHINKING GLOBAL LABOUR
After Neoliberalism

RONALDO MUNCK

© Ronaldo Munck 2018

This book is copyright under the Berne Convention.
No reproduction without permission.
All rights reserved.

First published in 2018 by Agenda Publishing

Agenda Publishing Limited
Bath Lane
Newcastle Helix
Newcastle upon Tyne
NE4 5TF
www.agendapub.com

ISBN 978-1-78821-104-8 (hardcover)
ISBN 978-1-78821-105-5 (paperback)

British Library Cataloguing-in-Publication Data
A catalogue record for this book is available from the British Library

Typeset by Out of House Publishing
Printed and bound in the UK by TJ International

Dai campi al mare, alla miniera
All'officina, chi soffre e spera
Sia pronto, è l'ora della riscossa
Bandiera rossa trionferà

Avantia Popolo, 1908

For Honor

CONTENTS

ABBREVIATIONS

ACE	advanced capitalist economy
ACFTU	All-China Federation of Trade Unions
AFL–CIO	American Federation of Labor – Congress of Industrial Organizations
AIFLD	American Institute for Free Labor Development
ATTAC	Association pour la Taxe Tobin pour l'Aide aux Citoyens
BRICS	Brazil, Russia, India, China and South Africa
CAW	Canadian Auto Workers
COSATU	Congress of South African Trade Unions
CUT	Central Única dos Trabalhadores (Unified Workers' Central) (Brazil)
ETUC	European Trade Union Confederation
EWCs	European works councils
FDI	foreign direct investment
FNV	Federatie Nederlandse Vakbeweging (Netherlands Trade Union Confederation)
FOSATU	Federation of South African Trade Unions
FTZ	free trade zone
GATT	General Agreement on Tariffs and Trade
GCIM	Global Commission on International Migration
GDP	gross domestic product
GU	Global Unions
GUF	global union federation
ICEM	International Federation of Chemical, Energy, Mine and General Workers' Unions
ICF	International Federation of Chemical and General Workers' Unions
ICFTU	International Confederation of Free Trade Unions
ICT	information and communications technology
ILO	International Labour Organization

IMF	International Metalworkers' Federation
IMF	International Monetary Fund
IOM	International Organization for Migration
ITF	International Transport Workers' Federation
ITS	international trade secretariat
ISI	import substitution industrialization
ITO	International Trade Organization
ITUC	International Trade Union Confederation
IUF	International Union of Food and Allied Workers
IWW	Industrial Workers of the World
JIT	"just-in-time" [production]
KCTU	Korean Confederation of Trade Unions
Mercosur	Common Market of the Southern Cone (South America)
MNC	multinational corporation
NAFTA	North American Free Trade Agreement
NGO	non-governmental organization
NHS	National Health Service (UK)
NIC	newly industrializing country
NIDL	new international division of labour
OECD	Organisation for Economic Co-operation and Development
ONS	Office for National Statistics (UK)
OPEC	Organization of the Petroleum Exporting Countries
RILU	Red International of Labour Unions
SAP	structural adjustment programme
SEWA	Self-Employed Women's Association (India)
SID	Specialarbejderförbundet i Danmark (Danish General Workers' Union)
SME	small and medium-sized enterprise
TINA	"There is no alternative"
TNC	transnational corporation
TUC	Trades Union Congress (UK)
TWN	Third World Network
UAW	United Automobile Workers (US)
UN	United Nations
UNEP	United Nations Environment Programme
VTsIOM	Russian Public Opinion Research Center
WCCs	world company councils
WCL	World Confederation of Labour
WFTU	World Federation of Trade Unions
WSF	World Social Forum
WTO	World Trade Organization

INTRODUCTION: THE ISSUES

We live in interesting times, yet sometimes our thinking is framed in terms from an older era. The world has changed dramatically over the last quarter of a century yet many paradigms for understanding it lack complexity and are constrained by a narrow nation-state optic. This book proposes to rethink global labour and boldly proclaim a new era of renewal and reinvention for the labour movement. What we call "globalization" or "neoliberalism" has meant, in practice, a huge expansion of market forces and a seeming reduction of space for alternative ways of organizing society. But this unparalleled expansion of capitalism has also led to an equally unprecedented emergence of a global working class, predicted by Karl Marx back in the 1880s, but usually dismissed as wishful thinking. Today the workers of the world are indeed unified under the same capitalist order even if their experiences of it are not the same and they do not yet act in concert.

In contrast to the dominant left-wing or progressive worldview that denounced globalization when it emerged as the dominant trope in the 1990s, I will argue that it opens as many doors for labour as it has closed for national governments: there are always alternatives. The processes of internationalization happen from above but also emanate from below: workers, women, peasants and students are beginning to unite across national frontiers in pursuit of global justice. Today there may yet be an opportunity to recreate the ethos of the early labour movement in the middle of the nineteenth century and to forge a new global labour movement that improves the lives of everyone wherever they are.

The world today is very different from the one in which the proletariat – free both of alternative means of sustenance and of extra-economic coercion – emerged. The world of work has been transformed for many and yet the capital/wage labour relation persists. Much work and many repressive social contexts are the same as they were in the first part of the nineteenth century. Our approach to the workers of the world today must, therefore, be historical, so that we can better understand the forces that have contributed to the evolution of labour

1

today and how it is likely to develop into the future. Labour is – or, at least, can be – a social movement and has an historic memory and a rich history of solidarity and innovation, as well as the more negative features that most observers focus on, such as its stale, male and bureaucratic ethos.

For too long there has been a widely shared assumption that "globalization" has created a new world order in which labour can only react to the circumstances that engulf it. But a long-term view shows us that the internationalization of capital in the 1980s and 1990s was, at least in part, a reaction to labour's considerable strength in the 1960s and 1970s. Workers are the authors of their own destiny, and it is their skills and their ability to cooperate and to inspire innovation that makes globalization what it is. Workers are dynamic agents of their own destiny, with their own identities, and can have alternative visions of society to those of the crass individualism that is based on a blind subservience to the market. Traditionally, both industrial relations theory and the somewhat pessimistic tradition of Western Marxism have a tendency to view workers as passive and trade unions as purely reactive organizations. Yet all the factors that have led to a decline in labour's power in developed countries – such as offshoring, restructuring and lean production – have also led to a recomposition of labour on an international scale and the creation of new forms of organization that challenge and resist the worst of capitalism's onslaught.

A long-view approach focused on labour agency also requires an integrated understanding of capital and labour's intertwined histories. Capitalism's drive to innovate is always related to its dealings with the recalcitrant "factor of production", namely flesh-and-blood workers. Its geographic expansion and continuous struggle to incorporate any lingering non-commodified (marketized) forms of production are testament to its creative-destruction nature. Capitalism's search for growth spawns a need to continuously develop new technologies and new products and is also related to the sometimes active, but more often muted, resistance by workers to exploitation. Moves to escape the clutches of the capital/wage labour relation are always contradictory and create as many labour opportunities as they do constraints. There is no one-way process leading inexorably towards "deskilling" or a "race to the bottom", in so far as capital needs labour, and workers can also learn, innovate and fight back, albeit with a delay while they adjust and labour's recomposition takes place, after the atomization that the free market policies create in the labour force.

We are now, arguably, entering a period "after neoliberalism", in which the hegemony of pro-market, pro-technology, pro-wealth ideas has been thrown into question by the 2007–9 crisis. Voices of discontent can be heard, and since 2010 a series of labour actions have shaken any complacency from above or pessimism from below that the condition of labour cannot be changed. What globalization has produced is a truly global working class for the first time. We may well see the workers of the world contesting exploitation and immiseration more frequently; moving around the world to seek better conditions and articulating their struggles with those of the counter-globalization movements that have emerged since 2000. Labour, as any social movement, takes time to recover from full frontal attacks on its well-being and even its very right to exist. We are beginning to see many signs of a multifaceted and flexible response to capital in all areas of the world, even in North America, once the pre-eminent home of the capitalist "dream". In particular, we see an openness towards the new social movements, as we saw in the trade union engagement with the Occupy movement. It is noteworthy that this new vision also extends to migrants, once viewed with open hostility by many established labour movements, which now recognize that all workers are part of the workers' movement. This process of recovery, recomposition and reorientation is, of course, uneven across countries and sectors and full of contradictions. But this uneven nature of workers' resistance is also combined, and now we can talk realistically of the "workers of the world" as a unified social presence facing the same problems and looking for similar outcomes.

Many commentators on the Left tend to forget the basic lesson taught by Michel Foucault, namely that a condition of power is resistance and that a reciprocal relation exists between them: where there is power, there is resistance to that power. For many commentators, the way to gain support for fundamental social change is to explain to people how bad things are and how evil the global power holders are. They end up with a fairly apocalyptic view that we are all doomed or that the end is nigh. What this book tries to do, instead, is to show how the changes in the global order since the 1970s have led to one massive wave of free market incursion into all aspects of social life (neoliberalism in short) being followed by a counter-movement in which society and social groups seek to regain control over market forces. Trade unions, for all their routine and bureaucracy, have played a positive role in organizing the workers of the world, including the marginalized informal, precarious and migrant workers. Those engaged with new social movements around ecology, feminisms, counter-globalization, and so on tend to think of unions and workers (at least 'blue collar' ones) as part of the problem, whereas I will try to show they are part of the solution, through their daily resistance and ability to create an alternative social order based on social control over the market and workers control over the workplace.

In the vast production of knowledge and debate around globalization and its contestation since 2000 there has been very little focus on workers and their organizations. The emphasis has been placed on what seemed new in terms of counter-globalization protests, for example. And labour was seen as an old movement, peripheral at best in the new era, its members bought off by the state and the trade unions hopelessly weakened and past their sell-by date. But, for all the new identity or place-based protests, a major feature of the era has been a continuous attack by capital on workers whether they are working in factories, fields or offices. The new global capitalism has an overarching objective of suppressing workers' wages and preventing the (re-)emergence of a powerful labour movement, which might constrain its ability to maximize profits. This will be a recurrent theme throughout this text. The World Bank in its 2018 *World Development Report* has recognized the problem posed by resurgent labour to the untrammelled rule of capital and calls for fewer regulations protecting workers, to allow for easier hiring and firing, especially in the global South, while promoting the informal employment model beyond the reach of state regulation.

There was a time, not so long ago, when the ringing call of *The Communist Manifesto* – "Workers of the world, unite; you have nothing to lose but your chains" – sounded faintly anachronistic to many in the developed world. This was the period in the 1950s in the global North when some workers had "never had it so good", according to the politicians. The problem was an excess of consumerism, not one of putting bread on the table. Yet now, after a quarter-century of pro-market and anti-labour policies, workers everywhere, including the developed Northern economies, are struggling to make ends meet. For the majority – in the global South – affluence was never a problem, and many continue to be affected by a brutality not really captured by Marx's term "extra-economic coercion". Today, as workers – be they settled or migrants, rural or urban – face an economic order that has had no clear strategy since the 2007–9 crisis, they are forced increasingly to seek alliances across geographical regions and gender, age, race and ethnic divides. By joining together, not only do they stand to lose their chains but they can also to be part of constructing another, more humane, world.

Structure of the book

In Part I I address the history of labour, starting the analysis in Chapter 1 with a wide-ranging survey of labour and capitalism that sets the scene for subsequent chapters and develops the themes and concepts that will be explored in later chapters. I examine the dramatic entry of the working classes or proletariat. Workers were "born in blood" in the original industrializing countries and in the colonial world, violence being at the very heart of this process. This is followed by the "great transformation", described by Karl Marx and Karl Polanyi, as the new capitalist mode of production took shape with the capital/wage labour relation at its core. Finally, I look at how the development of globalization – an unprecedented acceleration of internationalization and generalization of the wage relation – might be taking us back to the future. I question whether we are seeing a new dawn for a mobile working class that cuts across national boundaries, creates new solidarities and consolidates a liberatory identity to deal with a capitalism that seems unable to renew its dynamism.

Having set the scene for the emergence of a working class under the new capitalist mode of production, Chapter 2 addresses the "golden era", namely the period from the end of the Second World War up to the 1970s, when Western capitalism seemed to have secured a considerable degree of stability. Fordism was part of the labour process in the new factories, but it also ushered in a mode of labour regulation and social welfare provision that understood the benefits to capital of relatively good working conditions. It was the strength of the trade unions – and the shake-up caused by the Second World War – that was a major factor leading capitalism in the West to take that orientation. In the rest of the world colonialism was giving way to a post- or neocolonial world where the uneven development of capitalism continued to prevail, albeit without direct control by the West. In the early 1970s this Fordist/welfarist/developmentalist model of capital/wage labour relations began to enter into crisis. From this crisis a new order was born, the world of globalization and the internet, with neoliberalism as the dominant economic policy. This was to have a cataclysmic effect on labour and its organizations.

The era of globalization, covered in Chapter 3, was the dominant feature of the 1980s and 1990s. An unregulated market system went hand in hand with a recrudescence of unfree labour. Capitalism expanded globally and, in the 1990s, took under its wing the once socialist and once national developmentalist states. The doctrine of neoliberalism, by no means unified or as all-powerful as often presented, provided a rationale for this new "great transformation", every bit as dominant as the Industrial Revolution was in its day. What globalization also produced was a new, global working class that doubled in size from 1990 to 2005. It did not, of course, immediately challenge the new order but it did begin to develop as part of a broad social counter-movement to the unfettered market. The whole neoliberal model lost its hegemony during the 2007–9 crisis of capitalism, and things have never been the same since then.

In Part II I focus on the development of a global working class. The workers of the world were divided by colonialism and imperialism into "workers North", discussed in Chapter 4, and "workers South", as analysed in Chapter 5. In the North the dominant form of labour regulation gradually gave way to an ill-defined post-Fordism. For some analysts, this was even considered to be a progressive move that would lead to the emergence of a new transformative working class. What is less contested is the major impact of the collapse of state socialism – the Soviet Union and its allied/dependent states – after 1989. Vast layers of workers joined the global working class under the direct aegis of capital, but huge impoverishment and alienation in this region was also the result. This was the period in which the Western/Northern trade unions, and the international trade unions they sponsored, also began to face up to the massive crisis in terms of membership, strategy and even identity caused by the impact of neoliberal globalization and the technological revolution it had brought in its wake.

The workers of the South (Chapter 5) went from the colonial and then postcolonial situation of the 1950s and 1960s to what was called a "new international division of labour" in the 1970s. Basically, the old imperialist divide of an industrial North and an agricultural South began to break down with the development of "world factories" and free trade zones. There the outsourcing of Northern production lines reached a peak and saw a vast layer of workers in the South incorporated into the capitalist machine. A strong feature of this new wave of industrialization was the predominant role of women workers. This had the mixed effect of removing women, to some extent, from traditional patriarchy, while also increasing their exploitation and domination by the new capitalism. The other clear marker of this period was the rise of a new, more militant Southern trade unionism in countries such as Brazil, South Africa and the Philippines, where a social movement unionism, breaking with economism and political subordination, was first developed.

In Chapter 6, I turn to the idea of the "precariat", which offers a bridge between the expositions of North and South, and show how they are part of the same global order. I set the current interest in the notion of a precariat – a precarious proletariat – in terms of its antecedents, particularly in the labour studies of the South. Going back to the 1960s, we can see close critical attention to those workers who are deemed "marginal" to the capitalist order, in the sense that they do not even serve as a classic reserve army of labour. I also take up the later debates about informal employment that precede current concerns with precarious work. In conclusion, it seems clear that work is becoming increasingly precarious – both in the North and in the South – even if it is doubtful that we can discern a class or category separate (and even opposed) to the working class that we might call a precariat. The debate has enriched our understanding of the nature of work under late capitalism, however, and we may think of this "global precariat" as a concept symbolizing the fact that workers everywhere have the option of either accepting increased vulnerability and precarity or striving for the creation of solidarities and collective action that might protect them and form part of a new democratic and sustainable future for work.

Finally, in Part III, the book turns towards an analysis of new challenges for global labour, some of which are old problems as well as new ones. The thinking, action and policy-making around the labour movement and labour migration tend to be kept very separate, but in Chapter 7 I show how they are inextricably linked. The early formation of the working class at a global level is linked to internal and international migration patterns. Today the issue of migration is at the top of the political agenda not just in the North but also, for example, in China, in terms of its own internal migration. We need to consider what these labour flows mean to the labour movement. Trade unions have historically tended to take protectionist positions *vis-à-vis* the settled "national" workers they represent. Nevertheless, trade unions have also, on occasion, been at the vanguard of organizing migrant workers and defending their human rights. It is often said that human rights cease to exist at national borders, but trade unions are well placed to create a new social movement that places workers at the heart of the drive for global social justice.

Historically, the labour movement has had a wider remit than industrial relations in the workplace, having taken up social, political, cultural and community issues, and so it should continue. In Chapter 8 I examine some aspects of labour and its related "others" in the new social movements, starting with an emphasis on labour as a social movement. Most often, from a "new" social movement perspective, labour is written off as an "old" and totally incorporated institution. To give a focus to our discussion, I look at labour's often troubled relationship with environmental issues. Is it that we are seeing signs of a new systematic engagement by trade unions with climate change? What implications would that have? Finally, I turn to the broad issue of labour's engagement with global justice movements. Ever since the anti-WTO Seattle protests of 1999, when trade unionists and environmentalists came together in common cause, it has seemed at least possible that labour would join its "others" in a broad movement for social transformation.

In its origins labour was internationalist in its outlook, but it gradually became nationalized. Chapter 9 examines the high points and low points of labour internationalism, starting with the period of the First International. The carnage of the First World War put an end to early notions of proletarian internationalism. In the postcolonial period, and later in the 1950s, trade unions in the North often played a shamelessly imperialist role. Yet, gradually, as the internationalization of production gave way to globalization, as we now understand it, trade unions began to grapple once more with the international dimension. Only a transnational labour strategy could hope to contest a transnational capitalist strategy. The result, in terms of a movement towards global union formation, is patchy but it does, arguably, signal a turn in the labour movement away from single-minded reliance on the nation state to deliver reforms for workers. We can expect this dimension to increase in importance in the coming decades.

In the conclusion I turn to the progressive options before us, examining critically the problems that the labour movement has had in articulating a credible strategy for social and political transformation that would be fit for purpose today. There is an impasse in which the old way of doing business can no longer yield results whereas new approaches are only just beginning to gain traction. Arguably, we are in a transitional period, characterized by high degrees of instability and unpredictability that can be grasped only through a complexity theory lens. We need to establish whether, indeed, "Another world is possible", and, if so, what it would look like and how we might get there from a labour perspective. There are signs that we may be moving beyond the fragments of the various social movements contesting a now clearly failed economic model that can articulate a new strategy for democratic and sustainable social transformation. The new global working class is beginning to find its feet in the new world order and is also finding voice across the world. The global precariat that brings labour in the once affluent North and the new fast-developing South under the same regime of capital accumulation is not a new dangerous class but, rather, a layer of new workers that may yet revive and re-energize the old labour movement, to allow it to take up the challenges of today, which are so similar to those of the early Industrial Revolution, when it emerged in its first incarnation.

PART I
HISTORY OF LABOUR

To be able to understand the workers of the world today, we need an understanding of how the current state of affairs developed. This section of the book sets out the evolution of the capital/wage labour relationship and how the Industrial Revolution spawned a transformation in societal structures from which the working class sought to protect itself through resistance and collaborative organization, namely through trade unions, co-operatives and social movements. The postwar boom that dominated the Western industrialized economies until the mid-1970s was bolstered by the Cold War and underpinned by the social settlement wrought from Fordism and welfarism. Workers in the developed world enjoyed a brief period of stability and prosperity, albeit based on the exploitation of colonial or dominated territories and workers of the developing world. The collapse of that settlement ushered in a period of transition from which emerged the neoliberal dogma of the market that has held sway ever since. The strong unions of the North were defanged and declawed throughout the 1980s and 1990s, and their decline contributed to the ascendance of a new model of capitalism that reached beyond national borders. The age of globalization drew most of the world into its market for goods, workers and production as communism collapsed in eastern Europe in the 1990s. Since then a global working class has emerged that is characterized by increasing numbers of women joining the workforce and the insecurity of that work, brought about by capital's push for flexible labour. Organized labour's response has lagged these developments, but there are signs of a resurgence of grass-roots labour movements worldwide that aim to counter the dominance of the market and fight for workers' rights and welfare on a global scale.

1

LABOUR AND CAPITALISM

The study of the development of capitalism and the study of labour relations usually proceed along separate tracks, driven by different academic disciplines. In this book I follow an integrated treatment of capitalism and wage labour in the belief that one depends on the other. We begin with the way the working classes were, in Karl Marx's words, "born in blood", as capitalism and colonialism took over from the older social orders. Workers had to be violently separated from pre-existing means of survival to be "free" for capitalist employment. This process led to what Karl Polanyi called the "great transformation", which I examine to explain how the self-regulated market began to hold sway over society in general and over workers in particular. I conclude this opening chapter with a hypothesis that we are now moving "back to the future", as today's labour relations have much in common with the first era of industrialization in the 1890s, with a global market and a global working class that truly has "nothing to lose but its chains". The themes raised in this chapter will be explored in further detail in subsequent chapters, but a wide overview is necessary to pose the big questions. A labour approach to understanding the development of capitalism needs to foreground the capital/wage labour relation and the constant role of labour struggles in shaping that development.

Born in blood

"If money, according to Augier 'comes into the world with a congenital blood stain on one cheek', capital comes dripping from head to foot, from every pore, with blood and dirt" (Marx 1976 [1867]: 915). Thus spoke Marx towards the end of *Capital*, volume 1, when dealing with the "genesis of the Industrial Capitalist". The shift from merchant wealth accumulation to capitalism as a mode of production entailed a new mode of mobilizing social labour and nature and unprecedented levels of brutality to achieve it. The "primitive accumulation" of capital referred to by Marx required a new form of organization, and thus navies, armies and the capitalist state came into being. Expansion overseas was also essential to resolve the crisis of European feudalism, and so conquest, colonialism and naked pillage became an integral element in the development of capitalism. Above all, as Marx put it, "for the conversion of his money into capital ... the owner of money must meet in the market with the free labourer, free in the double sense, that as a free man he can dispose of his labour and that in his other hand he has no other commodity for sale, is short of everything necessary for the realisation of his labour power" (Marx 1976 [1867]: 271). Capitalist development entails the subordination of labour and is not an autonomous economic process.

Rosa Luxemburg, writing in 1913, saw Marx's vision as restricted because he did not acknowledge that the "primitive accumulation" he referred to was an ongoing process. For her, "'sweating blood and filth with every pore from head to toe'" characterizes "not only the birth of capital but also its progress in the world at every step" (Luxemburg 1951 [1913]: 364). The reasons she gives for this argument are debatable, because capitalism in the abstract might not require a non-capitalist hinterland to be able to reproduce itself. But, from the perspective of the globalized conflictual world order we live in today, the notion of "permanent primitive accumulation" has considerable purchase. Accumulation is not a purely economic process, and the transaction between capitalist and "free" wage labour is hardly an equitable one. "Force, fraud, oppression, looting are openly displayed without any attempt at concealment, and it requires an effort to discover within this range of political violence and contests of power the stern lens of the economic process" (Luxemburg 1951 [1913]: 365). In short, the capital/wage labour relation is born in blood, and violence continues to be at its heart.

It is important to stress, furthermore, that the capitalist mode of production was global from its inception. One clear example of this principle was the so-called "triangular trade", memorably brought to life by Trinidadian scholar and politician Eric Williams in his book *Capitalism and Slavery* (Williams 1944). This trade involved European manufactured goods sailing to Africa, where they were exchanged for slaves, who were then forcefully transported (the so-called "middle passage") to the Americas, from where plantation crops were taken back to Europe. This was a truly wondrous and productive profit-generating machine. While the precise historiography of Williams's critique has been contested by subsequent research, it still stands as a searing corrective to Eurocentric heroic narratives of the Industrial Revolution based on great inventors of machines. Above all, it demonstrates the integrated global character of the emergence of capitalism. It also reinforces Marx's much earlier point that "[t]he veiled slavery of the wage labourers in Europe needed the unqualified slavery of the New World as its pedestal" (Marx 1976 [1867]: 833). The combined and uneven development of capitalism was based on a similarly uneven development of labour subjection.

The development of capitalism was clearly inseparable in its genesis from the brutal subjection of the majority world through colonialism and imperialism. As John Smith puts it, "Imperialist domination and plunder was a necessary condition of the rise of capitalism in England, but it has taken the whole course of capitalist development for the imperialist division of the world to become internalized, to become a property of the capital relation itself" (Smith 2016: 225). Far from colonialism and imperialism (two sides of the same coin, really) being only part of capitalism's prehistory, they have become part of the DNA of the global capitalist order. As we shall see in a later section, the promise of globalization in the 1990s was that it would generate a "flat" world – a level playing field, as it were – but the reality has been a concentration of wealth in fewer hands and the deepening of structural inequalities between what we now call the North and the South. To recognize this basic fact does not lead inevitably either to what used to be called Third-Worldism or to the common interests of the workers of the world, despite divisions, oppressions and inequalities, being simply asserted.

Capitalism as a mode of production emerged first in Europe and, specifically, in England. The Industrial Revolution, based fundamentally on the textile mill and the steam engine, was well established by 1815 and was in full flow by mid-century. Cottage industry had to be totally destroyed to complete the separation of cultivators from the land. Once subordinated to capital, production made a great leap forward through technological innovations and a new labour process. Other competitors – such as the thriving textile industry in India – were also wiped out. Once the textile mills of Lancashire had been secured behind protectionist trade barriers, free trade was then imposed on the rest of the world, giving rise to the period of "free trade imperialism" that continued until the First World War. As Michael Barratt Brown concludes: "[B]y the middle of the nineteenth century, free trade had made Britain the workshop of the world. The fact was that British naval and military victories of the early nineteenth century, consolidated by Britain's industrial advance far ahead of any other nation, made the whole world, in a sense, Britain's colony" (Barratt Brown 1974: 53).

This is also the period in which an incipient international labour movement began to take shape, based on the common interests of workers. In its early manifestations, this social movement did not always take the form of organized trade unions. Various self-help or associational forms prevailed, such as the mutual societies and co-operatives. Mutualism has been defined as "voluntary arrangements, in which people make contributions to a collective fund, which is given ... to one or more of the contributors according to specific roles of allocation" (van der Linden 2008: 81). One of the most common ones was in relation to burial costs, whereby workers shared the cost of burying their family members with other working families, and thus a basic but nevertheless effective communal insurance system materialized. They might also act as communal pools of labour, for example in relation to rural tasks, in which labour is allocated according to need. The modern co-operative movement can also trace its roots back to these formative stages of the labour movement. Consumer co-operatives are associations in which budgets are pooled to make purchases at lower prices and then distributed to its members. These – and the producer co-ops that followed – also generated a rich associational life among their members.

The broad labour movement – in its multiple aspects – was part of what Karl Polanyi saw as the social counter-movement, which would emerge to temper the drive by the market to colonize all social relationships. Polanyi is also helpful in relation to the early phase of development through an instituted process and the mechanisms of integration. For pre-capitalist forms of integration, Polanyi points to two basic mechanisms: exchange occurs in an economic realm "disembedded" from social institutions; it is reciprocity and redistribution that prevail when the market is not all-embracing. The mutual aid societies and the co-operatives of the early labour movement were precisely organs of reciprocity (in which the social relationship prevails over the economy) and redistribution (in which custom-based rules are created by institutions, subordinating the economy and its logic to a social need and logic).

Until the last quarter of the nineteenth century we could refer to a pre-national phase of labour development before thoroughly national labour movements were formed, a process consolidated in Europe, as is well known, by the First World War. For Britain, in particular, the free movement of people across its empire was the natural counterpart to free trade. A particular Western European internationalism was the norm, following the practice of artisan movement across frontiers. Thus the First International, founded in 1864, was based on pre-existing solidarity discourses while also moving from the political domain to a more "economic" focus on the capital/wage labour relation. The rise of the First International, as Marcel van der Linden points out, "cannot be explained on the grounds of the rise of the factory system" (van der Linden 1988: 15); rather, it reflected the interests and the dynamism of the skilled artisan. As was frequently the case in labour history, these organizations were often transitional both chronologically and in terms of their functions between an older mode of production and a new order.

The First International developed a presence in parts of Latin America, particularly among European immigrants, but, overall, the reality of the colonized and postcolonial worlds was very different from that of Europe. So it was, for example, in Argentina, where the First International had a thriving section and where anarchism, anarcho-syndicalism and socialism had a strong presence. Karl

Marx, in correspondence with the First International organizers in Argentina, had an approach that can only be called Eurocentric, as he despaired of organizing in what he saw as "primitive" conditions. Argentina is an interesting case, because there were no pre-existing non-capitalist modes of production and the influence of African slavery was slight. "Free" labour prevailed in urban and rural areas (that is to say, labour that was free both of alternative means of sustenance and from extra-economic coercion). Nevertheless, coercion of labour was ever-present, with an 1815 law decreeing that individuals without property were deemed to be of the servant class and thus obliged to carry employment papers. Later citizenship was suspended for "wage servants, day labourers, soldiers and notorious vagrants" (cited in Munck, Falcon & Galitelli 1987: 56). When European migrants arrived en masse in the second half of the nineteenth century they were deprived of political rights, until 1916, and subject to arbitrary deportation.

What a purely European perspective lacked, to put it that way, was the element of race, ethnicity and national identity. The making of the working class in conditions in which colonialism, dependency or imperialism prevailed was inevitably bound up with the national question or national independence. We have already seen how the working class was anything but homogeneous and was riven by pre-existing and constructed divisions. Above all, as Caroline Knowles – among others – states, "[e]mpire is first and foremost a race story" (Knowles 2003: 119). Race was made by colonialism, but it also makes colonialism what it was and is. Race and ethnicity are at the very heart of working-class identity, structures and movements. We need only think of labour migration, for which race and ethnicity are central to the whole process. Why some people migrate and others do not, how people cross borders, how they obtain citizenship or do not are all questions bound up with race, as signifier of geographical origins and in its own right.

It might also be said that the labour activists and theorists of this period (and later ones) seemed to ignore the fact that the working class has two sexes. The commodification of labour and the exploitation of labour have, in fact, been gendered processes from the origins of the capital/wage labour relation. The analysis of the household, and reproductive activities more generally, have been weak points for mainstream and Marxist analysis alike, despite a few exceptions. For Alessandra Mezzadri, any vague reference to "intersections" between the two processes is but a descriptive analysis, and what we need to ask ourselves is "how do we understand class and class formation, once we account for forms of social oppression like patriarchal norms?" (Mezzadri 2016: 1890). It is hardly a question of asserting the "primacy" of class but, rather, of understanding class as a relational category marked by difference, experienced differently by diverse social groups and shaped by a multiplicity of social relations, resulting in a complex politics of transformation.

Reimagining the working class

What we need to take from this history, I would argue, is an expanded version of the working class, rather than the one common in mainstream and Marxist textbooks alike. Thus, for example, Marcus Rediker shows us another North Atlantic proletariat from that of the Industrial Revolution myth. It was in no way "free"; rather, it was *"terrorized, subject to coercion*. Its hide was calloused by indentured labour, galley slavery, plantation slavery, convict transformation, the workhouse, the house of correction. Its origins were often traumatic; enclosure, capture and imprisonment left lasting marks" (Rediker 2003: 120, emphasis in original). The institutions of labour – at work, at home and in relation to the state – were all built on violence. It is clear that we need to deploy a broader, more flexible and more global conception of the working class than we have so far (van der Linden 2008). The boundaries between free and unfree labour, economic and non-economic compulsion, the workplace and the household, class and race/ethnicity are far more porous than generally allowed for until recently. This insight is equally applicable in the present era, when we witness a rise of "new slavery" (Bales 2005) and all forms of trafficking of workers, who are, once again, uprooted and bought and sold in the global marketplace. It is also very much an expanded definition of the working classes we need today when traditional modes of exploitation are joined by "new" forms.

Finally, I must stress that the development of capitalism was based on the mobility of labour to meet its needs. The first wave of migrant labour was composed of those who left the land to work in the new factory mode of production in Europe, the second wave saw Europeans moving to the "New World" and the third wave was comprised of the various coerced groups taken to work the mines and plantations of the colonial order. So, for example, in the Lancashire cotton-producing town of Preston nearly half the population in 1850 consisted of immigrants, both local and from Ireland. A similar pattern applied in Prussia, where "in the 1830s the provinces of Westphalia, Rhine, Berlin and Brandenburg initiated their industrial expansion, attracting a large-scale flow of population from Prussia's eastern agricultural regions" (Wolf 1982: 362). The mechanization of agriculture further drove the flow of cultivators to the emerging factory system. Thus the mobility of labour was an integral element and a precondition for the development of capitalism.

The mass movement of European populations to the "New World" was a major feature from 1800 to the First World War, with more than 50 million people driven from Europe by a series of agricultural crises. This transatlantic migration operated as a safety valve in Europe but also provided a "white" labour force in North and (to a more limited extent) South America for the new industries. Female labour power mobility was more restricted during this period. The third wave of migration, consisting of contract labourers directed to the mines and plantations of the New World, built on the previous African slave transportation, which saw 12 million taken by force to the Americas between 1450 and 1800. With the gradual abolition of slavery other sources of labour needed to be found. This led to plantation owners resorting to "the tried and tested practice of employing migrants as indentured servants" (Wolf 1982: 98) as well as the Asian "coolie trade", which saw 2.5 million Chinese and 1.5 million Indian workers taken by force to the Antilles and South Africa in particular.

Labour migration, a topic we will return to throughout this book, is important both in its own right and for what it tells us about the nature of the capital/wage labour relation. As Eric Wolf has noted, "[A] hallmark of the industrial and plantation complexes constructed under capitalist auspices all around the world has been the juxtaposition of groups of different social and cultural origins" (Wolf 1982: 379). This is often taken as an explanation of heterogeneity between workers, but it can also point us towards the way the labour process is organized as the cause of labour heterogeneity. It is not pre-existing racial, ethnic or cultural differences that are the main issue, I would argue, but the way these were, and are, mobilized by capitalism for its own purposes. Thus, even as it unifies the world under the aegis of the capital/wage labour relation, capitalism also creates or constructs difference, segmentation and conflict in the working classes.

The great transformation

> The true implications of economic liberalism can now be taken in at a glance. Nothing less than a self-regulating market on a world scale could ensure the functioning of this stupendous mechanism.
>
> (Polanyi 2001 [1944]: 145)

In the 1940s Karl Polanyi wrote of the "great transformation" wrought by the Industrial Revolution in the nineteenth century. What we now know as globalization is simply this self-regulating market on a world scale. But Polanyi was referring to the Industrial Revolution, which he positioned in terms of the "disembedding" of the market from previous social and communal settings. While previous societies had been organized on principles of exchange, reciprocity and redistribution, now the market would become the sole logic of social and economic development. Markets had hitherto been subordinated to, and regulated by, various forms of social authority. Economic liberalism – the guiding principle of this new order – split economics from politics and from society. Henceforth, the market would shape society in its image, or, as Polanyi put it, "[a] market economy can exist only in a market society" (Polanyi 2001 [1944]: 74).

The self-regulating market was, for Polanyi, a "stark utopia", in the sense that it could never be achieved: "[S]uch an institution could not exist for any length of time without annihilating the human and natural substance of society; it would have physically destroyed man [*sic*] and destroyed his surroundings into a wilderness" (Polanyi 2001 [1944]: 3). In modern terminology, the self-regulating market was neither socially or environmentally sustainable. Counter-tendencies to those of disembedding could emerge, and Polanyi posited a "double movement" of market expansion and a societal reaction against it. No society could persist if labour in particular was treated poorly as a commodity, except for "the shortest stretch of time unless its human and natural substances as well as its business organization was protected against the ravages of this satanic mill" (Polanyi 2001 [1944]: 76–7). The "dark satanic mills" of William Blake were not only the factories of the Industrial Revolution but the infernal system that evolved to subdue workers and nature to the insatiable hunger of the new, unregulated market order.

Labour was to play a major role in this new economic order, according to Polanyi. That labour should become a commodity that could be bought and sold was essential to the logic of the market economy. Of course, as Polanyi stresses, "labour is only another name for human activity which goes with life itself" (Polanyi 2001 [1944]: 132), and thus its commodification would encounter resistance. Labour, for Polanyi, was but an "alleged commodity", mainly because it "cannot be shoved about, used indiscriminately, or even left unused without affecting also the human individual who happens to be the bearer of this peculiar commodity" (Polanyi 2001 [1944]: 76). At this level we could call this simply a moral critique of the great transformation, but Polanyi went on to discuss the role of trade unions under the new order, arguing quite clearly against reformist tendencies, stating that their purpose is precisely "that of interfering with the laws of supply and demand in respect of human labour and removing it from the orbit of the market" (Polanyi 2001 [1944]: 186). Thus, labour's inherent tendency to defend itself would lead to "decommodification", and this questioned the inherent logic of the new order.

The productivity and dynamism of the new order was not in doubt and seemed to confirm the hyperbole of Karl Marx and Friedrich Engels in *The Communist Manifesto*, in which they stated: "All fixed, fast frozen relations with their train of ancient and venerable prejudices and opinions are swept away, all new-formed ones are swept away before they can ossify. All that is solid melts into air, all that is holy is profaned" (Marx & Engels 1976 [1848]: 64). This system was subject to periodic crises, which would create upheavals for capitalists and workers alike, but the system was nothing if not inventive. New technologies and new ways of organizing labour would constantly renew the system. In the 1940s Joseph Schumpeter, the conservative economic historian who nevertheless learnt much from Marx, called this a process of "creative destruction" (Schumpeter 1994 [1942]). The Keynesian toolbox – which included the astute use of monetary policy to dampen the economic cycle and the manipulation of the minimum wage/workforce levels – did much to generate sustained levels of economic growth, an expanding working class and steadily increasing living standards for its members. It did seem that the "mixed economy" of the West was developing a formula that might diminish the attractiveness of state socialism, both in theory and in practice.

The twin pillars of this new labour regime in the advanced industrialized countries were Fordism and welfarism. The social regime of accumulation described by the term "Fordism" was based on domestic mass production and a range of politics and institutions supporting mass consumption, as well as the iconic assembly-line-type production of the early Ford car factories. It generated strong growth rates and the stable incorporation of a layer of the working class across the global North, with obvious regional variations. As to welfarism, it originated in Britain after the Second World War with the rise of the welfare state, in which the state plays a role in the protection and promotion of social welfare, as against the nostrums of the pre-war self-regulation market model. This model transfers resources through redistributionist taxation to provide services such as healthcare and education, as well as direct contributions to individuals ("welfare") who are unemployed. This model has been questioned since the 1980s and partly dismantled in the 1990s, but it played – and still plays – a pivotal role in assuring a level of social stability in the affluent North.

In labour history, and in the popular imagination, this period (from roughly 1945 to 1975) has gone down as the "golden era", or (in French) *les trente glorieuses* (the thirty glorious years). There is a great degree of mythology at play here, but for some workers in some parts of the world this was, indeed, a relatively secure period. The institution of the state and most political parties (including conservative ones) accepted that social incorporation was a more viable strategy than naked class war. The problem was that this particular constellation of economic, political and social forces was assumed to be universal by, for example, the theories of industrial relations then emerging. In reality, the "standard employment relationship" – based on stable, socially protected, legally binding, full-time jobs – on which the industrial relations discourse and institutions were built was neither universal nor even consistently applied in the North itself, where women and migrants fell outside its remit.

In the rest of the world the story of colonialism slowly unravelled, as British hegemony was finally displaced by that of the United States, following the Second World War. This part of the world had not experienced the effects of

Fordism and welfarism, except in small pockets. The core impact of the welfare state in the North was the link established between wage labour and social citizenship. The colonial and postcolonial economic orders could not deal with the "social question" in this way, not least as the extension of the welfare state and its provisions of a social safety net were specifically denied to UK colonial subjects. As Franco Barchiesi argues, outside the small circle of the advanced industrial societies there were no conditions to resolve the "social question" in the same way, in so far as employers and unions were much weaker and there was not the same incentive to equate wage labour with social citizenship (Barchiesi 2012: 13). Neither Fordism nor welfarism would apply in the countries of the South as they achieved (or consolidated) political independence in the postwar period, as the global free market expanded under US hegemony and imposed its logic of total commodification and exploitation.

There was, however, a move through the modernization theory, developed in the United States by Walt Rostow and others, to promote "development" in the colonial world through industrialization. While high mass consumption and full employment were not on offer for the workers of the world outside the protected North, there was a global reform element designed to integrate the South into the emerging new world order. As Arturo Escobar puts it, in the postwar period "the real struggle between East and West had already moved to the Third World", and it was "commonly accepted in the early 1950s that if poor countries were not rescued from their poverty, they would succumb to communism" (Escobar 1995: 33–4). Certainly, if it was colonialism that had created poverty in the majority of the world, it would be hard to imagine neocolonialism addressing this issue other than from the standpoint of its own interests, such as creating new markets and extracting raw materials. The development model created was one that generated some degree of industrialization but also deepened the ties of dependency through control of technology and the financial sector.

Since the era of globalization began, around 1990, the South was to go through an even more dramatic "great transformation", as it both industrialized and became more thoroughly integrated with the global economy. There had been a wave of industrialization in the 1970s and 1980s in the so-called newly industrialized countries, or NICs, but this time round the process was more generalized and signalled a world-historic shift in global capitalism. The "big picture" is that the global working class doubled in numbers between 1970 and 2000 to reach 2.7 billion workers, with the vast bulk of that number accounted for by the non-OECD or developing countries, where the number of workers rose from 1 billion to 2 billion over this period. Although industrial relations theory and practice, the International Labour Organization and the peak organizations of the transnational labour movement all continued to live in the era of the "standard employment contract", this new global working class was beginning to pose a challenge to orthodoxy, and to global capitalism itself in due course. The nature of the game had changed but many of the players were still playing by the old rules.

Around 1980 a clear-cut movement occurred, more or less globally, to decisively alter the historic compromise with labour through what became known as "neoliberal globalization". The new market-based social accumulation model had its origins in the brutal military coup in Chile in 1973. There, a mildly reformist government had been overthrown, with US connivance, and a Chicago-trained economic team committed to establishing a new development model was installed. The new Chilean minister of the economy declared that "the new democracy ... will have to be authoritarian, in the sense that the rules needed for the system's capability cannot be subject to political process" (cited in Taylor 1999: 42). That is to say, nothing from the political or social domains could intervene to moderate the workings of the free market. Within a few years key Northern governments came into power to implement just such a programme (Margaret Thatcher in the United Kingdom in 1979 and Ronald Reagan in the United States in 1981), albeit without tanks in the street and torture as a routine element – at least, not on the home front.

The 1990s became a period in which there was a virtual reconstruction of global capitalism along the lines of what Stephen Gill has called "disciplinary neoliberalism" (Gill 1995). This was not a term coined by the Left but one that emerged from the key promoters of the new model, such as the International Monetary Fund, which stated in 1997 that "the discipline of global product and financial markets applies not only to policy-makers via financial market pressures, but also to the private sector, making it more difficult to sustain unwarranted wage increases ... Markets will eventually exert their own discipline" (cited in Gills 2000: 4). The use of force by Reagan against the air traffic controllers in 1981 and by Thatcher against the miners in 1984–5 showed that market discipline would be backed by force when necessary. To create "investor confidence" there was a need to discipline those who did not submit to the new rules of the game, such as trade unions that insisted on using their collective bargaining strength – deemed illegitimate in the age of the individual – against the market and articulating an alternative logic, namely that of social protection.

In the global South the neoliberal globalization project led to a recrudescence of the primitive accumulation associated with the rise of capitalism in the North in the nineteenth century. David Harvey has dubbed it a process of "accumulation by dispossession", in which Marx's mechanisms of primitive accumulation were joined by new modalities such as "asset-stripping through mergers and acquisitions, and the promotion of levels of debt incumbency that reduce whole populations, even in the advanced capitalist countries, to debt peonage" (Harvey 2006: 147). Even newer mechanisms centred on intellectual property rights, whereby genetic materials could be patented by the pharmaceutical corporations to the detriment of traditional cultivators, effectively robbing original peoples of their traditional knowledge of herbs and other remedies. Education, health and other public assets that could be privatized would be privatized. Financialization went hand in hand with the offshoring of production, with the lowest wage being sought. Overall, in Harvey's words, "capitalism internalizes cannibalistic as well as predatory and fraudulent practices" (Harvey 2003: 148). We were seemingly returning to the era of Marx and, particularly, Luxemburg's prescient prediction of "barbarism or socialism", which is by no means overstated when we bear in mind the catastrophic consequences of unchecked climate change, which everyone today recognizes except for a few "climate change deniers".

If the workers of the Industrial Revolution were "dripping" in blood, so were those generated, exploited or cast aside by the globalization revolution almost 200 years later. In April 2013 an eight-storey building in Bangladesh's capital Dhaka collapsed, killing some 1,200 garment workers and injuring another 2,500. This tragedy could have been avoided; there had been ample warning that the building was unsafe and a number of shops and the bank had already vacated the building. But the mainly female garment workers were ordered back to work on pain of dismissal. The Rana Plaza massacre had repercussions across the world among other garment workers, but also with consumers. Just over 100 years previously the Triangle Waistshirt Company fire of 1911 in the US city of New York had killed 150 of the 500 young migrant women sewing items of clothing "by the piece", much as their counterparts in Bangladesh do now. In this typical sweatshop, the exit doors had been locked to encourage seamstresses to stay at their machines. The Triangle Waistshirt Company was acquitted of manslaughter but eventually paid the families who sued US$75.00 each.

Back to the future: a role for trade unions?

In 2006 the newly formed International Trade Union Congress declared a commitment to organizing workers that resonated with the founding principles of the First International in 1864, which pre-dated the emergence of strong national unions: "Congress highlights the need for working women and men to organise, now more than ever … [O]rganising [is] increasingly taking on an international dimension [and] solidarity requires that trade unions extend the opportunity of trade union membership to the unorganised" (cited in van der Linden 2008: 23). The labour movement had emerged in the middle of the nineteenth century in what was a pre-national form; that is to say, it was international in its concerns and perspectives. State formation and national consolidation would force labour into its national (even nationalist) format, but around 1850 we can discern a globalized labour condition that has a resonance with the globalization wave of the 1990s – hence our key theme of "back to the future".

From the 1830s onwards in Europe various associations of workers were formed with a clear transnational remit. Thus the International Working Men's Association declared its conviction in 1836 "that our interests – nay, the interests of working men in all countries of the world – are identified" and argued that "a federation of the working classes ... would form an admirable democracy" (cited in van der Linden 2008: 14). In 1848 a wave of democratic revolutions shook Europe and in the 1850s the technological revolutions of industrialization really took off. It was in this context that the First International (International Working Men's Association) was formed in 1864. It was, in many ways, a transitional organization, based partly on the traditions of the artisan and internationalism but also responding to the new capitalist mode of production. As van der Linden recounts, the First International was unlike its predecessors, which were predominantly political organizations; it was, rather, "to a high degree also an economic one, its rise and further development ... much more tied up with economic conditions and the fate of trade unions in the countries concerned" (van der Linden 1988: 14).

When we turn to the global South, as against the originally industrializing countries, we see that the "pre-national" period stretches well into the early twentieth century. Most analysts assume that labour in sub-Saharan Africa was also focused around the nation state. National boundaries and the national identification of workers are taken as a given. But that means eliding precolonial forms of ethnic identifications, massive migration flows and very significant regional political economies. For one critic of this perspective, Lucien van der Walt,

> transnational influences played a critical role in shaping working-class movements, which straddled borders and formed sections across the region and beyond it. Furthermore, ideological, ethnic and racial divides within the working class across Southern Africa played a more important role in constituting divisions than state borders.
>
> (van der Walt 2007: 223)

As with the European focus on the "standard employment contract", against which all others are measured, this is another case of a particular Western European pattern of state and nation development simply being taken to be universal. Any consideration of workers worldwide needs to use a more complex frame, open to the distinct patterns of capital accumulation worldwide.

Back now to the end of the twentieth century: we noted a resurgence of a whole range of social challenges to the free market order as the easy globalization facilitated by the collapse of communism in 1990 began to wane. Polanyi's problematic had posed the possibility that history moved through a series of "double movements", as mentioned above. This consisted of the drive by economic liberalism to extend ever further the self-regulating market, on the one hand, and the principle of "social protection", on the other, which would defend society from the deleterious effects of the market. This could be, according to Polanyi, through protective legislation or the formation of trade unions. At a later stage the welfare state in the global North and the developmental state in the global South would act as counter-movements, moderating at least the deleterious impact of the free market. While, for Polanyi, the counter-movement was "spontaneous", we can see how the system itself would develop mechanisms to protect the capitalist order from the effects of an unregulated market if taken to its logical conclusions.

It was not only the subaltern classes but also powerful capitalist interests that would be threatened by the anarchy of the market. The metaphor of the "double movement" allows us to grasp the diverse ways in which society reacts to the threats posed by the free market. There are a whole range of social and political forces – not least the working classes and their organizations – that seek to assert some form of social or democratic control over the market. And we should not forget that the rise of the modern labour movement was intimately tied in with the democratization of the absolutist state in the early bourgeois revolutions and the emergence of capitalism. Against the market-determined values of the first movement, the social counter-movement brings to the fore the social value of human activity. As Polanyi puts it for the middle of the twentieth century, "[T]he great variety of forms in which the 'collectivist' countermovement appeared [was attributable to] the broad range of the vital social interests affected by the expanding market mechanism" (Polanyi 2001 [1944]: 151). That is still the case today, with the added element that this counter-movement is a truly global one.

Globalization in the late twentieth century took Polanyi's "double movement" and scaled it up. National boundaries were clearly not as important as they had been in the mid-century period. As both Polanyi and Marx had predicted, the global extension of capitalism was inscribed in its very logic. Traditional or national barriers could not stand in the way of the ever-expanding market. Across the world, people were dispossessed of their traditional means of livelihood and pre-existing social networks and cultural values were eroded. The counter-movement of the early twenty-first century thus witnessed two major forms: one based on the greatly expanded working class of the South and the other based around those dispossessed by the market, which would include those driven from work and those in increasingly precarious work because of outsourcing in the North. We could call the first "Marx-type" resistance, reminiscent of the early days of the Industrial Revolution (for example, in China), and the second aspect of the counter-movement could be called "Polanyi-type" resistance by those dislocated by the second great transformation wrought by globalization (Silver 2003). The uneven but ultimately combined development of these two forms of resistance dominates the prospects for capitalism moving forward.

What does this mean for the organization of the trade unions and the wider labour movement? "Thoughtful trade unionists have come to recognise that playing safe is the most risky strategy. The present is either the end of the beginning or the beginning of the end" (Hyman 2004: 23). At the start of the twenty-first century many labour movement strategists and analysts would probably have thought they were witnessing the beginning of the end of labour as a major political voice. "There is no alternative" (to neoliberalism) was not just a slogan of the political Right but a palpable feeling in the general atmosphere. But in the first decade of the new century the mood began to shift, as the labour movement and trade unions regained some ground after the long neoliberal onslaught. Maybe we were now at the "end of the beginning" of a new era in which the workers and their organizations would begin to impact on the new global order they had helped to create. That is the premise of this book. It is not a falsely triumphal vision, however, but, rather, a realistic appraisal of the challenges of globalization and possible responses by the labour movement.

What we have begun to see from 2000 onwards is a clear recognition from the international trade union movement that globalization is a new paradigm that demands new strategies, tactics and organizational modalities, not least to deal with the new types of workers characteristic of the new information-based capitalism. In 1997 the International Confederation of Free Trade Unions had declared that globalization posed "the greatest challenge for unions in the twenty-first century" (ICFTU 1997). If the creation of a global economy was producing a global workforce then global unions might seem to be a logical development. But global economic power does not necessarily call forth a symmetrical global social counter-movement. The Netherlands Trade Union Confederation captured well the new mood when it declared that "the trade union movement must reinvent itself in order to deal with the challenges of the twenty-first century" (Kloosterboer 2007: 1). This will involve local, national and international action, basic organizing and engaging in the battle of ideas. We see signs of new forms of organizing in the wake of the 2007–9 global crisis and in response to the new more "flexible" forms of employment characteristic of the "gig economy". We need to assess both the achievements and limitations of this complex process of subordination and resistance of labour, especially now, after the virtual collapse of the neoliberal free market financial model.

While globalization undoubtedly signalled the end of "business as usual" for the nationally based trade union acting in isolation from the broader international labour movement, it generated a whole range of innovative responses (as well as steadily increasing analysis). This innovation has been seen at the local, national, regional and global levels. Sometimes the turn has been pragmatic and sometimes advances have been only partial. We can now say, however, that globalization has opened as many doors as it has closed, in so far as the nation state may have lost room to manoeuvre but workers have gained the ability to exchange ideas and even travel between countries, thus building solidarity We must also realize that labour responses at the global level are not in a zero-sum relationship with other national or local responses. There is no "one best way" for labour responses to globalization, with flexibility as the only given. The Dutch trade unions have argued persuasively for innovative trade union strategies to contest neoliberal globalization that

> will involve organising new groups hitherto underrepresented in the movement, local and transnational actions, a clear orientation towards social justice and coalitions with community groups and, last but not least, a vigorous engagement in the battle of ideas in terms of a vision for an alternative social order.   (FNV 2009: 2–3)

Of course, implementing this vision in practice is not so simple, it requires buy-in and a change of mindset at all levels of the workers' movement.

At the end of the twentieth century international trade unionism was confronted by a tragic paradox. There were more wage earners than ever before: around 3 billion, according to Richard Freeman (2008). The new International Trade Union Confederation and Global Unions together have more than 150 million members and cover more unions, workers and countries than ever before. This was on account of the incorporation of most of the formerly communist and national/populist unions. But neoliberal globalization implies the simultaneous weakening of traditional unionism's century-old national industrial base, the shift of that base to countries of the South (particularly China), the undermining of traditional job security and union rights and the decline, or disappearance, of support for social democratic parties, social reformist governments and the most powerful interstate agencies. Moreover, the unions were being confronted with a fact that – ensconced in their industrial, national or industrial relations cocoons – they had never previously felt it necessary to face, namely that in this globalizing world of labour maybe only one worker in 18 was unionized. Finally, with the disappearance of their competitors in communist or national/populist unions, the ICFTU/GU found itself not only in an alien and hostile world but ideologically disoriented. Previously it had been able to see itself not only as representing the most advanced union model but, as part of the "free West", opposed to both communist and national/populist unionism. Now it found itself left behind by the globalization of capital and the decreasing political interest of the international hegemons. From the perspective of the Great Financial Crisis (GFC) that began in autumn 2007, the trade union call for a "fair globalization" appears extremely limited and self-limiting indeed. When the theoretical organs of the financial bourgeoisie, such as the *Financial Times* and *The Economist*, openly proclaim the end of self-regulating market capitalism, it does seem pretty lame to call for "fair" globalization.

That the events in global financial markets in 2007–9 were unprecedented was clear to all concerned. The danger of a capitalist meltdown was real. In brief, as Robin Blackburn puts it, "The banks' needless pursuit of short-term advantage led to the greatest destruction of value in world history during the Great Crash of 2008" (Blackburn 2011: 35). This was clearly a systemic crisis and not just part of a normal business cycle. Unlike the situation in 1929, the major capitalist economies, and particularly their financial sectors, were so interlinked that there was no possibility of containing the crisis. The much-vaunted technological "New Age" had not materialized and capitalism had not escaped its cyclical boom-and-bust nature. The flotation of tech companies and the emergence of a renewable energy sector could hardly be the engines of a new phase of capitalism. In the past Schumpeter's "creative destruction" had allowed capitalism to emerge stronger and renewed from a crisis, as was the case after the 1930s. Now it seemed that the whole model of globalization, financialization and privatization was being brought into question, with no alternative on the horizon other than a managed or reregulated version of the same strategy.

The reaction to this unprecedented set of events was mixed. At first there was disbelief, some economists even arguing that the unregulated market regime had not been implemented systematically enough, but, on the whole, there was a full awareness that global capitalism was a systemic crisis. There was talk that we were "all Keynesians now", as the obvious need for state intervention to avert catastrophe was clear to everyone. All the international financial institutions and groupings of the leading economies met and agreed that measures needed to be taken to avert a return to national protectionism. In the event, as Blackburn noted soon afterwards, "[g]overnment rescue measures were to offer unlimited liquidity to the financial sector, while leaving the system largely intact" (Blackburn 2011: 35). For all the talk about the need to regenerate the financial sector to avert another catastrophe, after a few years it became clear that no major measures could be agreed transnationally. There was no political appetite to pursue root-and-branch reform, as national economies struggled to contain the recession and keep their own electorates onside. Soon it would be time for "back to business", with new schemes to make money out of money and handsome bonuses being paid to the architects of this dangerous machine.

One of the most interesting aspects of the global crisis was the new-found interest in the "emerging economies". For many mainstream economists, the BRICS countries and others would buck the trend and help the global economy get back on track. The former chief economist of the IMF even declared: "The situation in desperately poor countries isn't as bad as you'd think" (cited in Breman 2009: 30). Not only does this statement downplay the impact of the crisis across the global South, transmitted by all the networks created by globalization, but it also betrays a dangerous complacency. It is true that some countries, those less integrated into the dominant financial centres and their risky financial practices (such as Canada, for example), were less immediately and less severely impacted. It is also a fact that China, Brazil and India found some space to manoeuvre during the worst of the GFC, and they are the capitalist growth areas of the future. Overall, however, a global slowdown is bad for the South, for obvious reasons, and the economies there have diminishing capacity to take measures to protect themselves after 25 years of neoliberalism, during which the state's capacity to intervene has been curtailed.

It is, of course, too early to draw definitive conclusions around the long-term impact of the 2007–9 GFC on future global history. The parallels drawn with 1929 and the depression of the 1930s may have been overdrawn. And yet the business press continues to ponder the future of capitalism (no longer a term that polite commentators do not use) and refer to a new spectre haunting Europe (and the rest of the world), namely "the destruction of much of the institutional framework of globalization and undermining of the post-1989 international order" (Davis 2011: 2). It does now seem a very different world from that envisaged in 1989 by Francis Fukuyama, when the "end of history" was deemed nigh and economic and political liberalism was predicted to rule uncontested (Fukuyama 1989).

Although there has been a reorientation in reaction to globalization and the great crisis of 2007–9, international trade unions are also continuing their traditional efforts at union building, in defence of labour rights and in support of workers and unions internationally (Fairbrother & Hammer 2005). This seems to involve a new and more assertive language. An exemplar might be the International Transport Workers' Federation, the 2002 congress of which was devoted to the theme of "Globalising Solidarity". A turning point in its practical solidarity is indicated by, on the one hand, its failure to effectively support the Liverpool dock workers during the major lockout of 1995–8 and, on the other, its more effective support for the Australian dock workers during a related dispute later. But much national and international union solidarity activity is still carried out under the rubric of "development cooperation" and financed by the state or interstate organizations. At other times such activity is combined with union-to-union or worker-to-worker solidarity. It is notable, however, that most of this solidarity appears to be in a North to South direction. A more holistic, multifaceted and multidirectional notion of labour solidarity has yet to emerge, and the ICTU website reveals only an implicit recognition of the broader global solidarity movement.

What the historical parallels of the late nineteenth century and the emergence of the contemporary union movement teach us, however, is that this necessary shift will not be smooth and organic. It is more likely that alternative social forces (the "informal sector", for example) and geographical locations (the South, and in China in particular) will challenge and subvert the current structures and strategies. There are signs that trade unions are looking towards the new social movements – of migrants, women, the unemployed and others – for inspiration and support. Even in the United States, as Dan Clawson shows, "[l]abor's links with other [social movement] groups are denser and stronger than they have been for half a century" (Clawson 2003: 205), and this interaction has led to new, more progressive policies, as, for example, in relation to undocumented immigrants. Frances O'Grady, general secretary of the British Trade Union Congress, has recognized that "[g]rowing globalization has demonstrated ever more vividly that going it alone [for the unions] is not an option" (O'Grady 2004), and that not only do they need to engage seriously with the global justice movement but, if they wish to change the world, they will need to start by changing themselves.

The era of globalization has also became known as the "era of migration", and, in this element as well, we are perhaps going back to the future, as the original labour movement was, in part, a product of migration (see Chapter 7). There is now a sense that the current flows of migrant labour are fundamentally different from earlier forms of mass migration, in terms of volume and structural embeddedness. There are now 190 million people living outside their country of birth, which is approximately double the figure it was in 1980. We must also note the complexity of this new wave of worker movement. Contrary to media portrayals, only around a quarter of international migrants go from the South to the North, while nearly two-thirds of the flows happen within the global South. Furthermore, as was to be expected during the second great transformation, internal migration within China stood at 340 million workers between 1979 and 2009. In India two out of ten in a population that tops 1.2 billion are internal migrants.

In conclusion, I note that, in the current struggles to unify the working classes across ethnic, gender and skill divides, historical memories have had a powerful resonance. For example, we see mention in union debates of the Industrial Workers of the World (or "Wobblies"), formed in the United States in 1905, who articulated a revolutionary industrial unionism that cut across traditional guild and union lines. The grouping's promotion of the "one big union" concept is relevant today when unions again struggle to organize beyond the traditional workplaces. The model of workplace and other forms of grass-roots democracy brings back the notion of self-management, which may have relevance as people struggle to regain some control of their working lives. If unions do not seek to organize women, workers of colour or migrants, they cannot "represent the working class", as IWW leader Bill Haywood put it in 1905. The IWW ideology and principles revolved around the notion of solidarity, and the breaking down of the skilled/unskilled divide in particular. Today trade unions have a progressive role in responding to challenges and threats to society in its entirety, whether that be discrimination, pensions provision or education.

The next two chapters will explore in detail how work was shaped and how workers resisted in the postwar period (Chapter 2) and in the era of globalization (Chapter 3). As we have seen in this introductory chapter, the story of capitalism and the story of labour are inextricably linked. Workers and unions have been at the heart of social change and the democratization of the economy, society and the political order. It is not about a steady heroic advance: there have been many ups and downs. The point, however, is that capitalism cannot exist without workers, and that it is workers who "make the world go round".

2
THE GOLDEN ERA

Capitalism as a stable and seemingly sustainable mode of production came into its own in the aftermath of the Second World War. After this terrible, destructive period in human history, which began really in 1914, then continued with the 1929 crash and the slump of the 1930s, leading into the Second World War, a new vista of stable capital accumulation and harmonious labour relations opened up in the West. When the British prime minister, Harold Macmillan, in 1957 told people that "most of our people have never had it so good" he was not just politicking and he was not just speaking of Britain. We need only to recall that, between 1950 and 1973, output per capita in the industrialized countries rose *three times* more rapidly than the average of the previous 130 years. This new model capitalism created a new model of social regulation, which included Fordist production methods and the welfare state, at least for the advanced industrial societies. The first two sections of this chapter examine the basis of this unpredicted expansion of capitalism and its implications for the workers of the West. This was the heyday of national capitalism and corporatism, of the increased role of the state in economic affairs and in regulating relations between labour and capital. But, as the third section shows, the Third World, or developing countries, did not partake of the synergy and prosperity of the golden era. A new international division of labour, or NIDL, incorporated these countries into a global capitalist economy, but in a subordinate and uneven manner. The final section of this chapter examines the various versions accounting for the end of the golden era at some point in the early 1970s. My interpretation of the making and unmaking of the golden era, in both the North and the South, is specifically in terms of its implications for workers and the labour movement.

New model capitalism

The great crash of 1929, and the long depression of the 1930s that followed, provided a salutary shock to the economic and political leaders of capitalism.

It was recognized that free market forces would have to be tempered by state intervention if capitalism was to achieve a stable form, resistant to such shocks in the future. The central feature of this new model of "managed" capitalism was a generalized "acceptance of the so-called mixed economy – that is, a capitalist framework within which state enterprise was tolerated and the government held responsible for managing the economy" (Armstrong, Glyn & Harrison 1984: 193). Equally significant was the fact that "workers obtained certain rights and material benefits" (Armstrong, Glyn & Harrison 1984: 193) from this dispensation. At least in the core capitalist countries, as exemplified in the United States by the New Deal of the 1930s, workers had the right to jobs (and even pay rises), received welfare services and could join trade unions. Economic relations are always mediated through social relations, and in this new model capitalism, which consolidated itself in the postwar period, the labour/capital relation achieved a certain stability with consensus over its key parameters. In the then developing world the depression of the 1930s created the conditions for import substitution industrialization in some countries. The postwar period saw the definitive end of colonialism based on direct political domination and, in its place, the development of a neocolonialism based on economic domination. The capitalist world was becoming integrated into a coherent whole, albeit unevenly, and excluding those parts of the world under the sway of state socialist regimes committed to endogenous growth.

John Maynard Keynes had produced the macroeconomic tools to prevent a recurrence of the economic destruction and mass unemployment of the 1930s. The Keynesian toolbox is quite simple: it involves the use of monetary policy by the state to slow down or stimulate the economy, the use of spending and reserves to achieve the same objectives, and the manipulation of the minimum wage/workforce levels (Lipietz 1987: 38). This mode of regulation of the capitalist economy greatly facilitated the high and stable growth rates of the golden era. Keynes had, in his *General Theory* of 1936 (Keynes 1936), laid out the basis for this new institutionalization of aggregate demand management, but it was only after the Second World War (and his death) that the approach was actually implemented. The leaders of the capitalist economies in the West had noted a Soviet Union industrializing strongly during the 1930s while they were in depression. Even the economic success of Nazi Germany was a salutary lesson to the depression-marked capitalist democracies. As Stephen Marglin puts it, "[T]he Western democracies were put under considerable political pressure to prevent output and employment from being regulated by swings in private confidence" (Marglin 1990: 5). Keynes' "animal spirits" were going to have to be tamed and the vicissitudes of the market controlled, at least to some extent. Workers in the West had come out of the Second World War strengthened. Unionization had increased in quantitative terms but there was also a fundamental leap in confidence in the ability of the organized working class to run society for the common good.

It was the spectre of mass unemployment that was to haunt capitalist policy-makers as they moved out of depression and war into the golden era. Laissez-faire attitudes towards employment were not credible after the catastrophe of the 1930s. The new countercyclical economic policies prioritized the achievement of full employment, or, at least, the avoidance of mass unemployment. A social compromise between capital and wage labour would replace the free-for-all of laissez-faire economic dogma. High growth rates were matched by high employ-ment rates and rising living standards for most workers in the advanced capit-alist economies. Expansionary demand-side policies made sense to the capitalist elites, and workers granted the new "reformed" capitalism a certain legitimacy. In retrospect, though, the commitment to full employment was storing up problems for the system. Michał Kalecki, the Polish economist, who some assert came up with "Keynesianism" independently from Keynes, had argued that

> [t]he *maintenance* of full employment would cause social and polit-ical changes which would give a new impetus to the opposition of the business leaders. Under a regime of permanent full employment, "the sack" would cease to play its role as a disciplinary measure [and] "dis-cipline in the factories" and "political stability" are more appreciated by business leaders than profits. Their class instinct tells them that lasting full employment is unsound from their point of view and that unemployment is an integral part of the normal capitalist system.
>
> (Kalecki 1971 [1943]: 140–1)

This, arguably, would be a factor in the later shift by most governments to supply-side economic policies and contractionary demand policies.

The international dimension was also crucial in ensuring the stability of world capitalism in the postwar period. This was centred on the so-called *Pax Americana*, a world system in which political and military hegemony was vested in one power, namely the United States. In the postwar period a return to a pure gold standard for international finance was impossible, so the Bretton Woods Agreement of 1944 established a "flexible" gold standard. As the US dollar was the only con-vertible currency, this effectively made it equivalent to gold; as Michael Webber and David Rigby note, "[L]inking the dollar and gold was a boon to trade and the emerging postwar international financial system" (Webber & Rigby 1996: 27). Restrictions in the full flow of goods would be removed, and trade would reinvig-orate the capitalist world system. Bretton Woods created a system of fixed parities among the world's major currencies, to be adjusted through the new international body it set up, the International Monetary Fund. Although many of the 1944 agreements were never implemented, the Bretton Woods system created a certain degree of international financial stability until 1971, when it was unilaterally scrapped by the United States. The American "peace" was also ensured by force, which included open or covert military interventions in Korea (1950), Iran (1953), Guatemala (1954), Lebanon (1957) and the Dominican Republic (1965). Undisputed hegemony was shattered, however, by the ignominious defeat of the global power in Vietnam (1973), the effects of which were felt in the impunity with which the Organization of the Petroleum Exporting Countries raised the price of oil in 1973, thus hastening the demise of the golden era.

The *Pax Americana* also meant an unprecedented expansion of US business interests through the (in)famous "multinationals": the barely 7,000 overseas affiliates of US corporations in 1950 had risen to over 23,000 by 1966. During the 1950s and 1960s the growth rate of multinational investment increased dramatically, and they became the main agents of capitalist internationalism. The initial wave of postwar international investment originated in the United States, promoted by the Marshall Fund for Europe, and accounted for more than half the global total of foreign direct investment. The US corporations invested in and dominated much of the oil industry, mining and agriculture across the world. In the 1960s they also set up, behind protectionist barriers, to engage in manufacturing – for example, in Latin America. Later, European and Japanese international firms would become major players on the global stage. Thus, while the United States remained the largest overseas investor, its share of global FDI dropped from around 50 per cent in 1960 to 25 per cent in the mid-1990s. Although there was the occasional "multinational" from South Korea (Daewoo) and Venezuela (the state oil company) in the "top 100", the "vast majority of MNCs and FDI flows originate within, and move among, OECD countries" (Held *et al.* 1999: 248). It was among the "triad" of North America, Western Europe and Japan that real transnational power lay. In the postwar period MNCs became the main bearers of capitalist relations worldwide, and they arguably paved the way for globalization after the collapse of the golden era and the neoliberalism of the 1980s. They had risen to a position where they dominated the global production and distribution of many goods and services and were at the cutting edge of technological development.

The third pillar of the new model capitalism, after Keynesian macroeconomic management and the US-led international financial and investment regimes, was undoubtedly corporatism. Subject to a multiplicity of debates and definitions, theories of corporatism assert that unions, business and government come together to negotiate economic policies: "[U]nions are organized by the state and ... the conduct of industrial relations is structured through a system of compulsory arbitration" (Roxborough 1984: 3). For trade unions in the West it made sense to seek political representation for labour within state structures, as was the case with the paradigmatic formation of the British

Labour Party in 1900. The class struggle could be "managed" in the interests of labour as much as capital, or so it seemed. Representatives of the working class were at one and the same time fighting the capitalist system and striving for its continued expansion to the benefit of workers. Corporatism in some developing countries also allowed trade unions to "punch above their weight", as they engaged in political bargaining on the basis of fairly meagre social weight, as was the case in Latin America with workers who were crucial to the export economy, such as miners. The state capital/labour relation took many different forms, and the term "corporatism" may well be too flexible to be useful. The main point, as Philip Armstrong, Andrew Glyn and John Harrison make in their broad-canvas analysis of the making and breaking of the postwar boom, is that "the right of workers to organised representation was [an] important feature of the consensus" (Armstrong, Glyn & Harrison 1984: 199). Whether in the form of institutionalized collective bargaining, as epitomized by Britain, the co-determination system of Germany, Bolivian miners' co-management, French indicative planning or Japan's particular labour relations, there was a generalized belief in, and consensus around, the legitimacy of workers' representation and on the desirability of compromise over conflict.

It is important to note that corporatism also took an international form. The International Labour Organization was formed as a specialist UN agency in 1919 and was to become an integral element of managing labour/capital relations in the postwar world. In its origins it was a response of the Western powers to the perceived menace of the Russian Revolution. When US president Franklin Roosevelt presided over a major ILO conference in 1944 it signalled US endorsement of its role in terms of an international social policy. From its inception the ILO reflected the principle of tripartite representation, with representatives from government, employers and trade unions sitting down together. Its commitment to trade union freedom and collective bargaining during the golden era was part and parcel of US hegemony over the "free world". Robert Cox, in a significant critical insider account of the ILO, argues: "Tripartism can now be defined, in the perspective of the United States, as the reality of the corporative state veiled by the still vigorous myth of free enterprise" (Cox 1996: 427). Parts of organized labour would be allowed to sit at the "top table", with employers and governments, but at the cost of excluding the majority. Corporatism, at the international level, shifted from an understanding that the class struggle needed to be institutionalized to a quite non-conflictual version of tripartism in which managerial ideologies of production would exist unchallenged. A bitter fruit of this ideology, at its most extreme, was the long history of the US American Federation of Labor – Congress of Industrial Organizations acting as a labour agent of US imperialism, especially in its Latin American backyard. US labour acted effectively as an arm of the State Department, openly supporting "anti-communist" dictators repressing workers and their unions, to the extent that many trade unionists in the region articulated the view that CIO = CIA.

What the new model capitalism meant in terms of the world of work was, in the first place, a vast increase in the number of workers. In the advanced capitalist countries total employment rose by 30 per cent between 1950 and 1970. This was a significant increase in the size of the working class, but the degree of proletarianization was even greater if we take into account the decline from 30 per cent to 15 per cent of the self-employed, as a proportion of those officially classified as in work (Armstrong, Glyn & Harrison 1984: 236). The secular decline of agriculture and the rise of the new services sector marked a fundamental recomposition of the Western working classes. Increased mechanization and technological development led to increased skill and educational levels. Proletarianization led to an increase in unionization as well, with trade union members in the advanced capitalist countries increasing from 49 million in 1952 to 62 million in 1970 (Armstrong, Glyn & Harrison 1984: 238).

If we allow for a time lag of a decade for the so-called developing countries, we can see a similar process of proletarianization. Agriculture, once the main employer by far, declined in the "upper middle-income" developing countries from 50 per cent in 1960 to 30 per cent in 1980, and from 62 per cent to 46 per cent in the "middle-income" countries. The degree of industrialization was not so marked, yet the percentage of the labour force employed in manufacturing increased between 1960 and 1980 from 20 to 28 per cent in the upper middle-income countries and from 15 to 21 per cent in the middle-income countries. Although they were very unevenly spread across what became known in the postwar period as the Third World, capitalist relations of production were making considerable advances. There were few signs of a "social compromise" between capital and labour, and the process was more akin to the bloody "primitive accumulation" described by Marx, but it was the development of capitalism nevertheless. As Bill Warren once put it provocatively: "Whatever the new world being created in Latin America, Asia and Africa is to be, nothing can be gained from a refusal to recognise the existence of the developing capitalist societies already there" (Warren 1980: 255). With the emergence of a new international division of labour in the 1960s (see below), this development of a proletariat across the globe shifted from an extensive to an intensive mode. This was probably a necessary prerequisite to the development of globalization in later decades.

It is necessary to reiterate how uneven this undoubtedly dynamic capitalist period was. It looks more golden in retrospect than it actually was. It lasted for a mere 30 years and was fed and conditioned by a Cold War that threatened the world with annihilation. In a bold re-analysis of the long postwar upturn and its subsequent undoing, Robert Brenner (1998) has questioned in particular the view around harmonious capital/labour relations implicit in most versions of this history. Across the political spectrum there has been an assumption that workers were accommodated within the new regime of capital accumulation. For Brenner, on the contrary, it seems obvious that, for example, the postwar boom in Japan and Germany was "premised upon the suppression of labour and its consequent acceptance of low and (relative to productivity growth) slowly increasing wages" (Brenner 1998: 42), rather than on the consolidation of some capital–labour accord or compromise. In relation to the United States, Brenner is able to bring evidence to show that, "[c]ontrary to received wisdom, there was never anything approaching an 'accord' between capital and labour ... at any time during the post-war period" (Brenner 1998: 60). So, at most, we can place the labour–capital accommodation in relative terms (compared to the open class warfare of the neoliberal era), and then mainly for Britain and Western Europe. There was, of course, another side to the postwar boom, namely the peripheral Fordism of the developing world, usually instigated by highly repressive political regimes, committed to no form of accommodation with labour whatsoever.

Fordism and welfare

At the heart of the "new model capitalism" lay the Fordist labour process and the welfare state. When Henry Ford began producing his famous Model T motorcars in Detroit in the 1910s, he created a new work method. From the First World War F. W. Taylor's so-called "scientific management" had been introduced into most advanced industrial societies, based mainly on the separation between planning and execution in the workplace and the "one best way" to carry out a task. Taylorism, as it became known, really came into its own only when it was transmuted into Fordism. Ford pioneered the principles of mass production: introducing standardized products and working methods. His innovation of the assembly line enabled Taylor's "time and motion" method to be vigorously applied, as the machine henceforth dictated the work pace for workers and the level of skill required was reduced. Ford also introduced a daily wage ("measured day work") to replace piece rates, however, along with the famous "five dollar day", to attract workers to his car plants and to provide workers an income that would create a market for his goods. Antonio Gramsci, a contemporary observer of Fordism (as Lenin was of Taylorism), noted perceptively that its aim was "[t]o build up an organic and well-articulated skilled labour force or a team of specialised workers [, which] has never been easy" (Gramsci 1971b: 312). Fordism was seen by Gramsci as eminently rational, with a trade-off between higher wages and the associated rise in living standards, on the one hand, and a new labour process demanding an unprecedented expenditure of muscular and nervous energy, on the other. From its inception, then, Fordism was a form of capitalist production but also a mode of consumption. As Gramsci puts it in a striking way: "Hegemony here is born in the factory" (Gramsci 1971b: 285). This new logic of social transformation was to have profound effects on the social institutions and wage labour/capital relations during the golden era.

Fordism may be taken as an "ideal type" but, clearly, it had many variants across countries and across time. Robert Boyer refers appropriately to "one model, many national brands" (Boyer 1995: 27) in relation to Fordism. From this perspective he develops a typology of different national Fordisms, in a similar way to Adam Tickell and Jamie Peck's model (Table 2.1). What is particularly

Table 2.1 Variants of Fordism

Regime	Characteristics	Examples
"Classic Fordism"	Mass production and consumption by social-democratic welfare state.	United States
"Flex-Fordism"	Decentralized, federalized state. Close cooperation between financial and industrial capital, including facilitation of inter-firm cooperation.	West Germany
"Flawed Fordism"	Inadequate integration of financial and production capital at the level of the nation state. Archaic and obstructive politics identified by some authors.	United Kingdom
"State Fordism"	State plays leading role in creation of conditions of mass production, including state control of industry. *L'état entrepreneur.*	France
"Delayed Fordism"	Cheap labour immediately adjacent to Fordist core. State intervention had key role in rapid industrialization in 1960s.	Italy, Spain
"Peripheral Fordism"	Local assembly followed by export of Fordist goods. Heavy indebtedness. Authoritarian state structures coupled with movement for democracy; attempts to emulate Fordist accumulation system in absence of corresponding mode of social regulation.	Mexico, Brazil
"Racial Fordism"	Dualistic workforce. Privileged minority has North-American-style working conditions and remuneration levels that rely upon authoritarian state structures and "super-exploitation" of majority population.	South Africa
"Primitive Taylorization"	Taylorist labour process with almost endless supply of labour. Bloody exploitation and huge extraction of surplus value. Dictatorial states and high social tension.	Malaysia, Bangladesh, Philippines
"Hybrid Fordism"	Profit-driven expansion based upon modified Taylorism. Truncated internal market, societal segmentation and underdeveloped welfare state. Indirect wage indexation.	Japan

Source: Tickell and Peck (1995: 362).

interesting about this model is that it integrates the particular Fordist accumulation patterns with the Keynesian/welfare modes of regulation for each case. It is also a less Eurocentric model than those usually found in the industrial relations literature, with due attention being paid to "peripheral Fordism" and the "racial Fordism" typical of apartheid-era South Africa.

If there was one enduring legacy from the Great Depression it was the welfare state, that "safety net" to catch those who fell through the formal wage-earning structures of capitalist society. In Britain's paradigmatic welfare state, the 1942 Beveridge Report was premised on the notion of a "social minimum" of welfare, based on compulsory social insurance. While the origins of welfarism can be traced back to the turn of the twentieth century, it was in the postwar period that it was consolidated and generalized, in a way that commanded cross-party support. Coverage of previous unemployment schemes was broadened beyond full-time industrial workers. In relation to the Western European countries, Armstrong, Glyn and Harrison found that, "[c]omparing the situation in 1975 with the year of introduction ... the duration of benefits had doubled ... the delay before eligibility had halved ... and the period of disqualification had halved" (Armstrong, Glyn & Harrison 1984: 196). Far and away the most radical innovation was the British National Health Service, based on need, as of right and universal. Certainly, the welfare state never came close to eradicating poverty, even in the advanced capitalist countries. It did fundamentally reform the laissez-faire capitalism of the 1930s, however, and provide it with a "human face". To some degree it was only in retrospect, as the neoliberal age developed, that the welfare state acquired a more positive connotation. From the perspective of the developing countries, without even a rudimentary welfare state in most cases, or at best a formal system that did not deliver, the Western welfare state seemed desirable indeed to workers and their families.

The welfare state was probably not an unambiguous good for the working classes. A critical reading of the Keynesian welfare state, especially in its heyday, argued that it was designed to secure popular consent, to ensure the smooth "reproduction" of the working classes. It was seen as one of the repressive ideological mechanisms of the state, along with schools, housing departments and the family, an "ideological state apparatus" (see Althusser 1971) to match the "repressive state apparatus" of army, police, and so on. These were seen to work hand in glove to tame a rebellious working class – a case of an "iron fist in a velvet glove", as it were. Even when writers did not see the welfare state as an unambiguous offence against libertarianism, there was a tendency (in retrospect) to overstress its negative elements. As late as 1979 Ian Gough, author of an influential political economy of the welfare state, could argue that the welfare state "simultaneously embodies tendencies to enhance social welfare, to develop the powers of individuals, to exert social control over the blind play of market forces;

and tendencies to repress and control people, to adapt them to the requirements of the capitalist economy" (Gough 1979: 12). As the economic ideas of monetarism began to exert their grip on the Western political imagination, the welfare state began to be seen as an unaffordable luxury. As mass unemployment became the norm, it became harder to see a public health system and a welfare state "safety net" as somehow repressive social institutions "taming" a naturally rebellious working class.

If we now add up the ideas of Keynes, Ford and Beveridge (KFB), we get the basic ingredients of the "Fordist" social compromise that dominated across the advanced capitalist countries in the golden era. This KFB model not only dominated the economic scene, working relations and consumption patterns; it also shaped society as a whole and its particular postwar institutional arrangements. As Boyer puts it, "An unprecedented conjunction of political and social forces led to this new order" (Boyer 1995: 21). The rebuilding of war-torn societies took precedence over social and political differences, at least to some extent, and temporarily there was a paradigm shift. The Malthusian capitalist became a rational manager. The radical trade unionist took on board "scientific management" methods. Above these new "social partners" stood the KFB state, setting up the necessary public infrastructure and maintaining the countercyclical economic policy to keep things going. Managers would be allowed to manage by labour, and workers could expect a share of productivity gains as Fordism matured and to be "looked after" by the welfare state if necessary. The new production methods would be matched by new consumption patterns across the working classes, which helped legitimize the new order. The main point is that the KFB social order was an integrated whole, a seamless package with considerable synergies. As Boyer puts it, in summing up this virtuous circle, "It can be shown that a rather coherent accumulation regime has been built upon this genuine social compromise" (Boyer 1995: 22)

How did the workers of the West fare under Fordism? I have already mentioned the quantitative expansion of the Western working classes and the development or trade unionism. Yet, as Armstrong, Glyn and Harrison argue,

> [t]he increase in output was out of all proportion to the growth of employment. The number of people classified as in civilian employment rose by only 29 per cent between 1952 and 1973. So most of the extra production represented an increase in output per worker. Annual productivity doubled.   (Armstrong, Glyn & Harrison 1984: 168)

This great leap forward in productivity was not a result of longer hours worked, as these decreased steadily (albeit at less than 1 per cent per annum over this period). It was, rather, the quantity and the quality of the means of production that improved. There was, in essence, a veritable technological revolution during this period. According to Eric Hobsbawm,

> More than any previous period, the golden era rested on the most advanced and often esoteric scientific research, which now found practical application within a few years. Industry and even agriculture for the first time moved decisively beyond the technology of the nineteenth century. (Hobsbawm 1994: 265)

The language used by Hobsbawm to describe the golden era parallels that of Marx and Engels in *The Communist Manifesto*, who waxed lyrical on the capitalist revolutions of their day. It is well to remember, though, that, if the means or production per worker doubled in the advanced capitalist economies, this also meant that, effectively, "it was as though each worker was confronted by two machines where one stood before" (Armstrong, Glyn & Harrison 1984: 168).

There was a debate in the 1970s about "unequal exchange" between nations that also had implications for the position of Western workers in the global system. The original, if idiosyncratic, arguments for this analysis came from Arghiri Emmanuel (Emmanuel 1972), who applied a Ricardian international trade model to derive the notion of unequal exchange: basically, unequal quantities of labour were involved in international trade, to the detriment of the developing countries. The model involves the international mobility of capital and the international immobility of labour power. Emmanuel saw wages as an independent variable in this model (Marx's moral-historical element), which results in capital-intensive industrialization at the centre and labour-intensive methods at the periphery. The unequal exchange of their products in the international market results in uneven development. Other writers argued, to the contrary, that it was the uneven source of capitalism as a mode of production that led to wage (and productivity) differentials, and not the other way around. Emmanuel was also criticized for the divisive implications of his political conclusion that Western workers benefited from unequal exchange and thus were unlikely to engage in solidarity actions with their counterparts in the developing world. With hindsight, it is not so much the intricacies of the unequal exchange model that are interesting but the fact that there was a critical consensus that capital accumulation on a world scale was based on exploitation. Later the only consensus would be that all workers must be part of the globalization process and not suffer from exclusion.

Meanwhile, in Eastern Europe workers were labouring behind the Iron Curtain under what has been called the "iron age" (Lipietz 1995: 355). Lenin had been a great admirer of Taylorism's "time and motion" mechanical approach to work, and he once infamously defined socialism as "soviets plus electrification".

This was an industrial model of modernization that owed a lot to capitalism, in spite of a commitment to centralized planning as against the market allocation of resources. In the 1950s it seemed, from the prodigious Soviet growth rates, that the golden era had its Eastern counterpart. The drive to industrialize was paying off, even if the system was inefficient and the human cost huge. János Köllö characterizes Eastern Europe's "dark" golden era thus: "Disorder with a 'human face', not the strict Taylorian rule in the factory; anomie and slyness, not the Orwellian drill; informal bargaining and individual evasion of unfavourable local conditions, not the complete submission of workers" (Köllö 1995: 291). In the resource-constrained economies of Eastern Europe there was a rapidly growing level of employment. This was an extensive, rather than an intensive, pattern of capital accumulation. Unemployment rates were very low and workers had considerable rights not only to a job but also to social rights in that job. By the 1980s this model was in crisis, and the East joined the West's race into the globalization and deregulation new order. An interesting point is whether this crisis of modernization was more akin to the West's golden era crisis (see later in this chapter) or to the South's debt-driven crisis of the 1980s. We can probably surmise a third way into crisis even if the end result was, on the whole, a "Third-Worldization" of the East.

For Alain Lipietz, the "iron age" model of Soviet labour/capital relations was a cousin of the Fordist one, based on a menu of "Taylorism plus tenure" that allowed it to compete with the West in the 1950s (Lipietz 1995: 356). The extensive pattern of accumulation that ensued did not really require much flexibility, and it was well placed to absorb a surplus of rural labourers. In the transition from a non-industrialized to an industrializing economy this model was productive enough. Indeed, Leninism in the developing world generally took on the characteristics of a developmentalist ideology as much as those of a political philosophy. Wages grew only slowly and there was not a vast increase in mass consumption patterns, so that surpluses accumulated readily throughout this period. As Lipietz notes, however, "[T]he compromise of 'tenure with low wage' appears then as completely stagnationist" (Lipietz 1995: 356). There was a pressing need for more flexibility, even with the assumed parameters of the state socialist model. With a considerable delay compared to the West, the demands of "flexibility" nevertheless made themselves felt. So-called "external flexibility" – the right of managers to redeploy labour – meant the end of tenure. By the time this crisis in capital/labour relations came to the fore in the 1990s, the full-blown effects of political crisis were being felt. As state socialism collapsed, the social-democratic compromise of Fordism was no longer on offer and the workers of the East were brusquely introduced to the rigours of neoliberal flexibility under the aegis of globalization.

New international division of labour

If we take a global perspective on the long postwar boom in the West/North, perhaps the most noticeable transformation is the emergence of a new international division of labour. In the "old", or colonial, division of labour, Third World labour had been essential to the industrial revolutions in the West. This process of primitive accumulation led to plunder and forced labour across what was to become known as the Third World. The cotton industry of Britain, for example, was dependent on the slavery of the cotton-producing areas of North America. The growing mobility of capital – which began to penetrate all areas of the globe – was matched by mass migrations of labour, that unique and sometimes recalcitrant "factor of production". The keystone to capitalist "development" has always been labour. As Sydney Mintz writes in relation to the Caribbean, "[F]or most of the islands during most of their post-Columbian history, labour had to be impressed, coerced, dragged and driven to work – and most of the time, to simplify the problem of discipline, labour was enslaved" (Mintz 1974: 45). The sugar, cacao, gold, diamonds, wheat, beef and oil that fed the West's industrialization and population created for the non-West a subordinate role in a colonial division of labour sustained for centuries by force of arms. Imperialism was an integral element in the development of capitalism and helped shape its economic, political, social and cultural characteristics.

The basic argument of the NIDL theorists was that the traditional colonial division of labour, in which the Third World was relegated to the production of raw materials, began to change in the 1960s. Decolonization, and then the "economic imperialism" of the postwar period, began to generate pressures for change. For Folker Fröbel, Jürgen Heinrichs and Otto Kreye (1980: 13), three basic preconditions were required for this to happen.

- The breakdown of traditional social economic structures in the Third World, which led to the emergence of a vast pool of cheap available labour.
- The fragmentation of the industrial production process, which allowed unskilled sub-processes to be relocated to the Third World.
- The development of cheap international transport and communications technology, which made this relocation possible.

The NIDL is seen to have fundamentally restructured the relations of production in the Third World, with the emergence of a substantial manufacturing sector oriented towards the world market. The new "world market factories" engaged in a process of "super-exploitation" of their mainly female workers, recruited for their alleged submissiveness and "nimble fingers" (Elson & Pearson 1981).

This shift away from a purely agricultural and raw materials supply role, with all its limitations, was seen to create the conditions for the emergence of a classical opposition between capital and wage labour. For some of its most incisive analysts and critics, the NIDL also "contains the *possibility* of international solidarity between workers" (Fröbel, Heinrichs & Kreye 1980: 406, emphasis in original). We return later, in Chapter 9, to the issue of international labour solidarity but first we must examine the limitations of the NIDL theory.

The NIDL theory was not without its critics, even at the time (in the 1970s) when it appeared to reflect a changing global reality. Essentially, it focused on the world market, the level of circulation, to the detriment of changes at the level of production. As with the dependency theory of underdevelopment, to which it related in many ways, the NIDL thesis neglected the role of the state in the Third World. It was almost as if the "world market" had a life of its own and could impose its will across the globe. Furthermore, the NIDL thesis – at least, as articulated by Fröbel, Heinrichs and Kreye (1980) – seriously underestimated the level of industrialization that existed in the Third World prior to the 1960s. This led it to isolate the "world market factories" and the famous free trade zones as the main, even sole, sites of capitalist development in the Third World. In fact, if we take a broader perspective on Third World social formations, their importance is relative. If we take a more historical perspective on Third World industrialization, we also see that the "old" division of labour was in crisis in the 1930s and had probably reached its zenith at the time of the First World War. A final weakness of the NIDL thesis is the assumption, which is at least premature, that labour was achieving the same level of mobility as capital. In spite of these qualifications, a recast NIDL approach did direct researchers towards certain basic transformations in the global economy and the growing importance of Third World workers in the world system.

In reality, we can point to at least two phases of the NIDL. The first was typified by import substitution industrialization in the larger Latin American countries during the 1930s. For example, in Brazil the state had set up its first steel mill (Volta Redonda) and car plant in the early 1940s. This laid the basis for the expansion of capital accumulation in the 1950s, a process that acquired its own endogenous dynamic. State participation in fixed capital formation more than doubled between 1947 and 1960. It was only after this infrastructural basis had been laid by the national state that foreign capital became an important source of investment. By the 1970s manufactured goods accounted for more than a half of the total exports from Brazil. Some of these goods, such as textiles and shoes, were relatively labour-intensive but there was also a major automobile industry, in which the labour force was subsumed under Fordist methods of production. This pattern was typical of Argentina and Mexico too, but also applied elsewhere – India, for example. By the 1920s there were 4.5 million wage workers in the Indian manufacturing industry. By the 1960s, before the internationally generated NIDL was supposed to commence, these countries (and also the Philippines) possessed internally generated industrial sectors based on production for the home market. To view the Third World in its entirety as a simple reservoir of cheap labour (as the NIDL theories tended to do) neglects the dynamic development of capitalism across the globe.

The second wave of the NIDL saw the emergence of the East Asian newly industrializing countries in the 1970s, such as South Korea, Taiwan, Hong Kong, Singapore and Malaysia. The export-led industrialization of these countries since the late 1960s has often been associated with the establishment of FTZs, the modern equivalent of the nineteenth-century mining "enclaves". By 1975 there were some 80 FTZs across the Third World, of which 50 were located in East Asia. There were, of course, many more "world market factories" producing for the international market. Fröbel, Heinrichs and Kreye estimate that by 1975 there were 725,000 Third World workers engaged in this internationalized production sector, of whom more than half were based in East Asia (Fröbel, Heinrichs & Kreye 1980: 307). The NIDL led to a wave of relocation of electronics and textile plants from the West to the NICs. Thus, in the textile sector alone, the Third World share of total exports rose from 15 per cent in the mid-1960s to almost 25 per cent by the mid-1970s. The restructuring of the global electronics industry was even more dramatic, with the relocation of most semi-skilled manufacturing operations to the NICs. Through the "global assembly line" of the textile and electronics industries many more Third World workers (especially women workers) became an integral part of the world working class. By the 1990s these economies had become a leading growth area of the global economy and had also experienced their own capitalist crises.

If we take a broad retrospective view of the countries that entered the NIDL in the 1930s and then in the 1960s, there are two major characteristics of note. In the first place, this was mainly a *state*-led industrialization; and, second, it was part of a *national* development strategy. As Jong-Il You writes in relation to South Korea:

> The dominance of the state in guiding economic development ... is well documented. The state dictated the direction of production and investment activities with a variety of incentives and sanctions, thereby controlling and shaping the accumulation process. The state played a hegemonic role in shaping the capital–labour relations, too.
>
> (You 1995: 17)

This would be a general pattern, with differences of degree and format only, across both old and new NICs. The role of the state is important to note because it contradicts some of the *ex post facto* neoliberal myths about the East Asian NICs in particular. It is also well to recall, as against the neoliberal myth, that the big advance in the industrialization of the developing world occurred under the aegis of mainly nationalist regimes, albeit often authoritarian or openly repressive ones. Today, when "reform" is associated directly with the opening of these economies to the world market, we should stress the role of a certain degree of protectionism in the past. Indeed, all development theories until the 1980s, whether conservative modernization theories "made in the USA" or the radical alternative "dependency" theory originating in Latin America, conceived of development as *national* development.

As to the labour process that emerged under the NIDL, there are two main variants. The first is what Lipietz has called "bloody Taylorism" (Lipietz 1987). This is a Taylorism for the era of "primitive accumulation", a labour process guaranteed by repressive political regimes that maintained the regimentation of labour as much as the classical "time and motion" studies inside the plants. There is little attempt to construct a hegemonic type of labour process in which "acquiescence" is achieved through a "human relations" type of approach to workers. A premium is placed, rather, on the "adaptability" of the workforce to the demands of the Taylorist process, with the fragmentation of tasks and repetitive work routines at its core. The technological revolution in the West during the golden era led to a breaking down of the labour process, with less skilled elements being relocated to the Third World. While relative surplus value, according to Marx's criteria, is extracted from these workers, absolute surplus value is also important, given the lengthening of the working day, the employment of minors and the constant and direct compulsion by supervisors. As Lipietz writes,

> The results are as spectacular as the means used to achieve them. The rate of surplus-value rises sharply, whereas it remains stable in the central "Fordist" regime. The rise is due to the opening of the "scissors" between stagnant purchasing power and rising apparent productivity.
>
> (Lipietz 1987: 76)

This regime of accumulation proved extremely profitable to the NICs but it could not escape the basic Keynesian constraint that the home market was slow to develop only within this logic.

In some developing countries a genuine, if peripheral, Fordist system did emerge. For Lipietz, "peripheral Fordism" is a "true Fordism" in so far as it involves both mechanization and a growing consumer market, but it remains peripheral, in that the skilled jobs and production processes remain largely outside the South (Lipietz 1987: 78–9). This model fits countries such as Brazil, South Korea and

Mexico. The motor industries in these countries, for example, were sub-Fordist only in the sense that the auto workers did not reap the social benefits of Fordist factory life as they did in the advanced capitalist countries. At the level of the factory, though, the Fordist methods of the semi-automated assembly line, and the intensified division of labour, were fully implemented. Perhaps more typically "sub-Fordist" would be the average Third World textile plant of the 1970s, which adapted Taylorist principles but made no attempt to achieve the social integration of workers. This Taylorist labour process was complemented, however, by more traditional means of extracting surplus value, such as virtually unlimited working hours. Some of the most "modern" textile plants in the developing world are liable to practise subcontracting to small workshops, with outwork – once seen as a pre-capitalist labour process – finding a profitable niche in the late twentieth century. Such is the story of combined and uneven development in the lead-up to globalization.

As the golden era became tarnished in the North during the 1970s, the South was going through an ascendant phase. This was the period that saw the work of the famous "Brandt Report" (Independent Commission on International Development Issues 1980); it was also, in retrospect, a high point of international trade union influence on global development strategies. This enlightened programme for survival echoed many of the demands put forward by Third World governments at that time to promote a new international economic order. Countries would be taxed, on a sliding scale related to national income, to provide revenues for a World Development Fund. The unravelling of the golden era in the North did not immediately impact on the South on account of these moves towards a global Keynesian policy and the recycling of the petrodollar. Growth was uneven, but it appeared that peripheral Fordism would have as bright a future as its central counterpart had had for the glorious 30 years since the Second World War. From a political economy perspective, we can recognize, with Juliet Schor and Jong-Il You, that "the 1970s were a decade of ascendancy rather than setback as far as the South was concerned; economic growth continued, Vietnam defeated the United States, OPEC successfully raised oil prices, and the New International Economic Order was on the agenda" (Schor & You 1995: 5–6). It was only in the 1980s that the crisis became global as restrictive monetary policies in the North led to a massive increase in interest rates; this triggered the Third World debt crisis, with its catastrophic social and economic consequences.

Towards the end of the twentieth century an even "newer" international division of labour impacted on the countries and workers of the developing world. There was no longer a unified North and South, if there ever had been. We cannot even distinguish a centre, semi-periphery and periphery, as world-system theory did (see Wallerstein 1983). Although the new global economy is highly integrated, it is also extremely diversified. The network of the global information-led economy has integrated various parts of the world and its workers into its web. This is not done, however, by integrating national economies, which have become increasingly disintegrated. Thus, we can now speak of the "Latin-Americanization" or "Brazilianization" of the United States, or other once unproblematically designated advanced industrial societies. Pockets of development coexist with broad swathes of "underdevelopment" and human misery. Uneven development has always been a characteristic of capitalism, but what is striking today is the degree of development, on the one hand, and the utter disconnection of other parts of the globe, on the other. This newest division of labour relegates whole regions as surplus to requirements. Globalization has sharpened the process of social exclusion in all societies, and, indeed, has excluded some regions from even the dubious privilege of exploitation. Before we can turn to the effects of this new regime of accumulation on the workers of the world we need to unravel the precise nature of the crisis of the golden era.

We now live in a post-Fordist, post-welfare-state, post-interventionist-state, post-class-compromise era. The end of the golden era in the 1970s had far-reaching effects, leading to the hegemony of neoliberalism and the birth of the era of globalization. A critical understanding of how and why the postwar model of accumulation came to an end is crucial to a proper understanding of the new dispensation. Most analysts are agreed that the 1970s and 1980s were different from the 1950s and 1960s, but no clear paradigm has emerged such as that of the golden era. There is a recognition that many momentous events occurred in this period, such as the collapse of the Bretton Woods system of international finance in the early 1970s, the big increase in oil prices in 1974–5, the rise of Reaganism–Thatcherism, with its neoliberal economic policies, in the early 1980s and the collapse of state socialism at the end of that decade. It was also out of this period that the basic parameters of globalization emerged, to flourish fully in the 1990s. Where there is little agreement is on the pattern of causality in this set of events, and I will now seek to clarify some of the contending explanations.

At one level, the crisis that affected the advanced capitalist economies at the end of the 1960s and early 1970s is clear enough. The falling rates of profit in the ACEs between 1968 and 1973 were a clear indication that something was fundamentally amiss: profit rates in the United States, Western Europe and Japan were down one-third from their previous peaks. There was a wave of strikes across Europe between 1968 and 1970 that seemed to exacerbate this capitalist crisis of confidence. The expansion of the early 1970s was based on a massive US deficit and was fuelled by a rapid rise in inflation rates. As the economists of the time put it, the economies of the West were "overheating". When the crisis point was reached, in 1974, it coincided with a round of increases in oil prices by the OPEC countries, and the "greedy oil sheikhs" looked the likely and handy culprits. Certainly, as Hobsbawm puts it, "one of the reasons why the Golden Era was Golden was that the price of a barrel of Saudi oil averaged less than US$2 throughout the entire period from 1950 to 1973, thus making energy ridiculously cheap, and getting cheaper all the time" (Hobsbawm 1994: 262). This was undoubtedly one of the conjunctural factors triggering the crisis, but it was only part of a broader configuration of structural and conjunctural factors leading to a collapse of the postwar model. The golden era had begun to lose its shine nearly a decade before the "oil shock" hit it.

Another common explanation of the crisis, from both the Right and the Left, was the profit squeeze because of the power of workers to impose wage demands on capitalists. For Stephen Marglin,

> There was ... well before the oil shock, a general "full-employment, profit squeeze" throughout the OECD countries. This was not a phenomenon associated with business "cycles" ... but the result of a long period of sustained growth, rising wages, high employment, and increasing security for working people. The full-employment, profit squeeze had a direct effect on accumulation.   (Marglin 1990: 19)

The warning by Kalecki (see above), that full employment would remove fear of the sack and ultimately jeopardize accumulation, seemed to be coming true. Certainly, it is easy to see how a combative labour movement can, in certain countries and at certain periods, put a curb on profit rates. From there to deploying this argument as a full-blown explanation of the crisis is excessive, however attractive a class struggle perspective might be from a labour standpoint. For one thing, the timing is wrong, and it can be shown that the wave of labour militancy in the ACEs from 1969 to 1974 was more a response to the crisis of profitability, which had caused employers in the West to unleash a wages offensive on "their" workers. Even in general theoretical terms, as Brenner argues, it is hard to see how the full-employment, profit squeeze thesis "could account for an economic crisis, meaning a long-term reduction in the profit rate that produces a secular system-wide economic downturn" (Brenner 1998: 18).

For Brenner, in his commanding account of the crisis of the golden era, workers' action "may certainly reduce profitability in given locales, but it cannot, as a rule, make for crisis because it cannot, as a rule, bring about a spatially generalised (system-wide) and temporally extended decline in profitability" (Brenner 1998: 21). The crisis of the Fordist model extended into the 1980s, when the onslaught of the monetarists had successfully curbed even defensive workers' action in most of the ACEs. It is simply implausible that workers' action across the ACEs for a decade or more successfully thwarted all capitalist strategies for restructuring to escape the looming crisis. The political conclusion from that thesis as argued by some, namely that trade unions had become "too powerful" and that their rigidities were hindering technological innovation, is also lacking in credibility. An alternative explanation of the long boom and its demise would focus on inter-capitalist competition and its dynamic. The dense narrative and analysis advanced by Brenner focuses precisely on the uneven development of capitalism and the particular situation that emerged in the 1960s with the consolidation of German and Japanese exports to the United States. The United States was no longer as self-contained an economy as it had seemed, and the "latecomer" national blocs of capital were to become successful competitors. The outcome of declining profitability across the board would be a useful lesson for present-day gurus of "competitiveness" at all costs, a remarkably short-sighted growth strategy.

The international financial dimension is also a crucial part of the 1968–74 story. *Pax Americana* and the Bretton Woods system were cornerstones of the postwar dispensation. US hegemony in political, economic and military terms (not to mention the "cultural" dimension) was essential to global regulation. Now, not only was that hegemony being contested and the once all-mighty dollar seriously weakened, but the demands of the system were also changing. Although Bretton Woods had worked effectively in relation to monetary circulation, it was unable to control the new international credit system, which was emerging in a more "private" and unregulated way. As Elmar Altvater puts it, "Unregulated global credit was a factor of erosion of the (political institutional) regulation of the whole Fordist system" (Altvater 1992: 37). The United States inexorably pulled back from full convertibility of the dollar to gold, as per Bretton Woods, and then unilaterally abandoned the whole institution in 1971. What this signalled was also the abandonment by the United States of its leading international aggregate demand role. Although mild by subsequent standards, a real crisis of confidence in the international financial order ensued. The forces moving towards deregulation of the international financial markets were gathering strength. This chapter ended in 1974, however, with another oil price rise by OPEC, which, as Marglin notes, "triggered a new round of inflation which in turn catalysed doubts about the international order amid fears of a total collapse of the dollar-based financial system" (Marglin 1990: 24).

After the immediate impact of the 1974 crisis, Fordist–Keynesian policies continued to be implemented, but without solid Fordist institutions to sustain them. Thus, the 1970s were, in some way, a transition period; an interregnum in which the old had ceased to be effective but the new had not yet cohered. With the breakdown of the Bretton Woods system a two-decade-long process began in which the private financial market achieved its hegemony over state regulation. One indication of this battle is the simple fact that, by 1989, international bonds and interbank deposits totalled US$4.75 trillion, which was six times the total foreign exchange reserves of the central banks (Webber & Rigby 1996: 29). Finance capital was beginning to cut loose from the realm of production and the "real" economy. The other side of the coin was a concerted attack on organized labour, which also had to be disorganized to the benefit of the new capitalism. The 1980s were therefore marked by a consensus that Keynes was the "demon of profligacy incarnate" (Marglin 1990: 34). Supply-side economics completely obliterated any notion of demand management. Workers bore the main brunt of the monetarist onslaught but vast layers of society were affected by the roll-back of the welfare state. There was even a return to an aggressive US foreign policy, with the invasion of Grenada, destabilization in Nicaragua, the invasion of Panama, the bombings of Libya and Iraq, and so on, marking the comeback of the "terrorist state" discourse.

With this neoliberal onslaught of the early 1980s, a new regime of growth began to emerge in the ACEs. The era of organized capitalism – the large organization – gave way to a new-found faith in the operations of the free market, and a "disorganized" (in the literal sense) capitalism ensued. The organizations of the corporations, of the government and even of civil society had mainly enabled the market in the past, while being based on rational organizational principles themselves. Now the logic of the market was not only to dominate but to exert its logic over all sectors of society. Trade unions were not immune to this logic, and began to articulate the need to review their objectives to prioritize more the "services" that affected their members as individuals. Deregulation and the marketization of all aspects of social and economic life could not but have a profound effect on workers. For Michel Aglietta, author of one of the classic studies of Fordist regulation, this new growth regime led to uncertainty and instability:

> Increasing numbers of employees cannot find their place in the division of labour ... That is a measure of the depth of the malaise which has gripped wage societies in these trying times. The very principle of the integration of labour into the corporate structure, the progressive force behind the post-war boom, is now under threat.   (Aglietta 1998: 72)

It is not a question of donning rose-tinted spectacles when looking back at the Fordist golden era, but some social relations do become clearer with the benefit of hindsight.

After Fordism one gets post-Fordism, it would seem, but that equation is a bit too neat. In the ACEs there were a number of alternative wage labour/

capital relations emerging after Fordism but they cannot be given a clear "post-Fordist" label because no such dominant new paradigm has emerged. The policy of liberal flexibility in the era of global competitiveness has marked the domain of production as much as elsewhere. What seems to have emerged in many parts is a neo-Taylorism that is very much in the classical mould but without the social institutions and social compromise that went with high Fordism. At the other extreme is what Lipietz (1995) has called "Kalmarism", referring to the labour relations that prevailed in the now defunct Volvo plant in Sweden, which pioneered a negotiated involvement by the workforce. As Lipietz writes, however, "[C]ollective involvement of the workers is unlikely to emerge if there is no solidarity about goals between the forms and the workforce" (Lipietz 1995: 353). Certainly, there are a range of possibilities, and the "Japanese model", or "Toyotism", as it has become known, lies somewhere between neo-Taylorism and the Swedish model that was. The main point to make in concluding this chapter on the golden era of capitalism is that, after Fordism, this mode of production has not been able to generate a hegemonic paradigm to organize production and capital/wage labour relations in its central or core regions.

For the developing world, work after Fordism definitely did not mean post-Fordism. This is true equally for the South and for the East, which is rapidly becoming a developing capitalist area of the world system. In many ways, the after-Fordism shock has been greater here, because the state-led model of industrialization with the extensive deployment of labour was so dominant. Central planning and national development plans, typical of the East and the South in the golden era, are now defunct strategies. For Lipietz, a likely paradigm for the developing East is a form of "Taylorism and liberal flexibility", especially given that Taylorist principles were arguably never applied to their limits there (Lipietz 1995). As we shall see in Chapter 5, a whole range of possibilities opened up in the South. With demilitarization in South Korea, for example, we saw a transition from "bloody Taylorism" to a stunted but nevertheless real peripheral Fordism. It is hard to conceive of a democratic South Africa imposing a rigid anti-worker liberal flexibility regime on the trade unions and their members, who were at the forefront of the anti-apartheid struggle. In short, the future is still open in the after-Fordist era of globalization.

Back in the 1960s a capitalist from Detroit, who had become a US government functionary, declared (in)famously that what was good for General Motors was good for the United States. If somewhat brazen, this statement had a ring of truth about it. There was a certain synergy between transnationalist capitalist expansion and national capitalist state development. After the golden era, with the era of globalization taking shape and expanding, this position has not even got that degree of "truth" to it. As Tickell and Peck put it, there was a growing "contradiction between globalising accumulation and national regulation, or, more particularly, between the emerging unregulated global credit system and the fiscal integrity of the Keynesian welfare state" (Tickell & Peck 1995: 372). What had been a virtuous circle, involving the national and the international, accumulation and welfare, capitalist and worker, production and consumption, had now turned into a series of vicious circles. Monetarism was a response to this but also a symptom of the crisis, and ultimately unsustainable. For the new accumulation regime that emerged in the 1990s, based on accelerated internationalization, there would still be a need for a global regulatory order. This seems unlikely to emerge smoothly, as moves in this direction after the 2007–9 crisis ground to a halt and things reverted to the pre-crisis status quo. It is this search for global regulation to meet the economic and political disorder that underpins the next chapter and forms a key horizon for the international labour movement.

3

THE ERA OF GLOBALIZATION

Although the golden era of capitalism was primarily national, the last decade of the twentieth century saw a greatly increased transnationalization of economic, political, social and cultural relations. This led to a new era of globalization, which has had a decisive impact on workers worldwide, although much of the flourishing globalization literature seems to ignore the role of workers on the whole. This chapter seeks not only to introduce some of the major parameters of this new great transformation but also to explore its limits and contradictions from a labour perspective. A fundamental thesis is that workers and the workers' movement are, and will become, increasingly central to the new globalizing capitalist order. Capitalism is being reconstructed but so too are the world of work and the organizations of workers, as I show in the section on the new global labour force. I examine in particular the increased flexibility and feminization of this new global labour force. The final section on the global social movements explores the extent to which globalization has created the conditions for a new social movement for workers worldwide.

A new great transformation

Globalization, whether viewed as a panacea for the new century or demonized as the source of all our evils, had become the new "common sense" for our era from around 2000. In a relatively short period of time the term "globalization" spread across academic disciplines, spawned multiple research centres and generated a vigorous counter-movement. It is a most labile term, fluid and slippery in its meaning and its political implications. As a starting point we could do worse than Paul Drache's (only slightly tongue-in-cheek) conclusion that "[t]he simple truth is that one-third of the globalization narrative is over-sold, one-third we do not understand because it is a process unfolding and one-third is radically new" (Drache 1999: 7). Globalization appeared as a new grand meta-narrative, just as we were being told that the meta-narratives of labour and socialism were dead. It is presented in much of the academic literature – not to mention more popular outlets – as a homogeneous, irreversible and all-encompassing process. It can mean everything and anything, or, it seems at times, nothing at all. So, I propose a brief review of its economic, political and social/cultural aspects, from a labour perspective.

The main debate at the economic level is whether the increased importance of the TNCs (transnational corporations, as the "old" MNCs are now called) and of international trade represented an increased internationalization of capitalism or the birth of a new globalism. For the globalists, we were now moving into a borderless world (Ohmae 1990) in which the TNC rather than the nation state rules supreme. This is seen as part of a secular process of international integration, viewed as part of the inevitable story of human progress, as in the modernization theory of the 1960s. This discourse is based on a very real internationalization of production, financial and consumption flows since the 1970s. It also rests on the substantial upsurge in investment by TNCs, which have developed an increasingly global remit over the 30 or so years. For Kenichi Ohmae, these "stateless" corporations were the genuine movers in the interlinked economies of the "triad", comprising the United States, the European Union and Japan in the 1990s. The decision-making process of the TNCs – and sovereign "consumer choice" – is seen by Ohmae to be at the heart of rational resource allocation at the international level. If the TNCs are able to shake off the antiquated restraints of the nation state and its interfering bureaucrats, they can enter the brave new world of globalization as "knights of the road" on its electronic highways. This open and global economy is presented as the epitome of the "level playing field", as against the particularism and biases of corporatism. It is the international market that, for Ohmae and his followers, provides economic coordination, not only for development on a world scale but also for effective global mechanisms, given its self-interest in policing itself. Ohmae's messianic vision is, of course, but another perspective on the nightmare scenario presented by the anti-globalization gurus (see Falk 1999).

For those concerned to demystify the programmes and the politics of the globalists, Paul Hirst and Grahame Thompson (1996) make a considered and, to some extent, persuasive case. Their overall conclusion is that "the globalization of production has been exaggerated: companies remain tethered to their home economies and are likely to remain so" (Hirst & Thompson 1996: 17). Essentially, they would prefer us to stick with the title of multinational corporations (MNCs) rather than transnational corporations (TNCs), which implies a global rather than an international capitalist enterprise. The quantitative data sets used in this debate are complex and undoubtedly subject to different interpretations. Yet the basic point is that international firms still have a "home base" and are thus also subject to political control in that nation state. There is a historic element to this debate too, with an argument that under the gold standard (up to the First World War) the advanced capitalist countries had less autonomy than they have today. It is important to note that, for the anti-globalists, or demystifiers such as Hirst and Thompson, the main point of the debate is a political one. For these authors, "globalization is a myth suitable for a world without illusions but it also robs us of hope" (Hirst & Thompson 1996: 6). They were keen to undermine the "global-ization excuse" used by governments such as Britain's New Labour as an alibi for not playing a more active role in taking social control over the global economy. International firms are not "footloose and fancy-free"; they are not above the law; and nation states can and should take steps, individually and collectively, to seek regulation of the new economic order.

At the political level, the main debate in the globalization literature is the extent to which internationalization of the economy has led to a decline of the nation state and its decision-making powers. For the globalists, the day of the nation state has simply gone: "The uncomfortable truth is that, in terms of the global economy, nation-states have become little more than bit actors" (Ohmae 1990: 12). The nation state, for Ohmae, is simply a "nostalgic fiction", and it makes no sense to talk of Italy or China, or even the United States, in an era characterized by global capital flows. Even production is multinational, and no one can tell where our cars, clothes or food have been produced. Nationalism, according to these globalizers, has become the refuge of the losers: "[W]e don't hear much about feverish words of Hong Kong nationalism, but the people in Hong Kong seem to live rather well" (Ohmae 1990: 13). By contrast, the nationalisms of the ex-USSR states do not seem to put food on the table. Today's borderless economy is seen to have reconfigured the nation state out of existence, following up the job that the "footloose and fancy-free" MNCs had begun in the 1970s. So-called national interest is seen as a flag of convenience for outmoded pro-tectionist economic policies, and also as a total illusion in a knowledge-driven economy that does not require a national base. This is a strongly economistic set of arguments based squarely on the illusions of traditional modernization and convergence theories, which ignored differences in wealth and power between nation states and the social groups within them.

Contesting the "death of the nation state" thesis, Linda Weiss (1997) makes a number of important points. First of all, tendencies towards economic inter-nationalization do not mean that globalism has been achieved. One might also ask the pertinent question of whether globalization would have materialized without the active designs of powerful nation states and the consent of others. Second, as Weiss puts it, "globalists tend to exaggerate state powers in the past in order to claim feebleness in the present" (Weiss 1997: 13). The golden era (see Chapter 2) was not characterized by omnipotent national states. Nor is the

construction of national helplessness in the face of the cold winds of globalization an innocent political act. Globalization is, in short, a political ideology as
much as a socio-economic phenomenon. Third, the globalists "have not only
over-stated the degree of state powerlessness. They have also *over-generalised*
it" (Weiss 1997: 16, emphasis in original). Against the illusions of the convergence theorists, even the imperatives of globalization have not led to a "one best
way" for capitalism to develop. Instead, we have national capitalisms and differential state capacities to adjust to the demands of international competitiveness (Berger & Dore 1996). Weiss even goes so far as to see national differences
increasing rather than diminishing. It does seem unlikely that the nation state
changed suddenly from being a bulwark of national capitalism in the 1970s to
being a mere transmission belt for global capitalism some time in the 1980s.
We may question, however, whether in demystifying the "myth of the powerless
state" the globalization sceptics may not be ignoring some fundamental transformations in the world order. It would probably be sensible to assume that the
contemporary nation state is neither "powerless" nor the same mythical body
that national sovereignty theory has assumed since the seventeenth century.

If the economic and political debates around globalization have too often been
artificially polarized between the globalists and their demystifiers, this is less true
in the cultural domain. In some ways this area has produced some of the most
original and thought-provoking analysis of the present epoch. First of all, it is
important to note the perception that while "culture, as an arena differentiated
from economics and politics, has never been totally globalized it has nevertheless shown a greater tendency towards globalization than either of the other
two arenas" (Waters 2001: 124–5). We need only think of the universalizing
tendencies of religions in order to see some truth in this statement. And the so-
called global culture of McDonald's and Coca-Cola gives it an even more contemporary ring. In some ways, globalization seems to be simply the emergence
of a global culture. As Fredric Jameson puts it, "[H]ere what begins to infuse
our thinking of globalization is a picture of standardization on an unparalleled
new scale" (Jameson 1998: 57). More specifically, we operate with an image of
"the world-wide Americanization or standardization of culture, the destruction
of local differences, the massification of all the peoples on the planet" (Jameson
1998: 57). From a labour perspective, we can actually see a lot of truth in this
image too. Managers fly around the world accessing the same news media, stay
at the same hotels, indulge in the same pastimes. Workers across the world live
under the aegis of the same neoliberal globalization discourses, work under
similar labour regimes characterized by "flexibilization" and often watch the
same television programmes. Managers and workers alike live in the era of globalization and are equally part of the communications revolution and the network society. Labour strategies of transformation need to be cognizant of these

new realities, if they are not to do battle on a terrain already vacated by labour's opponents.

One of the main images we need to overcome in understanding the global dimension is that the global is dynamic and fluid, whereas the local is embedded, static and tradition-bound. From this powerful image Manuel Castells derives the notion that capital and labour live in different places and times. While capital is global, exists in the space of flows and lives in the instant time of computerized networks, labour inhabits the local, exists in the "space of places" and lives by the clock time of everyday life (Castells 1996a: 475). This image certainly reflects a strong element of what is going on around us, but it is something of a binary opposition. Ash Amin has developed a more satisfying interpretation of global-ization "in *relational* terms, as the interdependence and intermingling of global, distant and local logics, resulting in greater hybridization and perforation of social, economic and political life" (Amin 1997: 133). This more fluid concep-tion of globalization as something not just "out there" but "in here" too seems to owe a lot to the notion of hybridity, as developed in cultural studies, espe-cially postcolonial studies. Its relational emphasis is also congruent with Marx's continuous emphasis on the capital/labour *relation*, as against the worlds of business and workers taken in isolation. What our unpacking of the economic, political and social-cultural dimensions of globalization points us towards is a more open, multipolar and, indeed, hybrid set of solutions to the problems posed for progressive social transformation by the era of globalization.

One of the main themes in critical analysis of contemporary capitalism became the necessary social "embeddedness" of its institutions. Complex production systems cannot be based exclusively on impersonal market mechanisms; they require individual and social trust. J. Rogers Hollingsworth and Robert Boyer point out: "Trust is an important lubricant in a capitalist economy ... As consumer demand becomes more diversified, technology more complex, and the economy more centralised, there is potentially more uncertainty among actors and there-fore trust may erode" (Hollingsworth & Boyer 1996: 24). Yet only high degrees of trust can sustain the complex systems of production that the new capitalism is creating. Flexible specialization requires coordination and cooperation between economic actors. There has now been a swing against the conception of TNCs as "footloose and fancy-free", which stresses precisely how they are embedded in social and political relations. The governance of large firms is now understood to include "traditional" family ties as well as regional and even feudal links. As Boyer and Hollingsworth argue, "[T]he social embeddedness of relationships in capitalist societies permits actors to circumvent the limits of pure rationality and the interaction of anonymous markets" (Boyer & Hollingsworth 1996: 451). Even a good economic performance, if it is to be sustainable, requires a favour-able social setting and an enabling political environment. National economic institutions must also be part of a more complex regional and international mode of regulation of capitalism, however. Its main characteristic is its multi-polar nature, with no single level self-sufficient. These variable configurations are typical of the more fluid patterns that globalization is creating in terms of economic development and governance.

A perspective based on social embeddedness, in many ways following the tradition of Polanyi, also allows us to see the variations in governance systems possible in the global era. In the international arena it is not just capital units that confront one another but whole social systems of production. Convergence has not occurred under globalization any more than it did in the 1950s in the era of modernization. There are national capitalist paths and forms of governance in which the role of labour varies markedly. Hollingsworth and Boyer note percep-tively that "economic competition is increasingly becoming competition over different forms of social systems of production, and competitive pressures for better economic performance are more and more often translated into pressures for broad societal change" (Hollingsworth & Boyer 1996: 38). So what is com-peting is not capital but capitalist social systems. This throws new light on the role of labour, which can now be seen as more central to the concerns of capital. There is certainly scope for arguments to situate global competition in this way. In these terms, a "race to the bottom" in relation to labour conditions is not the only, or even the most rational, response, and gearing up the social system of production to take the "high road" of high productivity and good wages in a cooperative environment is a perfectly plausible way forward.

It is important, finally, to recognize that globalization may not be uniformly negative for democratic political and social forces. John Agnew and Stuart Corbridge argue: "Globalization is not only a synonym for dis-empowerment: it creates conditions for democratization, decentralization and empowerment as well as for centralization and standardization. Globalization opens as many doors as it shuts" (Agnew & Corbridge 1995: 219). Globalization has led to – or, at least, accompanied – a certain degree of decentralization of production and work methods. Politically, it has tended to "hollow out" the national state (as traditional government competencies are delegated both upwards, to supra-national bodies, and downwards, to private companies, as part of the logic of neoliberalism) but, perhaps, made it more porous regarding social initiatives. At the cultural level, it is now accepted that globalization has not led to standardiza-tion (or Americanization) but, rather, has created multifaceted, multidirectional and hybrid flows and cultural formations. It can thus plausibly be said that glo-balization may "open doors" or create the conditions for a new wave of social advance. For a long time now the responses to globalization have opposed total acceptance with total rejection. It is now recognized, however, as Weiss points out, that "neither resignation nor resistance define the real range of options"

(Weiss 1999: 127), which include a whole series of institutional reforms and policy actions. Globalization can be "managed", as Weiss points out, but it can also be controlled socially, as an analysis building on that of Polanyi would show. Globalization is still subject to the demands of governance, for its own survival, apart from anything else, as we have seen above.

Labour and globalization

In the world of labour, the positive potential of globalization has not been missed. Thus Denmark's Specialarbejderförbundet i Danmark, in a bold trade union manifesto, has declared: "The time has come for trade unions to use the positive sides of globalization to the advantage of workers and poor people all over the world" (SID 1997: 23). The question of will or agency is usually ignored in analyses of globalization, but here a major trade union says simply that "[i]t is time to change our own defensive attitude" and go on the offensive both nationally and internationally. Some of the positive aspects of globalization detailed include the effects of the ICT revolution in terms of providing workers and unions with instant information from around the world. It is not just that information has become more accessible; it is also that "[t]here is more transparency, monitoring and control of what is happening around the globe than ever before" (SID 1997: 29). The ICT revolution can be seen to create, to some extent, a new democratic equivalent, allowing for better international communications, technically, socially and politically. Thus, for example, we have the emergence of the political or ethical consumer, keen to support moves to make MNCs respect basic human rights and environmental norms.

This section has forced us to reconsider the way we view globalization as a context for work and workers in the twenty-first century. We need to reject totalizing and messianic views of its implications. For too long radical political economy has tended to reify what we call globalization and ascribe to it a logic and coherence it simply does not have. This way of thinking of globalization makes it very difficult to "think" of an alternative to it or imagine another future and work towards it.

It is important for us to have a very clear understanding that "[g]lobalisation in its modern form is a process based less on the proliferation of computers than on the proliferation of proletarians" (Coates 2000: 256). If capital is understood as a social relation (between the owner of capital and the worker) then, clearly, its worldwide expansion will inevitably spell a global expansion of the working classes. This is not just a quantitative expansion; it also entails a series of qualitative shifts in the nature of work and the global labour force in both social and spatial terms, as we shall see in Chapters 4 and 5, on workers in the North and

South. Globalization has not just occurred because capital suddenly became more mobile in the late 1980s. It also responds to the needs of the capital accumulation process, not only to expand but to subsume more and more workers under the capital/wage labour relation.

The most significant impact of globalization on the capital/wage labour relation has been to practically double the numbers of the global working class. Quite suddenly, in the early 1990s, the workers of China, India and the ex-Soviet bloc became part of a single world market based on capitalism and the market. The size of the global labour market, according to Freeman's calculations, increased from fewer than 1.5 billion workers to just under 3 billion (Freeman 2008: 1). This quantitative leap, as labour previously outside the direct sway of capital was globalized, is matched by a substantial shift in the composition of that global labour force, as we can see in Figure 3.1.

The figure shows quite clearly that a major divergence opened up after 1980, with the so-called developing world's share of the global industrial force increasing dramatically while that of the more developed or originally industrializing countries declined, not as dramatically but still decisively.

This world historic shift and the trends in the size and composition of the global labour force have had a massive impact on labour. On the one hand, capital flowed to countries such as China and India, where economic growth was

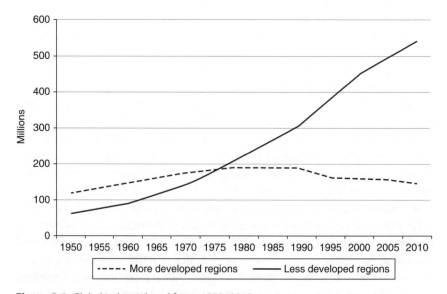

Figure 3.1 Global industrial workforce, 1950–2015
Source: Smith (2016: 103), based on the ILO's KILM (Key Indicators of the Labor Market) data.

occurring in a low-wage context. While real earnings of urban China nearly doubled in the 1990s, workers in other countries suffered directly. This new model capitalism, particularly in Latin America and sub-Saharan Africa, was based on an expansion of the informal sector rather than on the growth of what were called "decent jobs" by the ILO. But the main impact of China, India and the ex-Soviet bloc entering into the labour market was to reduce the ratio of capital to labour greatly. As Freeman puts it, quite bluntly, "This has shifted the global balance of power to capital" (Freeman 2008: 2). This is when outsourcing began in earnest, as capitalists in the affluent North chose to relocate to low-wage regions or used that threat to drive down wages and conditions at home. The lack of capital in poor India, state-regulated China and the non-sustainable socialism of Russia led to a decisive shift in the balance of forces between labour and capital internationally. The transnationalized corporate elite were told that, "just as managers speak of world markets for products, technology and capital, they must now think in terms of a world market for labour" (Johnston 1991: 115). In 1991 William Johnston argued categorically that "the globalization of labor is inevitable" (Johnston 1991: 126). The logic was a simple one: to make the best of all resources, including "human resources" (labour), wherever they might be.

In terms of the regional distribution of the global workforce (Figure 3.2), Asia and the Pacific accounted for 60 per cent of the world's labour force in 1990, but this proportion will decline to 55 percent by 2030. The proportion of

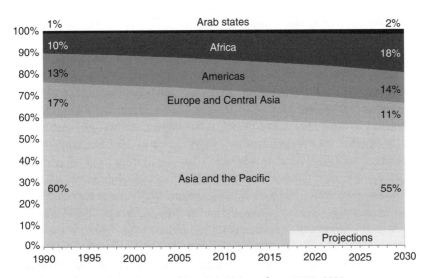

Figure 3.2 Regional distribution of the global labour force, 1990–2030
Source: ILO (2017).

the global labour force in Europe and Central Asia is also declining. While the share of employment in the Americas will increase slightly the most dramatic change will occur in Africa, where its share will increase from 10 percent to 18 percent.

In terms of the gender distribution of the global labour force, we note that, by the mid-1980s, more than half the working-age women across the world were in paid employment. Women represented more than one-third of the total labour force, and considerably more in the North, although we may question, to some extent, the validity of the data on female paid employment in the South. The implications for the economy of increased entry by women into the paid labour force are considerable. Johnston argues, for example, from a management perspective, that, "[i]f other conditions are favourable, countries with many women ready to join the workforce can look forward to rapid economic expansion" (Johnston 1991: 118). From the point of view of women workers, these economic transformations may have a significant impact on their role in the wider gender division of labour in society. Of course, like any broad process of social transformation, what is referred to as the "feminization" of the workforce has a mixed impact. Thus, as Brigitte Young argues, "[t]he flexibilisation of the labour market has produced greater equality between educated middle class women and men while creating greater inequality among women" (Young 2000: 315). For every professional female post there are probably quite a few more 'menial' female posts created.

The gender gap in labour force participation varies greatly according to region, and is most pronounced in North Africa, the Arab states and Southern Asia. Overall, the gender gap stood at 26.5 percent in 2017, compared with 28.6 percent in 1990, but it is due to increase again to 26.6 per cent in 2030. Female participation rates in high-income countries have reached their peak and are declining; in China, India and Russia they have stagnated; and they are increasing steadily in the so-called developing countries, sometimes halving the previous gap, as in the case of Brazil.

Returning to the question of a global labour market, we may now reconsider the argument that we actually have one. Analysts, such as Johnston, seem to work with a largely unilinear scheme whereby "what was once a local labor market became regional, then national, and finally international" (Johnston 1991: 123). This process of extension has been much more uneven than is recognized by the modernizing perspective, both in spatial and in temporal terms. That is to say, for example, that it ignores the question of unfree and semi-free labour in the South (and in the North as well); nor can any but a small minority of today's lead sector workers be part of a truly global labour market. Castells is undoubtedly correct to argue that "[l]abor markets are not truly global, except for a small but growing segment of professionals and scientists" (Castells 1998: 93). Castells also goes on to argue, however, that "labor is a global resource", in so far as corporations may go anywhere in the world to seek the labour they want, highly skilled labour will be imported from anywhere in the world by those same corporations and, lastly, workers are driven by economic necessity, war and famine to seek work across the globe (Castells 1998: 93). Maybe we *are* moving towards a global labour market, but not in a simple, unilinear and optimistic fashion.

What we all probably can agree on is that globalization sets new parameters for the labour force today and that there is a tendency towards the creation of a global labour market. We live and we work in an increasingly integrated global economy. Certainly, labour is not as mobile as capital, but it is not immobile and capital is still embedded in national societies. The labour process is also increasingly part of an integrated transnational network, as are the corporations that create such networks and recruit workers to them. Some leading sectors of the labour market – for example, information and communications technology – are already part of a unified labour market. Others are increasingly affected by the operations of a global capitalism that constantly seeks to devalue labour power. This process has, even in one key country, the United States, helped to break the national unity of US capital and US workers in pursuit of the imperial interest. A sensible conclusion on the global nature of workers' horizons is that of Mihály Simai, who argues: "Workers and their unions ... have come to an understanding of the internationalisation of the main processes influencing employment, wages and conditions and social policies" (Simai 1995: 27). Gains that may have been achieved on the national terrain will, increasingly, be lost or maintained within the parameters of the global capital/wage labour relation.

With regard to the overall effect of globalization on labour, we could do worse than begin with the World Bank's authoritative 1995 report *Workers in an Integrating World* (World Bank 1995). In it, the World Bank, with undisguised glee, predicts accurately that by the end of the century less than 10 per cent of the world's workers would be outside the global capitalist economy, compared to the one-third of the global workforce that twenty years earlier was told it was building socialism or the national development state. The driving forces of global integration were seen as unstoppable by the World Bank, and the world's workers had no option but to submit – or, in the World Bank's own words, "[g]lobalization is unavoidable – the welfare of Joe, Maria and Xiao Zhin is now more closely linked than ever before" (World Bank 1995: 54). These "representative" workers were seen to face risks, but deeper international integration (i.e. globalization) was seen to hold positive prospects "for those countries and groups of workers with the capacity to respond" (World Bank 1995: 188). Of course, the Bank acknowledged that increasing international competition and "freewheeling" capital would not only cut jobs and wages but would, effectively, wipe whole nations and regions off the economic map. It understood that the scenario of workers' fortunes worldwide converging was less likely than growing divergence. In brief, according to the World Bank, "[g]lobalization offers opportunities but also exacerbates risks" (World Bank 1995: 124). This served as a maxim – and possibly the epitaph – for a new era of global capitalist expansion from around 1990 to 2007.

Perhaps one of the more interesting asides in the World Bank report is the argument that "the lives of urban workers in different parts of the world are increasingly intertwined" (World Bank 1995: 1). There was rapid change under way in the global political economy – "revolutionary times", said the World Bank. For workers, it meant many things; not all positive, but it has created an objective community of fate, in so far as workers' futures in different parts of the world are becoming more integrated. There are also, against dire predictions of the "end of work" in the era of computers, more workers entering the labour market. As Castells points out, "Workers do not disappear in the space of flows and down to earth work is plentiful" (Castells 1996a: 474). Indeed, it is calculated that the world's workforce doubled in the last three decades of the twentieth century. Work is expanding, and so are the working classes. This labour force, increasingly integrated by the internationalizing tendencies of globalization, is also changing its centre of gravity. It is the maelstrom of development of the capital/wage labour relation that is generating what truly might be called a second "great transformation".

The World Bank painted a largely realistic picture of the transformations that have and are occurring in the world of workers worldwide. It clearly and expectedly took for granted that things would continue as they were, however. While it was concerned about the "downside" of globalization and argued for a stronger role for the state than desired by market fundamentalists, the projection of globalizing trends was seen as inevitable. As Diane Elson (1996) notes, the World Bank view of globalization suffers from technological fetishism (technology as the driver of globalization), the invisibility of capital (not seeing how capital drives this process) and the "fallacy of composition" (the belief that all countries would have benefited had they decided early on to take advantage of the opportunity). What are then seen as "transitional costs" for workers adjusting to the new global order may well become permanent costs because the World Bank simply assumes that it will all work out for the best in the end. The negative effects of globalization, actually built into the process and not just potential risks, are largely ignored by the World Bank. The World Bank report was even behind the times in not recognizing the need for better international coordination and regulation of market mechanisms. The series of international capitalist crises since this report was issued is ample testimony to the continued validity of Polanyi's perspective regarding social regulation of the market.

Flexibility and feminization of labour

Many issues are opened up by the analysis above, but I prefer here to concentrate on just two "global" issues, namely the "flexibilization" and "feminization" of labour. The dominant theme in the labour flexibility debates is that it leads to economic growth, which in turn creates more jobs. According to the OECD, the flexibility of labour takes five main forms.

- External numerical flexibility – number of employees adjusted in accordance with employers' needs.
- Externalisation – part of the firm's work is put out through subcontracting.
- Internal numerical flexibility – working hours and their "delivery" adjusted according to employers' needs.
- Functional flexibility – workers' jobs modified according to employers' needs.
- Wages flexibility – labour's reward according to productivity and market conditions (cited in van Dijk 1995: 223–4).

If we added spatial or geographical flexibility we would have a fairly comprehensive picture of the model worker at the end of the twentieth century. Flexibility, in its multiple but interrelated guises, is probably the defining characteristic of labour in the era of international competitiveness. The drive towards labour flexibility – which is a global one, albeit taking different forms given the particular national forms of embeddedness of the labour market – is leading to smaller workforces, fewer rules in the workplace, weaker unions and wages being tied to the business cycle.

Labour flexibility is a social process but it is also a discourse, a contested political terrain. As such, it exemplifies the importance in the "era of globalization" of critically examining – deconstructing, perhaps – the dominant discourses of work. If flexibility is read simply as deregulation, then its negative effects will inevitably prevail. But it is possible to see the drawbacks of this implementation not only in equity terms but also in terms of efficiency. What may be good for the firm (at least in the short term) may not be good for the national economy. Thus, in terms of global economic growth – the mantra of the competitiveness advocates – there could also be a contraction of world demand if this policy is followed unilaterally. As Boyer puts it, "In a nutshell, the pursuit of flexibility, a rational response to the crisis, may actually exacerbate it, by undermining international trade" (Boyer 1988: 251). The increase in more precarious forms of employment is an obstacle to increased productivity as well, of course. A consensual or "concertation" approach to labour flexibility would not be based on the assumption of labour market rigidities. Instead, it would focus on growth, but also on better levels of education and training for workers. Above all, it would develop new forms of regulation, as required by the new internationalized production systems and the more flexible labour markets that have developed. Effective production restructuring and innovative forms of competitive advantage have usually emerged in situations in which trade unions are strong and labour is treated as a human resource, and not just another cost to be cut.

Governments are ambiguous in their approach to what has become known as the "gig economy" in recent years, a sector that, in the United Kingdom, embraces over 1 million workers. A catch-all term, it denotes various forms of ad hoc labour arrangements: it ranges from the "self-employed" who work as minicab drivers (Uber) to takeaway delivery workers (Deliveroo) to freelancers, casual labourers and workers in a whole range of services on zero-hour and temporary contracts. There is official recognition that frequently their declared self-employed status belies that they have one sole employer and that they should be accorded regular workers' rights, such as sick pay, pension payments and a minimum wage. Given that 45 per cent of UK employment growth between 2008 and 2017 has been in this sector, it is a major issue, not least because of the persistence of in-work poverty, which undermines much of the austerity programme of the government *vis-à-vis* welfare. Employers complain that any change in status for gig economy workers would increase unit labour costs by 20 per cent. In the event, new legislation to "regularize" this sector was shelved in 2018, amid fears that it would face right-wing Conservative opposition in the context of Brexit negotiations.

The gig economy has become synonymous with labour exploitation in the United Kingdom, affecting all aspects of the economy. The very notion of "zero-hour contracts" – workers are on call but not guaranteed work – would have been inconceivable in another era. Now, while employment growth masks the impact of the 2007–9 crisis, workers are taking the brunt in terms of austerity policies and steadily deteriorating working conditions. Workers' livelihoods and quality of life have been impacted, with surveys showing that over a third of workers do not earn enough to keep up with the cost of living and that workload, stress and mental health issues are climbing (CLASS 2018).

The gig economy is anathema to union activity. In recent years, however, trade unions – or similar organizations – have made significant inroads in terms of organizing and representing these workers. For example, in 2016 in New York Uber and the International Association of Machinists and Aerospace Workers Union jointly announced the formation of an Independent Drivers Guild to represent Uber drivers. In Seattle the city council has also passed a law allowing app-based drivers to bargain collectively. This challenged Uber's business model, which classified its drivers as "independent contractors", thus avoiding laws that allow workers to unionize. In 2018 Europe's largest airline, Ryanair, a pioneer of just-in-time, union-free air transport since 1985, was forced to recognize and negotiate with a pilot's union that had been informally in existence for some years, supported by the international trade union organizations. The power of organization can still overcome the atomization sought by the new and emergent forms of work and management typical of the precariat.

Related to the "flexibilization" debate is that around the "feminization" of labour, which could potentially have more far-reaching social consequences. Throughout the 1970s and 1980s there was a marked increase in the number of women entering paid formal employment in many regions. Most noticeable was the upsurge in female employment in the electronics industries of South Asia, Mexico and other regions, entering the "new international division of labour" (see Chapter 5). In the 1990s we saw the development of a theme encapsulated by Guy Standing as "global feminisation through flexible labour" (Standing 1989; 1999). With deregulation, the retreat of the state from economic affairs, and "flexibility" as the new watchword in labour relations, we could expect a shift in gender patterns of employment. Standing found that, overall, "[w]ith many more women continuously in the labour force or finding it easier to move in and out of it, or combining labour force and other work, more women are remaining in the labour force until a later age" (Standing 1999: 588). What was noticeable was that these tendencies increased in the 1990s, as export-led industrialization gave way to a more profound internationalization. To some extent, the apparent increase in female participation in the paid workforce reflects a decrease in male rates of employment, especially in the formal sector (see Chapter 5).

Overall, the 2007–9 global financial crisis reversed previous trends towards reducing gender-based inequality in the labour market. Initial impacts on industries such as construction (predominantly male employment) dominated the longer-term impact globally, for example in the services sector, which were predominantly "female" sectors. Public sector cuts, the decline of tourism and job losses in the textile industry all impacted women workers primarily. The gender gap in terms of employment and in terms of pay began to worsen, not least in the OECD countries, where some closing of the gaps had occurred since the onset of globalization in the 1990s. The underlying issue is that women's participation increased dramatically just when the neoliberal regime was at its height, "deregulation" was the dominant drive in the labour market and atypical, precarious and badly paid jobs became the norm.

The gender pay gap in the United Kingdom received considerable public attention in 2017 in relation to the BBC and the medical and banking sectors. A number of high-profile cases led to a focus on pay discrimination. A number of research projects were undertaken to uncover the causes of the nearly 10 per cent gender pay gap in contemporary Britain. The UK Office for National Statistics (ONS 2018) has found that, indeed, some of the pay differential could be explained in terms of there being more men in senior roles with higher salaries. Universally a somewhat higher proportion of women work part-time, paid at a lower rate per hour. Once these factors had been accounted for, however, they could explain only one-third of the gender pay gap. The ONS was at pains to say that domestic caring responsibilities that their modelling exercise did not take into account could play a role but it also admitted that pay discrimination might be part of the explanation. Of course, men and women already knew this, but it was finally receiving statistical backing.

The "feminization" of global labour thesis is by no means unproblematic. In the first place, the term seems to conflate the increased participation by women in the paid labour force with informalization and other forms of labour destructuring under late capitalism. In Standing's own use of the term, he refers to how "the type of work, labour relations, income and insecurity associated with 'women's work' have been spreading, resulting [in] a transformation – or feminisation – of many jobs traditionally held by men" (Standing 1989: 1077). Yet what constitutes "women's work" is socially constructed and varies across societies. Nor is it clear on the evidence that women's share of employment in traditionally "female" sectors, such as textiles, has actually been increasing. In fact, it is to the contrary. In that much-vaunted female employer, the electronics industry, trends in the 1970s have since been reversed, with women losing jobs more rapidly than men on the whole. Elson's persuasive conclusion is that "[t]he gender division of labour, which tends to confine women to relatively subordinate and inferior positions in the organisation of monetised production, is not overridden by 'flexibilisation'" (Elson 1996: 40). Indeed, it tends to set the parameters of how "flexibility" operates in a gendered fashion. What is also gendered is the "take" on "flexible" modes of production, by which women have been able to carve out some advantages, while men tend to view them as uniformly deleterious.

We must always remember that women make up approximately 80 per cent of home-based workers worldwide, according to the ILO. In this sense, flexibilization and feminization are nothing new. This "hidden" workforce also highlights the problems with traditional trade union notions centred on the male worker in a factory and the "family wage". The linkages that have occurred in many developing countries between factory workers, homeworking campaigning groups and women's organizations are now occurring at the international level. This has even moved beyond networking and information exchange to the organization of concerted activities – for example, in the Women Working Worldwide campaign (see www.poptel.org.uk/women-ww). The processes of global restructuring of labour that are occurring have created the need (but also the opportunity) for what Amrita Chhachhi and Renée Pittin refer to as strategies and policies that are "multi-faceted, utilising interlocking industrial, economic and political structures and processes" (Chhachhi & Pittin 1996: 21). One could also add the cultural dimensions to get the full picture of multivalency, which now characterizes labour responses to globalization at their most progressive or transformative. The link between workplace, household and community has become most clear in relation to research and action around women's work worldwide. The creative forms of organization, the refusal of binary oppositions (e.g. reform or revolution) and the links with other social movements may well be characteristics that will spread.

Global social movement?

The main problem with most of the literature on labour and globalization is that it tends to conceive of labour as a passive victim of the new trends, the malleable material from which globalization will construct its new world order. Capital is seen as an active, mobile, forward-looking player in the globalization game while labour is seen as static, passive and basically reactive. The game has changed, and labour seems to have few cards. Only rarely will someone point out, as Andrew Herod does, that "workers and unions have been actively involved in shaping the processes of globalization ... both by modifying the impacts of capital's activities and by shaping internationally the very possibilities for these activities" (Herod 1998: 40). The reality is that labour has been back centre stage since the mid-1990s at least, and clearly so since the turn of century. General strikes have occurred in many parts of Europe, in Latin America, in Canada, in South Africa and in South Korea. The disorienting changes suffered by the labour movement in the first decade of globalization seem, at least in part, to have been overcome. Change was a slow but organic process, often initiated by the activists and shop stewards, rather than the rank and file. As Kim Moody recounts, "The unions took on new roles: as champions of the interests of the working class as a whole, not just as representatives of their members, and as political surrogates for failed parties of the left" (Moody 1997: 14).

We increasingly find trade unions as the formal institutional manifestation of labour representation moving beyond the factory gates and breaking with a narrow, economistic conception of trade unionism. Historically, economic unionism has focused on representing workers as economic actors. As George DeMartino argues, in relation to the United States, there was once a powerful left-wing workerist orthodoxy that "grants privileged status to workers in an enterprise, [as] they alone are empowered to determine when and how to struggle, and for what?" (DeMartino 1991: 31). The broader community could express its "solidarity" when called upon, but could not interfere with union "autonomy". Today it is widely recognized in labour circles that unions are not simply about defending workers' rights at the place of work, and the artificial barriers between workplace and community are not so impregnable. Thus we see the emergence of a "social unionism" that recognizes workers as citizens and consumers and not just economic actors. Unions can also take on a "political unionism" strategy, particularly in the Third World, where the traditional "Northern" economic unionism may not be effective. Unions therefore become political or even "populist" campaigning organizations, from South Africa to Latin America, but also from Poland to the United States, where they have developed a more fluid view of how to pursue their struggle under contemporary capitalism. The emerging social movement unionism is an active, community-oriented strategy that works with a broad conception of who the working people are. It breaks down the binary oppositions between workplace and community, economic and political struggles and formal-sector workers and the working poor. When workers adopt this orientation they often find allies among the "new" social movements and, in particular, in NGOs. The ICFTU campaign against child labour with its broad alliance strategy, including active collaboration with the relevant NGOs, is in its own way a reflection of the growing power of social movement unionism in the trade union imaginary. The clearly perceived diminishing returns of "business as usual" strategies lead even sectarian and bureaucratic trade union leaderships in the direction of social movement unionism.

It is always wise to take a long-term perspective on labour, especially in its conflicted relation with capital. Giovanni Arrighi makes the useful point that there has always historically been a considerable time lag in terms of labour's response to capital's restructuring (Arrighi 1996). Looking back to the previous period of global financial expansion in the late nineteenth century, Arrighi finds that there were 25 years of organizational instability, with more defeats than victories, and then it took another 25 years "before the ideological and organisational contours of the world labour movement became powerful enough to impose some of its objectives on world capitalism" (Arrighi 1996: 348). We can now expect that, thanks to the current condition of "time–space compression", the labour revival this time will not take 50 years to materialize. Indeed, the signs of this revival have been there since around 2010, as a number of labour struggles worldwide signalled a very real social recomposition and political revival of the labour movement. What is also clear is that this revitalized labour movement will be much influenced by the example of the "new" social movements that have come to the fore over the last 30 years. In this sense, labour will increasingly become a social movement once again. Current labour activity worldwide is no longer confined to desperate rearguard actions against neoliberalism, as was the case in the 1980s and early 1990s. While still weakened by the ravages of the long neoliberal night, the international labour movement has since 2000 entered into a process of recomposition. The first reactions of fear and insecurity in the face of the forces unleashed by globalization have given way to a more settled and confident mood.

When considering the role of trade unions in a global world, the first thing we need to consider is the variety of unionism, which, just like "varieties of capitalism" (see Coates 2000), recognizes that there is no one model. Thus, when faced with the challenges posed by globalization, unions coming from a business unionism background will respond differently from those ensconced for many decades in a social democratic or corporatist model. Thus Lowell Turner argues that trade union revitalization may combine a range of strategies depending on its history, including "organizing, labour–management partnership, political action, reform of union structures, coalition-building, and international solidarity" (Turner 2004: 114). Trade union revitalization is clearly context-dependent, but we cannot ignore how, in the era of globalization and fluid transnational communications, we may well see hybrid strategies emerging; unions may "skip stages" and adopt strategies from other locations and times. Whatever forms emerge in response to conditions, in all cases there will be a need for trade unions to get back in touch with their grass roots, listen much more to their members, who can be drivers of innovation, and connect more with the general issues affecting workers without being restricted by traditional notions of the role of trade unions.

The other major framing concept to bear in mind is the spatiality of labour in all its aspects. The "spatial turn" in the social sciences belatedly had an impact on labour studies. Now, as Susan McGrath-Champ, Andrew Herod and Al Rainnie show, the vision of Ohmae and others of a "flat world" (Ohmae 1990) under neoliberalism was wrong, and we recognize how labour markets are regulated in place-specific ways, social relations are constructed over space, and workers are subject to what we might call a "socio-spatial dialectic" (McGrath-Champ, Herod & Rainnie 2010: 6–7). The triumphalist visions of Ohmae and others that globalization meant the end of distance/space, and the pessimism of others who saw labour mired in a static local world, were now being replaced by a more complex understanding of the various interlinked scales on which labour was formed, organized and struggled, from the local to the global, through national, subregional and supraregional, not excluding the domestic level. Workers could also, in this regard, "skip scales" and take local labour struggles to the transnational domain.

There is now a growing interest in the "global unions" generated as a response to globalization but with origins back to the start of industrialization. On the face of it, the global unions are a formidable social force, and, I would argue, a clear example of the Polanyian counter-movement, whereby social forces react against the destructive impact of the unregulated market. If neoliberalism dominated the 1990s and early 2000s, since then we have seen a less decisive dominant strategy and an increase in labour organizing. Global Unions is an umbrella organization embracing the 176-million-strong International Trade Union Confederation formed in 2006, the Trade Union Advisory Committee of the OECD and ten powerful global union federations, the successors to the old international trade secretariats. Transnational trade unionism has now become normalized as part of the repertoire of the unions. We see, for example, in 2008 the alliance between the United Steelworkers in the United States and UNITE, the UK union, and in 2009 the creation of Nautilus International through a merger of Nautilus UK and Nautilus Netherlands, representing professional maritime staff.

There is a huge diversity in the way transnational unionism organizes and the activities it undertakes. It can operate between different union executives or at grass-roots level. It may be workplace-oriented or involve NGOs in campaigning around labour issues. It may successfully bridge the local/global divide or political divisions, but that is not automatic and there will be occasions when it may not be able to do so. Successful transnational unionism is able to negotiate complexity and to leverage its own multi-level modes of operating. We have, for example, seen the successful exercising of workers' power in apparel value chains. Mark Anner (2011) describes one such campaign against sweatshops in the apparel industry, showing how direct action by students in the United States aided workers organizing in Honduras. Garment workers in global value chains are usually considered weak up against hypermobile high-profit companies such as Nike. Such corporations are vulnerable to boycotts, and when transnational union resources are focused on a particular industry or country they have considerable resources and power.

Ultimately, we need to recognize that it is not a question of the onward march of labour simply restarting after it was halted by neoliberalism. The complexity of transnational labour organizing is fraught with contradictions and pitfalls. There is the usual contradiction between limited resources and unlimited labour issues to take up. Organizing new layers of workers may, in fact, reduce the capacity of unions to take action. There is a huge problem with the transnational collective bargaining approach of the 1970s, in so far as it ignored the majority of the informal or precarious global labour force. Political lobbying and labour education have a valuable place in a global strategy, but they do not resolve the organizational or representational deficit the unions now face. Labour market activity (around codes of conduct, for example) can be mounted in association with the NGOs but the contradictions between two organizational logics are ever-present. Without wishing to appear glibly optimistic, however, I would concur with the conclusion of Richard Croucher and Elizabeth Cotton that "[t]he global unions are the only institutions that can develop the collective experience, articulation and collaboration between unions in the way demanded by globalization" (Croucher & Cotton 2009: 119).

From the International Confederation of Free Trade Unions to the smallest local union, there is now a well-established understanding that globalization represents one of the severest challenges to the labour movement since its inception. At its 16th world congress, held in 1996, the ICFTU's main position paper argued: "The position of workers has changed as a result of globalization of the economy and changes in the organization of production" (ICFTU 1997: 4). So, at the very centre of its strategic concerns was the question of globalization and the need for transnational action, once the lonely call of far left groups on the fringes of the labour movement. Now the ICFTU – still bureaucratic, but with a new post-Cold War identity – could state quite categorically that "one of the main purposes of the international trade union movement is the international solidarity of workers" (ICFTU 1997: 51). Perhaps symbolically marking the entry of the ICFTU into the era of globalization and the information society, the 1996 world congress also saw the launch of the organization's own dedicated website.

"International solidarity must become a natural reflex throughout the union movement" was the bold proclamation of the then ICFTU general secretary, Bill Jordan (2000). When Jordan, a cautious (not to say conservative) ex-leader of the British Engineering Workers' Union, stated that international labour solidarity (not just on May Day) was the order of the day, something had changed. I believe it is mainly that the objective conditions created by globalization demanded a concerted international trade union strategy. Furthermore, in terms of the changing organization of production outlined above, the ICFTU has become aware that the Western, urban, male, full-time, permanent worker is no longer the only, or even the core, member of the trade unions. The ICFTU now proclaims a new orientation towards women workers and young workers. It addresses the issue of the informal sector, both in developing countries and in the advanced industrial societies. The ICFTU has even begun to understand that it must work with far less traditional NGOs and campaigning groups on issues such as that of child labour. There are, of course, limitations to this sea change in traditional ICFTU policies and practices, but the shift is a comprehensive one.

The international trade secretariats have, for a very long time, played a strong international role. These organizations trace their origins back to the turn of the last century and embrace national unions in a particular sector – for example, transport, the food industry, mining. One ITS, the International Federation of Chemical, Energy, Mine and General Workers' Unions, argued that the dramatic increase of internationalization since the mid-1980s demanded a coherent international labour strategy. The move towards international trade union action should not be seen as a last resort (when action at the national level has failed); rather, "action has to be planned on the international basis right from the start" (ICEM 1996: 55). Fire-fighting, or wheeling in the international dimension when all else fails, is simply seen as an inadequate trade union response when capital has become so mobile in its activities. The ITSs are also keenly aware that their members, such as in the food industry, exist in commodity chains stretching from the supermarket through to the fields of the developing countries. The ITSs also have their weaknesses, however, as pointed out by Dan Gallin, himself a former general secretary of an ITS, the International Union of Food and Allied Workers. Although Gallin believes that the ITSs are the most effective international trade union organizations around, for him their weaknesses include being based on national unions that think in national terms, their financial and personnel constraints and the fact that "they hardly ever co-ordinate, do not communicate much and rarely co-operate" (Gallin 1999: 7). Compared to the resources of an MNC, the average ITS has a small contingent of 15 to 20 staff members coordinating global strategy from Geneva, albeit with an increased outreach potential because of the communications and transport revolution of the last 20 years.

At the regional level, trade unions are increasingly beginning to develop a coherent joint strategy. This is necessary and not surprising, given that one of the main effects of globalization is, in fact, an increased regionalization. The "triad" of the United States, the European Union and Japan has increased the importance of the regional dimension in all three areas. Thus, in 1973, the once fervent Little Englanders and rejectionists of all things "continental" in the British trade union movement became enthusiastic supporters of the European TUC and, much later, became key supporters of the Remain position during the Brexit debate. There is, of course, considerable debate on the effectiveness of European bodies such as the ETUC. For one, it is dependent on the Commission of the European Union for three-quarters of its budget, which hardly augurs well for its independence. Likewise, the effectiveness of the European works councils initiative is highly questionable (see Wills 2001). Yet, even if a pale Europeanism, based on semi-mythical notions of "social dialogue" or partnership, prevails over internationalism, there has still been significant cross-national union cooperation across Europe in the last decade.

In North America there was a fierce trade union debate in the United States, Canada and Mexico on how to respond to the North American Free Trade Agreement in the 1990s. Nationalist responses by the three labour movements moved closer to a common position, albeit partially and hesitantly, in relation to this major step towards capitalist rationalization. Establishing a community of interests among the workers of North America was not easy, and it did not do away with particular national interests. The US unions' orientation towards the "upward harmonization" of labour rights and standards in the region was by no means unambiguously welcome in Mexico, where different priorities probably prevail. It was also noticeable, however, that the Canadian unions, which previously knew little about labour conditions in Mexico, developed a remarkably sophisticated and sensitive policy towards transnational cooperation with Mexican workers and unions. Careful study of this whole experience can help move us beyond the sterile counter-position between the globalization blues and an abstract internationalism. Some of the ambiguity (and hopefulness) of the new transnational labour discourse can be discerned in the statement by American AFL–CIO president Lane Kirkland:

> You can't be a trade unionist unless you are an internationalist. You can't be a real trade unionist unless you think of workers wherever they happen to be, and unless you realise that substandard conditions and poverty anywhere in the world are a threat to good conditions and comparatively good standards anywhere in the world.
>
> (cited in French, Cowie & Littleham 1994: 1)

The conflictual, but ultimately productive, interaction between US, Mexican and Canadian trade unions over NAFTA may yet be undone by the protectionist policies of the Trump regime but the lessons learnt will not so easily dissipate.

National union centres are also changing under the impact of globalization. The limitation of nationalist, economistic and corporatist strategies are plain to see. In Denmark, the General Workers' Union has not only expanded greatly to embrace around a quarter of the country's workers but has put forward a remarkable programmatic statement (SID 1997). The Danish union calls for a bold "new global agenda" that argues: "We must use our global strength to force TNCs to have much more moral and ethical standards, to respect workers' rights, to have codes of conduct and to accept the establishment of international workers' councils" (SID 1997). There is a keen awareness here of the pressing international political issues raised by globalization. There is a feeling that this statement reflects more than just pious declarations, as many ICFTU statements seem to do. That is because the Danish union does not think in purely trade unionist ways and recognizes, for example, that

> NGOs are an important voice in civil society. As trade unions we must be more open to enter into strategic alliances not only with our political allies, but with NGOs such as women's and youth organisations, social welfare, development and human rights, and environment and consumers' organisations who share our general objectives.   (SID 1997)

The question arises as to whether these diverse labour organizations constitute a social movement, let alone a global social movement. For Castells, in his authoritative three-volume study of the new capitalism, "[t]orn by internationalization of finance and production, unable to adapt to networking of firms and individualization of work, and challenged by the engendering of employment, the labour movement fades away as a major source of social cohesion and workers' representation" (Castells 1997: 354). The rest of this book will seek to demonstrate that, while the challenges to labour are well diagnosed, that prognosis is, at the very least, outdated. It ignores the way a social movement can, by definition, learn and change to meet new situations. It assumes that capital and labour live in two watertight compartments, one in real-time fluidity, the other in boring clock-time stagnation.

In terms of who the workers are that the trade unions are organizing, or need to organize, the new global capitalist order has seen the nature of work changing rapidly, but there have also been many myths constructed around this transformation process. We have not witnessed the "end of work" and we are not all ICT workers. Massive proletarianization is at least as much a feature of globalization as the increased mobility of capital. Another feature often missed in media and academic emphases on the "new" in terms of "teleworkers", "cyberworkers", and so on is the survival – and, indeed, expansion – of "old" forms of work. Although the new informational economy is having profound effects on the world of work, it is well to recall that fully two-thirds of the world's workers still work in the fields of the South.

For the vast majority of the world's workers, the much-vaunted informational economy has had only a negative effect. For every worker who benefits from the "knowledge economy" there are many more still being super-exploited in agriculture or catering. It is worth taking India as an example, because it is that country's government, employers and some trade unions that have led the campaign against the "social clause". Why they take the stance becomes clearer when we realize that over 60 per cent of India's GDP is currently contributed by the country's massive unorganized sector, which accounts for around 80 per cent of employment. A third of the working population and two-thirds of the landless agricultural workers live below the official, fairly basic, nutrition-based poverty line (Harriss-White & Gooptu 2000: 90). When referring to an "unorganized" sector, we need to be clear what this means. There is a distinction between the "organized" capitalism of the early twentieth century and the "disorganized" capitalism of the late twentieth century. For India, Barbara Harriss-White and Nandini Gooptu make clear that while "most work may be unregulated by the state ... the markets for their labour are far from 'unstructured'" (Harriss-White & Gooptu 2000: 90). In fact, the workers and their labour are closely regulated by the reconstituted "traditional" structures of class, caste and gender.

The situation of those not benefiting from the "new" global economy has been taken up by the ILO with its "Decent work" campaign. For a whole historical period the ILO had focused mainly on male workers in formal economic institutions. At the turn of the century, however, it began to reorient towards the broad mass of the working poor and took up a strong gender stance. The ILO recognizes that "[t]he agenda for 'decent work', resting as it does on complementarities and new synergies between the social and economic aspects of development, requires new analytical frameworks" (ILO 1999: 3). The organization advocates a concept of "social efficiency" to match or balance the economic logic of globalization. The informal sector is recognized as a crucial area in which organized labour needs a strategy, particularly in the South. Women workers are made more visible through its new perspective, and the particular situation of migrant and child workers can be prioritized. The concept of "decent work" is, of course, a social construction, and varies across cultures. What the ILO has done is to introduce an ethical element into the "jobs debate", recognizing that the quality of employment is as important as the quantity.

At the other end of the work continuum are the "teleworkers", the networkers and innovators of globalization, the workers of "turbo-capitalism". These highly skilled, self-sufficient new employees are seen as the harbingers of future work practices and a categorical break with the traditional workers of capitalism. These "symbolic analysts" are the flip side of the fast food chain worker in the North, with whom they are more or less on a par in terms of numbers. They represent the beginnings of a true global labour market. They are, indeed, different from the industrial worker who actually "made" things, in so far as they "think" about things. It is less clear, however, that this form of work represents any sort of break with the "traditional" capital/wage labour relationship, based on exploitation. Ursula Huws writes: "It is apparent that a new cybertariat is in the making" (Huws 2000: 20), referring to the new front-line information workers of the North (and parts of the South) who are rapidly becoming proletarianized. There is, indeed, no certainty that the labour process of the new cyber-workplace, at Google, for example, is any more worker-friendly (in essence, as against image) than that of their 1950s counterparts, who wore grey suits to the office and had a job for life, however boring that might have been.

There is a common conception that these "new" workers cannot be organized by the "old" labour movement. This problem is recognized acutely by the trade unions, and thus a British trade union leader declared in 2000 that "[t]he whole future of trade unions depends on us demonstrating our value in [the] new sectors. We cannot just rest on our traditional heartlands of manufacturing and the public sector" (Morgan 2000). The new ICT professionals are much younger than the average trade union member, and their memory is of the neoliberal era and not of the golden era in which the unions had a certain social weight. Nevertheless, the "flexibility" of the new labour regime spells insecurity for its workers, and its much-vaunted speed of operations leads directly to stress for its operatives. This is creating some inroads for the unions, particularly when "old" unionized companies set up "new" economy offshoots. There is still a feeling that it is not only employer resistance that unions face but the perceived irrelevance of traditional trade unionism for the "new" workers. Sitting in the dot.com sector with a good salary, tempting share options and even employee "chill-out zones", why would you need a union?

In practice, the trade unions have begun to make considerable inroads into the "new" economy. This is hardly surprising if one recalls an earlier "new" capitalism when office workers came on the scene. They were considered "different" from their factory-floor counterparts, but by the middle of the twentieth century white-collar workers were one of the bastions of the labour movement in many countries. For Seumas Milne, the initial skirmishes between managers and union organizers in the dot.com sector "suggest the workings of the new economy may turn out to be more familiar than previously imagined" (Milne 2000). In short, the new economy still suffers from old problems. The famous Amazon online bookshop was the site of a fierce unionization battle in 2000, led by the Communication Workers of America for the customer service representatives and by the United Food and Commercial Workers Union for those who parcel up the books ordered on the internet. And it is the internet that has been the logical place to organize for many computer programmers. Thus in France employees of the UbiSoft video games producer set up the first "virtual trade union" in 2000 to defend their working conditions in a sector that does not believe in human relations departments, let alone trade unions.

The "new" knowledge workers may not seem so novel if a long-term view of the changing nature of the labour process is taken. Workers have nearly always used knowledge as well as physical effort to get the job done. The early workers in the auto industry had precisely such a knowledge of the labour process that Taylorism had to separate the tasks of conception and execution to create white-collar employees and blue-collar workers respectively. Today, for every "upmarket" flexibilized knowledge worker, there are three "downmarket" flexibilized workers. What is technically possible in terms of "future work" is unlikely to materialize in a social system still (or even more than ever) dominated by private profit and social divisions. As Standing points out, "In terms of work, the growth areas of the late twentieth century have been care and voluntary and paid work in non-governmental service organisations, usually non-profit, welfare-oriented groups" (Standing 1999: 395). Yet this work is not socialized; it has not become part of the mainstream of society. The denigration of non-profitable activities will probably diminish in the decades to come as the obsession with "social capital" increases.

We perhaps need to reconsider at this point the relationship between work and technology, in so far as it is crucial to all debates on the future of work. In the sociology of work there is a long tradition of technological determinism going back to Marx, who once said: "The hand-mill gives you society with the feudal lord; the steam mill gives you society with the industrial capitalist" (Marx 1976 [1867]: 166). Marx may well have regretted this statement, and, indeed, elsewhere he broke with this type of determinism, but the tradition lingers on. Thus, from at least the 1960s, there has been a tendency to argue that "computers give you a post-industrial society". All work will be carried out by computers and robots, and this will spell the end of work as we know it. In the real world, however, technology is mediated by social and political structures that make this scenario unlikely. New communications technology may soon mediate all economic transactions, but the underlying social structure is still a divided one. While technological innovation will most certainly impinge dramatically on the world of work, this will be mediated by capitalist organizational imperatives, and, for that matter, by the nature of workers' responses to them.

Finally, when considering the future of work, we should also recall with Chris and Charles Tilly that "[f]uture work will continue to depend on struggle – muted, routinised or openly contentious" (Tilly & Tilly 1998: 264). The repertoires of action in the diverse workplaces of capitalism have always been shaped by the continuous interplay between employers and employees. This is a dance that always has two partners, even though one or the other may lead at specific points in time. Class struggles have certainly changed format and modalities since the early days of capitalism but there is nothing to indicate that struggle has vacated the contemporary workplace. Indeed, there is every indication that globalization is proving to be as powerful an agglutinating factor as classical capitalism was in terms of unifying different social struggles against a common enemy. The repertoires of contention deployed by today's future workers may be different – and an element of individualism is undoubtedly more important than in the heyday of collectivist ideologies – but they are emerging and helping to shape the future of the globalized "new economy" as well.

PART II

DEVELOPMENT OF A GLOBAL WORKING CLASS

Since the emergence of capitalism the world has been divided into rich and poor, colonialist and colonized, First and Third Worlds, developed and developing countries and now, as they are termed, the Global North and Global South. This dichotomy is beginning to shift, as the globalization of capitalism is beginning to create a global labour force that increasingly experiences the same precarity wherever it is located. Whether it becomes a fully developed global working class, conscious of its own interests, depends on the internal struggles within the labour movement as much as on the development of the global economy.

I start with an analysis of the progress experienced in the North by the working class since the Second World War under the New Deal and the welfare state, the gradual unpicking of this settlement with the advent of neoliberal market policies and the impact of the collapse of the Soviet Union in the 1990s, up to the present-day gig economy. The following chapter takes up the story of the workers of the Global South in the same timeframe from the postcolonial 1950s to the new division of labour in the 1970s, which saw a massive increase of the working class and its ability to impose some improvements in labour standards. Finally, I chart the emergence of a new labour scene in the 1990s, which saw the North and South fading as the dominant analytical paradigm, to be replaced by that of the "global precariat": a precarious proletariat, with a global constituency. It is the struggles of this "global precariat", as part of the working class and not opposed to it, that will decide whether there is a new global working class in the decades to come.

4
WORKERS NORTH

As the workers and labour movement of the Global North began to suffer under neoliberalism, the emerging new era of globalization reduced Fordism to an almost mythical status. Under the guise of "flexible specialization", new work practices almost completely transformed the world of work. This chapter begins by examining the new model of flexible capitalist development. I also survey the newly important dimension of regionalization, both in North America and in Western Europe, which seems to go hand in hand with globalization. The key issue this chapter raises is whether in the North we now have a stable post-Fordist social regime of accumulation. Is there likely to be a new virtuous circle of capitalist growth and worker prosperity emerging in the capitalist heartlands? What have been the implications of bringing the workers of the once communist East into the capitalist orbit? Finally, what has been the trade union reaction to the new capitalism? We show how, after an era of disorientation, disorganization and demoralization during the 1980s, some new patterns of worker resistance emerged towards the end of the last century.

Flexible financial capitalism

The new growth regime that followed the collapse of the Fordist golden era was to be characterized, above all, by the dominance of finance capital. Whereas under the Fordist regulation model (see Chapter 2), in which national governments to a large extent determined financial matters, now the financial domain seemed to acquire a life of its own. The deregulation and opening up of financial markets across the West in the 1980s set up a contradiction between an unregulated global financial system and the fiscal role of the Keynesian welfare state. The booming stock markets and credit systems in the 1990s created a widespread mood of optimism about the future of capitalism. The "new economy", as it became known, would sweep away all before it, including trade unions, and generate a new knowledge-based society. That trade unions might be seen to be part of the "old economy" based on manufacturing is testified to by the fact that in Britain in 2000, while the average age of all workers was 34 years, the average age of trade union members was 46 years. It was only slowly that the trade unions would realize that the new economy and the "imperialism of finance" (Tabb 1999) would necessitate new strategies, tactics and, indeed, mindsets.

If financialization ruled in the "new economy", the term "flexibilization" came to dominate the labour market and the labour process. The discourse of labour "flexibility" dominated throughout the 1980s and into the 1990s. Poor economic performance in the West, particularly in Western Europe, was blamed on labour "rigidity" in terms of wages, labour conditions and constraints on capital imposed by trade unions. Flexibility became synonymous with dynamic change, and an ability to adapt to pressures and incentives. It did not appear to be either socially or politically smart to argue for the opposite of "flexibility". What the much-vaunted strategy actually entailed was a reduction in wages ("labour costs flexibility"), a reduction in the number of workers ("numerical flexibility") and an increase in the number of tasks the remaining workers had to perform ("functional flexibility"). Overall, by the end of the 1990s, across the North, the "flexibility" offensive had created a workforce that was much more insecure and had seen many of the welfare rights gained under Fordism wiped away.

The transition to the "new economy" could not, however, be seen as a panacea for capitalism. After all, economists and capitalists had also thought that the golden era would last indefinitely. Yet the virtuous circle of Fordism turned vicious as the internationalization of production put pressure on wages in the North, which in turn impacted on levels of consumption. To some extent, the "new economy" of flexible financial capital can be seen as a response to this crisis; it was not necessarily a stable new regime of accumulation. Tickell and Peck argue that the restoration of sustainable economic growth had not occurred by the late 1990s and that "the search for a new institutional fix continues" (Tickell & Peck 1995: 373), a gap still evident today. From this perspective, neoliberal globalization can be seen as "a symptom of continuing political-economic disorder" (Tickell & Peck 1995: 375) rather than as a harbinger of a new order. In particular, there is nothing to suggest, especially after the debacle of the 1999 Seattle WTO ministerial meeting, which did not reach a consensus, that stability in the capitalist order can be achieved without setting up a widely acceptable and credible global regulatory order.

An assumption running through most of the debates and polemics around globalization and the new financial capitalism in the early 2000s was that national economic policy-making was now ruled out. If that were to be the case, national governments would simply become pawns in the big game of globalization, and workers' organizations would be bereft of any viable strategies at the national level. The TNCs were seen to be "footloose and fancy-free", roaming the world for the best locations. Increasingly globalized markets were seen to lead to the logical corollary of open world labour markets. Thus, an influential article on "Global Work Force 2000" in the *Harvard Business Review* (Johnston 1991) argued: "The globalization of labor is inevitable ... As labor gradually becomes international, some national differences will fade" (Johnston 1991: 126). With capital globally mobile and labour rapidly becoming so, the role of the nation state in regulating capital, labour and the capital/wage labour relation would, quite obviously, fade away. That there have been tendencies in this direction seems clear enough, but it is also the case that they can (and do) simply serve as an alibi for national governments that want to "go with the flow" of globalization rather than take a national development path.

Now that the first wave of globalization has passed, it is less plausible to see the irreversible decline of the nation state as attributable to exogenous techno-logical changes. To a large extent, the portrayal of the nation state as anachron-istic has been part of the disempowering rhetoric of globalization. From this perspective, as Manfred Bienefeld puts it, "[g]lobalization is treated as beneficial and inevitable, [while] demands for national sovereignty are dismissed as mis-guided and foolish" (Bienefeld 1993: 415). The optimism, arrogance and ahis-torical blindness of the globalizers have given rise to a counter-movement of progressives calling for a return to nation state hegemony and a reaffirmation of sovereignty (and even of protectionism). Apart from Bienefeld himself, the most articulate case comes from Paul Hirst and Grahame Thompson, who not only argue, with considerable statistical support, that the globalization of production has been exaggerated but also suggest that, "far from being undermined by the processes of internationalization, these processes strengthen the importance of the nation-state in many ways" (Hirst & Thompson 1996: 17). The role of the nation state in crafting a recovery from the 2007–9 global financial crisis has shown, in practice, that the "death of the nation state" was somewhat premature, if not just wishful thinking on the part of the globalizers.

It is probably not a question of simply steering a middle course between the "globalizers" and the "nation-staters", I would argue. As with development theory more generally, there is always an interplay – or "dialectic" – between internal and external factors in explaining employment patterns and inequality trends. The answer is never simple, as Glyn shows in a careful statistical ana-lysis of "internal and external constraints on egalitarian policies" (Glyn 1999), which does not lead to any conclusive answers. Certainly, no one should ignore national histories, modalities of class struggle and the responsibilities of national governments. The regulation school analysis of the Fordist era always stressed national trajectories, and in development theory this led to a healthy "internal causation" reaction against dependency theory. Under the regime of flexible financial capitalism, however, the space for different models has diminished. As François Chesnais puts it, with regard to the regulation approach, "The modalities of integration into the international system of the globalised regime of accumulation with financial predominance [our flexible financial capitalism] are both infinitely more constraining and more homogenising than they were in the Fordist accumulation mode" (Chesnais 1997: 297).

Future of work

Another underlying assumption of, for example, the 1999 Seattle protests against the WTO is that globalization will lead to a "race to the bottom" in terms of labour standards. While the globalization optimists were predicting an equalization upwards of wages across the world (as predicted by the Heckscher–Ohlin model of international trade), the sceptics were claiming a "bargaining down" by national governments and the spread of "social dumping". With competitiveness the watchword across the world, cost minimization strategies by businesses are bound to have an effect on labour. As we shall see below, however, there is no clear, universal and irreversible tendency for wages to decrease and inequality to increase. Likewise, only a small proportion of the world's workers are part of what might be conceived of as a "global labour market", in the sense that they are fully mobile and can transfer from location to location. This really applies only to the top business elite, frequent-flyer class. Thus, our analysis needs to be disaggregated and cannot be based on "global" trends alone.

Nor should we accept the simplistic thesis that the "new economy" spells the "end of work". It has been argued by some that manufacturing jobs will disappear in the face of the new information technology in the same way that agricultural jobs were decimated by Fordism and urbanization in the past. A shift of occupation to the services sector is also ruled out because of the increasing impact of automation in that sector. Society, it has been suggested, will divide up into workers and non-workers, with social exclusion becoming more important than economic inequality. As Castells notes, however, the forecasters of a jobless society "do not provide any consistent, rigorous evidence of their claims, relying on isolated press clippings, random examples of firms in some countries and sectors, and 'commonsense' arguments on the 'obvious' impact of computers on jobs" (Castells 1996a: 255). What is ironic, over and beyond the lack of any clear link between automation, robotics and joblessness, is that these predictions were issued in the United States in the mid-1990s, a period in which 8 million jobs were created over a four-year period.

The new economy – flexible financial capitalism, as I have called it here – is characterized by combined and uneven development, in the same way that the old one was. Yet there are also elements pulling in the opposite direction: the need for the social and political embeddedness of economic standards remains. The need for some social regulation of market processes increasingly makes itself felt, particularly in the wake of the 2007–9 global financial crisis, which even fervent supporters of globalization put down to a deregulation process that had gone too far. Boyer, for one, is extremely sceptical of the suggestion that current transformations will lead to the emergence of a totally novel regulation mode based on a finance-led accumulation regime (Boyer 2000). As in the past, with Fordism, institutional configurations and institutionalized class compromises will vary across countries and regions, and a universal "new economy" is not likely to materialize. For Boyer, in a similar way to the combined and uneven development option, the result is likely to be a form of "hybridity", with different forms in different countries according to their diverse social and political legacies, creating what we might call "varieties of the new capitalism".

What is not in question throughout these debates is that the era of globalization is having profound effects in the world of work. In Chapter 3 we saw the extent to which "marketization" is bringing more and more workers across the globe directly under the sway of capitalist relations. While in the 1970s around one-third of the world's workers lived under central planning regimes (the "socialist" camp), by the 1990s they were under fully (if "primitive") capital accumulation regimes. Such giants as Russia, India and China have now entered the domain of fully marketized societies. The cutting edge of the new economy is, of course, the information technology sector, and here international mobility and flexibility have reached a peak. This technological revolution and associated drops in the cost of communication and transport have been the drivers of the increased economic integration that is at the heart of the globalization process. Workers in this sector in particular have become part of a global labour market. But what about the two-thirds of the world's workers still on the land and the industrial workers of the "old" North?

It would seem that it is the industrial workers of the old smokestack industries who are one of the main losers in the globalization race. Economic theory (in the shape of the Heckscher–Ohlin model) would tell us that increased North–South trade should lead to a fall of wages in the North and an increase in the South as markets integrate. But both sets of workers are said to gain in terms of efficiency. Leaving to one side, for now, the picture in the South, we should consider here the impact of globalization on Northern workers. The main losers are undoubtedly the "unskilled" workers of the North, such as those in the US Rust Belt who voted for Donald Trump, who were hit hardest by the practical disappearance of the labour-intensive section of the North's manufacturing sector. The optimistic reading of current trends is that the increased efficiency resulting from market integration, referred to above, will eventually pay off and that a new golden era will emerge for labour too. For the pessimists, there is a large global labour surplus, and increased trade with the South exposes vulnerable sectors of the North's economy and workforce to competition it cannot deal with. Inevitably, wages and conditions will go down and unemployment will go up. Any gains from increased economic integration will go to capital and not to labour, especially the traditional working class outside the high-tech sectors.

Adrian Wood considers the effect of increased North–South trade on employment and inequality and concludes that, at the very least, the "optimists" above "greatly underestimate the adverse side effects of this trade on income inequality in the North" (Wood 1994: 4). At the same time, though, he berates the "pessimists" for advocating a retrograde protectionism in which all workers across the globe will lose. It is thus not a matter of labour losses generally and across the board in the North; rather, the issue is that, while skilled workers have gained from the "new economy", the traditional unskilled workforce has invariably lost out. Less costly than protectionism would be government intervention to assist those sectors affected by this process. The European Union's discourse of "social inclusion" has precisely that function, while in North America the rhetoric of "flexibility" rules supreme. The much-vaunted increase in employment in the United States during the 1990s (referred to above) was extremely precarious, and badly paid jobs were typical of this process. Perhaps more important than North–South comparisons for workers of the industrialized countries is the competition between the US and European social regimes of accumulation, which are the real elements in competition and not the largely fictional "national" economies.

Regional models of capitalism

If we take a balanced look at the new internationalized, information-based, flexible capitalism, we see that it is not so much global as regional in its impact. Regionalization is not a counter-tendency to globalization but, probably, an integral element in its operationalization. Regionalism even more so than globalization is an elusive concept, often just described geographically. For some analysts, the European Union, the North American Free Trade Agreement, Mercosur and the Asia-Pacific Economic Cooperation organization operate with a different logic from the multilateral system that has guided economic relations since the end of the Second World War. But most regional institutions can also be seen to foster economic openness and bolster the multilateral system. In both the Global North and the Global South there are varieties of regionalism, just as there are varieties of capitalism. Regional blocks can be defensive as well as offensive and have different relations with the global capitalist system. This results in both conflict and cooperation at the same time, under a regime of non-hegemonic interdependence at the global level.

United States

We begin our analysis of the different regional models of capitalism inevitably with the United States, given that Fordism was also the "American epoch". During the long postwar boom American capitalism shaped the global economy in many ways. After the reconstruction of Europe and the re-emergence of Japan as an economic power, however, its hegemony was no longer uncontested. After the collapse of the golden era, US capital sought to restructure itself on a profitable basis, mainly through an attack on the workers. A startling statistic is that, between 1950 and the mid-1960s, while US employers had accepted nearly a half of all petitions for trade union elections, this proportion fell to 26 per cent in 1970 and 16 per cent in 1973 (Brenner 1998: 109). Following the 1974–5 oil-crisis-driven recession, the employers' offensive deepened. Work practices were shaken up with draconian "productivity drives", anti-welfare and austerity drives were mounted and the safety net of social services virtually disintegrated. The weaker traditional sectors of industry, established in the "Keynesian" era, were also ruthlessly undercut. So, was a new and prosperous "American model" the result of this drastic surgery, as promised by its promoters?

According to many commentators, the United States in the 1990s entered a period of sustained economic growth that seemed set to pull the world economy along in its wake. Certainly, by the mid-1990s US manufacturing had recovered to the profitability levels of 1973, but it was still far short of the levels in the 1950s and 1960s (Brenner 1998: 187). Yet there was little to justify faith in a "new era" other than the Wall Street stock market's sustained boom. To a large extent, the claims for a new turbo-charged capitalism come from the new economy sectors, in which productivity is notoriously difficult to measure. The rise, and subsequent dramatic decline, of the e-commerce sector (the dot-com bubble of the late 1990s and early 2000s) is testimony to how difficult it is to make confident predictions for the new capitalism. Brenner argues that even "the low rates of inflation and unemployment of the late 1990s are 'unremarkable' based, as they are, on an 'extraordinarily slow growth of both demand and wage costs'" (Brenner 1998: 249). Neither GDP growth rates nor those of aggregate demand point towards a dynamic US model of capitalism, capable of launching a new golden era matching the postwar boom.

US regionalism in North America, as concretized in NAFTA, is entirely consonant with the advance of free market liberalism since the 1980s. Although regionalism in the Americas had effectively collapsed in the 1970s, thanks to the debt crisis and an absence of an agreed development paradigm, that subsequently changed. Erstwhile economic nationalists in Latin America have turned their backs on national development to fully embrace economic integration with, albeit subordinate to, the North. While no one believes that textbook economics will prevail and that working conditions and rewards will equalize across the Americas, there is a belief that integration is not a zero-sum game and that less powerful economies may also benefit to some extent. From the perspective of the North, the NAFTA process points towards the limits of an independent economic policy for a country such as Canada. It also indicates that the United States retains the option of applying "open regionalism" in its own sphere in such a way that it discriminates against non-members, for example in Europe or Japan. The history of the Trump administration so far has confirmed that the United States will choose whatever international path it considers best in the short term and is not wedded to the global free market ideology.

Europe

The European "model" of capitalism and industrial relations is often contrasted favourably with its US counterpart, as being somehow more "social". There is an implicit contrast between a US-model "low road" to capitalism and a European "high road" based on high skill levels, productivity and wages. Once human resources are recognized as a crucial economic input, it makes sense to increase expenditure on education and training and to ensure minimal health and social security provisions as a safety net for those who fall out of the labour market. While deregulation and flexibility were the watchwords in Western Europe throughout the 1980s, this did not necessarily conflict with corporatist arrangements when those successfully regulated capital/labour relations. Whether it was neoliberalism, neocorporatism or even some notion of social consensus or partnership, the overriding objective was to "modernize" European capitalisms to make them more "competitive" in the era of globalization. It is important always to realize that behind the European "model" lay a diversity of national configurations and distinct pathways.

Certainly, Europe provides interesting material for the debate as to whether globalization would promote convergence or diversity between national societies (Berger & Dore 1996; Crouch & Streeck 1997). Overall, the pattern of change in the social systems of production and industrial relations in Western Europe since the 1970s points towards a prevalence of diversity, albeit a renewed or revised diversity. Thus, for example, Boyer finds that, in the race for flexibility in the 1980s, specific national factors re-emerged, to the extent that "one of the main lessons to be learnt from this international comparison is that each country [in Europe] has its own way of adapting to a lower, less stable, rate of growth" (Boyer 1988: 212). The uniformity of the Fordist era, underwritten by steady rates of growth, gave way to greater instability and diversity. The specific history, structure, even "custom and practice", of each country's capital/wage labour relations sets the context of how an overriding imperative such as "flexibility" is dealt with, modulated, possibly even subverted, in practice.

As to the European Union, it has been inherently contradictory in its policies in the last decades. The drive towards the single currency and deregulation is a major element in the neoliberal revolution, but concern with "social Europe" (although resisted in the United Kingdom) points towards a more socially integrationist model. The European Union has expressed a concern to balance "flexibility" with social security and to ensure that the drive towards competitiveness does not lead to wholesale social exclusion. A crucial question is the extent to which an expanding European Union will maintain this tendency and not create a two-tier Europe as divisive as was the north–south split in Europe during the 1970s and early 1980s. There is a clear tendency for the continuation of the welfare state to be sacrificed at the altar of competitiveness. As Castells notes, however, "The political debate and the social conflicts around the ways to control, and guide, the transformation of European societies throughout their gradual integration into an increasingly globalized economy" (Castells 1996a: 325) have now opened, and it cannot be reduced to the brave new digital globalizers versus the old bureaucratic public sector. It remain to be seen what impact Brexit will have on the rest of Europe but we can assume that the debates raised here will continue albeit without the United Kingdom holding things back.

Japan

The last leg of the "triad" of the global North is Japan, home of "Toyotism", and sometime model and sometime culprit for other capitalisms. The postwar transformation of Japan is one of the success stories of contemporary capitalism. The social and cultural embeddedness of Japanese economic institutions has been a key to this success. Nor can Japan's long enduring economic crises of the 1990s justify the apostles of neoliberalism, who use it to proclaim the superiority of non-institutionalized, free market capitalism. Not only did the state play a key role in promoting economic development but firms continued to act as "institutional companies", exercising a degree of regulation. Against the fashions of current development theory, Japan has always been characterized by a national development strategy and a strong developmental state. High rates of investment have been associated with rising living standards for the working population. As Castells outlines, this remarkable economic performance "relied on social stability and high labour productivity through management–labour co-operation, made possible by stable employment and by seniority-based promotion, for the core labour force" (Castells 1998: 219). The "Japanese miracle" entered into crisis in the mid-1990s, however, and no longer seems such an attractive option. Inevitably, the rise of China since the mid-1990s, with its economic reforms, has to some extent marginalized Japan in the region.

The regional dimension of Japan within the Pacific-Asia region is extremely significant, pointing towards what Castells has called "a powerful, semi-integrated Asianpacific economy that has become a major centre of capital accumulation in the world" (Castells 1998: 169). Indeed, up until the 1990s this appeared to be the only dynamic growth area in a generally stagnant capitalist world economy. Since then, of course, China has emerged as the major economic power in the region, eclipsing the East Asia NICs and Japan while building on their success. Whether this will lead to a new "Pacific era" for global capitalism, to match the "Atlantic era" of the twentieth century, is open to question, however. Castells, while optimistic that this new economic network will be the harbinger of a new multicultural global economy, somewhat contradictorily says that there can be no Pacific epoch because "there is no Pacific region as a separate or integrated reality" and its process of development "has been, and is, enacted by parallel nationalisms" (Castells 1998: 308). China's role in the new global economy seems to confirm this verdict, in so far as we see few signs that China aspires to replace the United States as global hegemonic power, focusing instead on the development of its particular variant of state capitalism.

The Great Financial Crisis of 2007–9 led to a general recognition that a process of global realignment had occurred since the end of the Cold War. The likely endpoint of the shifting positions between the major imperialist powers is as yet unclear. We are unlikely to witness anything as comparable as the shift from a UK to a US global economy that occurred after the last major capitalist crisis in the 1930s. Most analysts would probably agree with Andrew Gamble's verdict that "the United States may be suffering a further relative decline – many of its capacities and its structural power are weaker than they were – [but] there is still no clear challenger to take over" (Gamble 2009: 139). Although the European Union has an economy of a similar size its ever-continuing political divisions (not least the complex impact of Brexit) make it an unlikely contender to take on the role of new global hegemon. As to China, its economic potential is of course huge, and on its present course it will probably emerge as the world's largest economy quite soon. China does not seem posed for global leadership as the United States was in 1930 (or even earlier), however, and it faces the massive social and political contradictions of its classical-Marxist-style industrialization and urbanization processes.

In summary, we have passed from the sometimes abstract concept of globalization to its unfolding through regionalization, a process that picked up steam in the 1990s. While this process may well complement liberalization, it may also undermine liberalization, and lead to reconstituted forms of (inter)national pooled sovereignty. Regional development policies, in Europe, for example, are well able to deal with and constrain the allegedly all-powerful transnational corporations. What European integration also points towards is the advantages to capitalism of social stability. The "other side" of globalization as a driven, dynamic and despotic process is what Kathleen Thelen and Ikuo Kume, writing on Germany and Japan, refer to as "employers' heightened dependence on stable and predictable relations at the plant level" (Thelen & Kume 1999: 478). Not only are production networks much more tightly integrated today but the demands of just-in-time labour processes (see section on after-Fordism below) also point towards the limits of deregulation. The destabilizing effects of the neoliberal-driven process of globalization impact upon capitalists as much as upon workers and can drive them back towards more cooperative relations with the workforce. Of course, unexpected events in the political domain may derail this tendency and lead to a renewal of inter-capitalist rivalries, but, I would argue, these underlying tendencies continue to operate.

What we need to consider from this perspective is the issue of the social embeddedness of economic relations, a theme derived from the early work of Polanyi. Contrary to the nostrums of neoliberalism, markets exist within society and firms are embedded in social relations. The different national and regional models of capitalism examined above are all distinct social systems of production. The high tide of neoliberalism has passed and the once unlikely terms of "trust" and "cooperation" are returning to rational long-sighted capitalist discourse. What is particularly important to note, again with Hollingsworth and Boyer (1996: 46), is that in the era of global competitiveness it is not "economies" that are competing but, rather, social systems of production. The very nature of a country's social and political fabric is being tested in the era of globalization, and, while this may well have destructive effects, it also presents an opportunity for progressive social and political transformations.

Capitalism in the former communist Eastern Europe

What made capitalist globalization a plausible prospect was, above all, the collapse of the alternative socialist, state capitalist or bureaucratic-collectivist mode of production that had prevailed in the East. The reintegration of Russia's, Eastern Europe's and then China's workers into the capitalist world economy represents a fundamental social transformation in world history. These so-called "transition" economies have moved from "Marx to the market", without medi-ation, in a dramatically short time span. The World Bank, in its influential 1996 report entitled *From Plan to Market* (World Bank 1996), pushes the line of a "short, sharp shock" to build capitalism in the East, but admits: "More Russians are dying during transition. Male life expectancy fell by six years between 1990 and 1994 (from 64 to 58) and that of women by three years (from 74 to 71)" (World Bank 1996: 120). The box text, cheerfully entitled "Is transition a killer?", looks around for contributory causes, such as an increasing consumption of vodka, but, while stressing that it is still "the subject of continuing investigation", effectively concludes, in all fairness, that "the transition itself is a direct cause" (World Bank 1996: 128).

It is important to understand why the socialist model collapsed in the Soviet Union, because this has serious implications for the future of workers in these countries – and elsewhere, for that matter. Basically, I would argue that it collapsed under its own contradictions, primarily the failure of the statist indus-trialization model to adapt to the new capitalism emerging in the 1970s and 1980s. As Castells puts it, the crisis of the Soviet economy and society from the mid-1970s onwards "was the expression of the structural inability of statism and of the Soviet variant of industrialism to ensure the transition towards the infor-mation society" (Castells 1998: 7). While the Soviet model of industrialization was able to some extent to compete with industrial capitalism, it lacked the dyna-mism and flexibility to make the leap into post-industrial information capitalism. There was a need to shift from an extensive to an intensive model of develop-ment, and the system simply collapsed under the pressure. It was a similar tran-sition to that which many developing economies, particularly in Latin America, had to make in the 1970s, namely from the collapse of the import substitution model of industrialization to the export-led, more intensive model that prevailed from then onwards.

Once the old statist model had collapsed, and with it the welfare state that it represented to workers, capitalism had to be constructed. As with the ori-ginal emergence of capitalism in the West, its Eastern variant had to engage in a process of what Marx called "primitive accumulation" to create a capitalist class. Workers were "freed" from welfarism to create a pool of proletarians and the nomenklatura was given free rein to loot the state so as to acquire cap-ital. The free market advisors brought in from the United States to oversee this process were ostensibly shocked to see the development of a "gangster capit-alism" quite unlike the serene model of capitalist development their textbooks suggested would occur. The World Bank finds that liberalization led to "rampant corruption and rent seeking" (World Bank 1996: 23) but still stresses the need to ensure private property rights: "Property rights are at the heart of the incentive structure of market economies ... They determine who bears risk and who gains or loses ... [T]hey spur worthwhile investment [,] promote work effort [and] reward effort and good judgement" (World Bank 1996: 48–9). It is now debated openly in Western financial centres whether "good judgement" was displayed by those who encouraged the development of "gangster capitalism" in the East, which even on its own terms is proving unviable.

It was an integral part of the logic of this transition that it was the workers in the transition economies who would suffer most. In just a few years industrial employment was cut by one-third and wages fell by almost two-thirds. The ILO notes the emergence in all the "transition" economies of high and long-term unemployment and that "[t]he worst aspect of economic restructuring is the appalling growth in the number of people living in poverty" (ILO 1995: 111). Women workers were particularly hard hit, as they were driven by the new capitalism back into the home. The general picture is that in the Soviet Union there were 100 million people living below the official poverty line by 1991, and in 1992, after a bout of hyperinflation, it was officially reckoned that 80 per cent of the population had incomes that put them below the poverty line (ILO 1995: 112). Since then there has been some recovery but many workers, if they were lucky enough not to lose their jobs, were pushed into precarious, low-income jobs, with the concept of a minimum wage seen as a quaint relic of the past. The welfarism that "actually existing socialism" represented in practice for workers was also an increasingly patchy or simply rhetorical affair. The workers of the East were in an extremely fluid and uncertain situation as they came into the capitalist domain. Castells is surely right when he argues that "the most enduring legacy of Soviet statism will be the destruction of civil society after decades of systematic negation of its existence" (Castells 1998: 68). There were no dense networks of activated civil society to call on in reconstructing the world of workers after the collapse of real socialism. Individual survival strategies were no match for a globalized capitalism in full flow seeking to incorporate the uncolonized lands of the East. In these fast-moving economic flows of "globalization", the reconstruction of a Soviet cultural and political identity proved very hard. The social and economic devastation, with a particularly hard impact on women, youth, elders and the disabled, created a social wasteland. The ILO understates the situation when it declares that these issues "threaten the political stability of the new nations, bring the risk of social discord much closer and undoubtedly contribute to a substantial worsening of socio-economic inequality" (ILO 1995: 111).

As Mikhail Gorbachev began his fateful policy of perestroika in the second half of the 1980s the Russian labour movement became reactivated. In 1989 the powerful miners' union began an all-Russia strike, which, according to Kirill Buketov, "awoke the country from its lethargic slumber. For the first time in many years, hundreds of thousands of workers gave notice of their dissatisfaction with their wretched position and of their unwillingness to remain mute slaves" (Buketov 1999: 100). Perestroika then began to operate within the trade unions as the old statist apparatuses – "transmission belts" of the Communist Party line, according to official doctrine – came under pressure from below and from the broader economic and political transformations under way. New independent trade unions, outside Party control, were formed in many sectors. The 1989 miners' strike thus prompted a massive reorganization of the trade unions and brought the workers' movement to the fore in the process of political change. Nevertheless, while the strikes of 1989, and a reprise in 1991, were instrumental in bringing down the old regime, Simon Clarke is right to note that "the workers had neither the time nor the space in which to constitute their own organisations, and consequently have had a very small part to play in the unfolding of the crisis" (Clarke 1992: 26).

The Soviet trade unions had conceived of their role from 1917 onwards as "transmission belts" between the Communist Party and the working masses. They came to play a crucial role in maintaining the stability of the Soviet system, oiling the relations between workers and the state. Now, with the collapse of the Soviet model and the rapid process of economic transformation, the very *raison d'être* of the trade unions was called into question. The drive towards marketization imposed the logic of a capital/wage labour conflict on the situation very abruptly, albeit mediated by the specific features of the Soviet transition. The trade union leadership sought, naturally enough, from its point of view, to carve out a role for itself under the new dispensation, under the banner of "social partnership". Thus keying into a dominant Western paradigm, the accumulated economic, political and social weight of the trade unions under communism could be reconfigured in the nascent capitalist order. The extent to which that mission has been successful is debatable, but the point is that the trade unions did not just shut up shop and go home.

It is not a "normal" capital/wage labour relationship that emerged in Russia, in so far as the trade unions tend to ally with their direct employers against the government and the new "raw" capitalist measures. Notwithstanding the lingering concept of a "labour collective" and the nostalgia for a productivist capitalist model, the new capitalism has become a reality. Significantly, in mid-2000 a Moscow court ruled that McDonald's had improperly disciplined one of its employees who was seeking to establish a trade union. Yevgeny Druzhimin, a forklift truck operator on the ruling body of the huge multinational's small union, had been disciplined six times in as many months, in an attempt to cow the union. Russia's official labour code was still worker-friendly enough to prevent the company from disciplining an employee without the union's permission. Significantly, a broad survey of popular opinion conducted by VTsIOM found that 58 per cent of employees were owed back wages, 60 per cent said they had lived better under socialism and 82 per cent blamed the new "economic system", rather than "drunkenness or laziness", for poverty under the new regime.

Worker organizations did not just dissolve when faced by the new capitalizing logic of the market. Whether in the shape of the Polish Solidarity, workers' councils or bureaucratic statist trade unions, workers' organizations played a role, albeit sometimes a negative or passive one. Very few just fell into line with the wishes of the mainly Western neoliberal economic gurus advising the proto-capitalist class of the East. One Polish commentator refers to "the persistence of *homo Sovieticus* – the attitudes and habits of passivity, welfare dependency, poor labour discipline, disrespect for the law, etc." (Edmund Mokrzycki, paraphrased by Bryant 1994: 66). Over and above the unduly negative perspective this list betrays, there is the undoubted truth that the social conditioning of 50 years could not dissolve in five years, however frantic the pace of economic developments. A study of workers in Hungary during the transformation phase (Burawoy & Lukács 1992) also shows how flexible and resourceful workers have been in the East when faced with the whirlwind of capitalist neoliberal globalization.

If we stand back from the fast-moving pace of economic, political and social transformation in the East, we can see how Polanyi's notion of a "great transformation" might help us understand the underlying dynamic. For Polanyi, himself Hungarian, "[s]ocialism is, essentially, the tendency inherent in an industrial civilisation to transcend the self-regulating market by consciously subordinating it to a democratic society" (Polanyi 2001 [1944]: 234). In the East, going through a second great transformation as dramatic as the first, nineteenth-century version described by Polanyi, this was not happening. Instead, democracy was being curtailed and deformed to allow the so-called "free market" (which is not spontaneous but created) free rein over an atomized society. The destruction of society in a very real sense is a precondition for the creation of a market society. The question to ask now is whether Polanyi's counter-movement, a conscious social regulation of market mechanisms, has emerged in the East. I tend to agree with Maurice Glasman's verdict that "Polanyi underestimates the moral attractiveness of the market as a foundation for freedom and prosperity – a crucial part of its appeal in Eastern Europe at present" (Glasman 1994: 200).

The choice facing the East was posed starkly as either state or market, as in the World Bank's report *From Plan to Market* (World Bank 1996), in which the transition is seen as simple, unequivocal and totally positive. Yet, when democracy is denied and stable social associations are derided, even the much-vaunted market reforms become vulnerable to corruption, as has occurred under Vladimir Putin's Russia with the consolidation of the oligarchy that became rich through a wave of privatization and the emergence of a "wild" capitalism. Polanyi, at one point in his analysis of a market unmediated by the social, declares that, in this situation, greed becomes "elevated to a moral principle" (Polanyi 2001 [1944]: 84).

In theory, maybe, an unrestricted global market would provide the optimum match between security and freedom. As the World Bank puts it: "The freeing of markets is the basic enabling reform from which all the potential benefits of transition flow" (World Bank 1996: 7). Although the organization calls for "stabilization" as a vital component of liberalization, so as to prevent hyperinflation and promote productivity, it has not grasped Polanyi's nettle and understood that a social "counter-movement" is necessary even to ensure the sustainability of the market reforms.

We need to understand the critical importance of the remaking of the working class on a global scale over the last 30 years or so. The dynamic (yet destructive) nature of this system is evident not least in the rise of the BRICS countries as vibrant centres of capital expansion and accumulation in a "classical" mode. New working classes are being forged in these regimes, and the future of class struggle will depend largely on their outcome. As Mike Davis puts it laconically, "Two hundred million Chinese factory workers, miners and construction labourers are the most dangerous class on the planet. (Just ask the State Council in Beijing.) Their full awakening from the bubble may yet determine whether or not a socialist Earth is possible" (Davis 2011: 15). What we need to add to this classic Marxist perspective, however, is an understanding of how "primitive accumulation" continues to operate through "accumulation through dispossession", a "Third-Worldist" perspective articulated before its time by Luxemburg against Lenin and the other orthodox Marxists of her day.

After Fordism?

After the collapse of Fordism comes post-Fordism – or maybe not. The debate on the nature of the labour process in the advanced capitalist countries is a crucial one, both there and in the developing countries, where it will inevitably impact (see Chapter 5). Having examined the main contours of the social system of production in the West and in the former communist bloc we must now turn to what Marx termed the "hidden abode of production", namely the labour process that generates production and wealth. I begin with a broad-brush debate on the transition from Fordism (see Chapter 2) to post-Fordism, then go on to the specifics of "lean production", the "feminization" of labour and the prospects for a new form of social regulation. It is important to note at the outset that these debates are about more than just the technical organization of work; they go to the core of how we live in contemporary society. The workplace is embedded in social, cultural and political institutions, discourses and visions of how we should lead our lives. At the moment the undisputed hegemony of the market in regulating these processes has been challenged but the ultimate outcome is uncertain.

Table 4.1 Fordism and afterwards

	Fordism	*After*
Economic regulation	Keynesian	Monetarist
Markets	Mass	Niche
Lifestyle	Conformist	Pluralistic
Systems	Centralized	Decentralized
Organization	Bureaucratic	Dehierarchized
Regulation	National	Global
Lead sector	Consumption	Finance
Skills	Deskilling	Multi-skilling
Workers	Mass	Polyvalent
Characteristics	Rigidity	Flexibility
Production	Assembly line	Flexible
Society	Welfarism	Privatization
Driver	Resources	Demand

If we take a wide-angle view of the transition from Fordism to post-Fordism as paradigms of social systems of production, it would look something like Table 4.1. It is important to bear in mind, though, that these are ideal types, and probably do not exist in reality in such a neat form. The list in the table could be extended but the general picture is clear. Fordism, as described by Gramsci in the 1930s, was a new industrial lifestyle based on the "American way", but it came into its own during the postwar boom. Its methods, its philosophy and its prescriptions for the "one best way" to organize work spread across the world. Post-Fordism emerged in the 1980s, partly as a way to think through a coherent alternative to the dying Fordism that would be more progressive socially than the then dominant free market liberalism of Thatcher and Reagan.

To flesh out the broad paradigmatic shift beyond Fordism, we need to examine the specific delineation of the new workplace and the social system of production. The new post-Fordist configurations would have serious effects at the level of industry, production and the division of labour. Industries move towards a horizontal deconcentration, production processes deal with uncertainty and unpredictability through flexibility, and the division of labour moves from a focus on the individual worker to flexible work teams. There is also a shift from economies of scale to economies of scope. Production norms also move from standardized products to specialized ones, hence the term "flexible specialization". The productive process shifts from an emphasis on quantity to a focus on quality. It is ironic that Benjamin Coriat, after drawing up this model and arguing that "[f]lexible specialisation practices or strategies of dynamic flexibility [as he prefers to term them] open certain opportunities to create profitable niches or segments of markets", can only conclude realistically that on current trends "there is only a very slight probability that this model will become a reality" (Coriat 1992: 155).

If we now look at what happened in practice in the North, we will find that, apart from the odd experiment in Sweden and elsewhere, it was in fact a form of neo- (as against post-) Fordism that prevailed. Certainly, increased automation of the workplace and some of the new "flexible" work practices offered some resolution to the crisis of Fordism. Flexibility of production could be nothing other than an improvement on the rigidity of Fordist and Stalinist mass production methods. Yet in a sense all this did was to give a new lease of life to Fordism, so at most it can be termed a neo-Fordism. For Aglietta, who in many ways launched the contemporary analysis of Fordism, neo-Fordism involved "the transformation of the totality of the conditions of existence of the wage-earning classes" (Aglietta 1979: 168). The attempted renewal of US capitalism in the 1970s, to cope with its loss of undisputed hegemony, led directly to a shift from a regime of extensive accumulation to one of intensive accumulation, in which work was intensified through an application of the new information technology and automation. This regime also spread from industry to schools, hospitals and the leisure industry.

If neo-Fordism prevailed in the 1970s, a post-Fordism was being detected in the 1980s. As already mentioned above, the main drive of the after-Fordist work practices was "flexibility", and a major model was the Japanese one, sometimes known as Toyotism. The Toyota experience was codified and generalized by a Massachusetts Institute of Technology (MIT) study entitled *The Machine that Changed the World* (Womack, Jones & Roos 1990). This study extols the virtues of "just-in-time" (JIT) production – to reduce stocks and work in progress – and the dramatic productivity increases of Japanese car plants during the 1980s. The authors dub this approach "lean production" (which, for workers, also meant "lean" pay and conditions) and seek to generalize it across industries, arguing that its requirement of skilled and committed workers made it equally attractive to labour and to capital. Subsequent studies (e.g. Williams *et al.* 1992) show this picture to be oversimplified even for the car industry, in so far as it overrates the difference between "Japanese", "European" and "American" work practices. Nor is it plausible to establish such a binary opposition between bad old mass production and good new lean production in this way, as real workplaces are both more complex and more conflictual places.

The "Japanese" model has now, of course, lost much of its shine since Japanese capitalism has shown itself vulnerable to the contradictions of the species. Nevertheless, as Tony Elger and Chris Smith note, many commentators in the West "remain mesmerized by idealized contrasts between production paradigms or broad-brush conceptions of Japanization" (Elger & Smith 1994: 12). As with "Fordism", Japanization – or the more specific Toyotism – has tended to suffer from conceptual inflation. It has also become a contested discursive terrain, with different commentators stressing more the technical elements (JIT) while others emphasize the more autonomous worker supposedly required. Certainly, the concept of Japanization acquired a life of its own, especially the claim by a MIT study that a Japanese car was produced with half the amount of labour and material its US counterpart required (Cusumano 1992: 23). Whether this was a myth or not, lean production spread across the globe in the 1990s, although in different versions and with varying degrees of compliance from the workers concerned.

We can only conclude that life after Fordism could follow many different paths. For some analysts mass production is set to decay steadily and progressively and eventually fall away (see Hirst & Zeitlin 1989), whereas for others a major element of mass production will remain central in the economies of the North (Coriat 1992). A new virtuous circle of productivity growth based on flexible production in its benign form seems at least unlikely. A reversion to Fordism may be entirely logical in situations of stagnant economies with a large labour surplus. In terms of the broad social system of production it thus seems unwise to predict that any one work regime, such as flexible specialization, will become the "one best way", as Fordism was in its heyday. While the new principles are generalizable – no one can argue against "flexibility" in principle – older systems of production may be too well embedded to change. A pattern of uneven and combined development of the old and the new thus seems most likely, the main criteria always being the same, namely productivity and profitability.

A flexible workforce

Flexibility, as we have seen, has come mainly to mean deregulation; it is part and parcel of the drive to remove the state and society from any role in regulating the capital/wage labour relation. The flexibilization of work in the North in the 1980s and 1990s also coincided with its "feminization", even if there was no direct correlation between the two. We do know that, of the extra 29 million people who entered the recorded labour market of the European Union between 1960 and 1990, 20 million were women (Rubery & Fagan 1994: 146). We also know that the steady growth of the service sector in most countries of the North since 1970 is associated with the growth of female employment. The conclusion of Jill Rubery and Colette Fagan in relation to these trends, however, is that "[t]here is no mechanical relationship between the growth of atypical employment [part-time, temporary or other 'flexible' forms] and the increasing participation of women in the economy. Likewise there can be no simple equation between feminisation and employment flexibility" (Rubery & Fagan 1994: 159). As with other issues, we need to set employment relations within the broader societal context, in this case the particular national configuration of gender relations shaping the contours of employment. The increase in the proportion of women in the formal labour market is related to changes in social attitudes in the postwar era, the emergence of equal pay legislation and the decline of the male "family wage". It cannot be attributed to the rise of temporary part-time work as part of the flexibilization drive, but we do need to recognize the gendered nature of that drive.

What is clear is that "[l]abor market flexibility is both a racialized and gendered concept" (Peck 1996: 136). Flexibility is as much a political as an economic concept and is set in the context of segregated or segmented labour markets. Thus "flexibility" can spell "responsible autonomy" and "multi-skilling" to the white male core worker of the new capitalism and, at the same time, create insecurity and even harder work for the woman or black worker. Women do not come into the labour market simply as workers but within the parameters of societies that discriminate against women in different ways. And, of course, behind the new male "flexiworker", giving his all to his high-powered city job, lies someone (usually female) who, in a very "flexible" way, is also caring for their household needs while trying to earn a living. In the social construction of work at the turn of the century it is thus necessary to bear in mind that "[n]ew forms of labor flexibility are associated with new forms of labor control, new forms of labor exploitation and, by implication, new forms of gender and racial oppression" (Peck 1996: 136).

Flexibility means deregulation and the removal of the state from the capital/wage labour relation. But this is not a policy without contradiction, and it is subject to the Polanyian counter-movement whereby society seeks to regain some control over blind market forces. In particular, it is now widely accepted, even by the OECD, that eliminating state interference in employer/employee relations will not in itself generate more jobs, as textbook economics had predicted. The so-called rigidities of the labour market – strong unions, labour protection legislation, high wages – are no longer seen as the main culprits of unemployment. Governments are increasingly being drawn in to curb the rogue employers of the gig economy and they are reconstituting institutions such as government-backed apprenticeship schemes. If deregulation is not a simple answer for governments, then it follows that they may be persuaded to regulate the working day, holidays, leave entitlements, temporary employment and the infamous zero-hour contracts. It is noticeable that the critique of deregulation is coming not only from those concerned with equity but also from those motivated by efficiency. The instability in employment that results from deregulation conspires directly against productivity, after all, and precludes a long-term training programme as well.

Trade union responses to the new model capitalism

Trade unions, and labour movements more generally, are not just passive mirrors of capital's transformations; they are constantly renewed and reconfigured in their identity and strategies. As social movements, they can be reflexive, learn from mistakes and setbacks, rethink accepted nostrums and develop a more productive approach to the problems they face.

One way of entering this complex and developing terrain of debate would be through a review of some of the political and organizational changes undergone within the US labour movement, once considered the epitome of conservatism, if not of corruption, within progressive labour circles. The victory of the "New Voice" slate in the 1995 AFL–CIO elections marked a significant turn in US labour politics. A once large and vibrant labour movement (particularly in the 1930s and 1940s) had slipped into decline and was virtually moribund by the 1980s. Its numbers had been reduced by nearly half and its strategic vision was almost non-existent. A whole range of factors, from capital's offensive (alluded to above) to the weaknesses of the labour leadership, were responsible for this; but what was to be done?

The post-1995 union leadership set in motion a process of change, which is still continuing. Much of the change was straightforward enough, such as a massive recruitment drive and a much greater, and overdue, focus on gender and "ethnic" issues. What was probably most significant, though, was a major emphasis on unions as organizers of a social movement. Breaking with the language of corporatism, the US unions began to speak the language of democracy. Above all, in a perhaps unknowing borrowing from the experience of Southern unions (see Chapter 5), the AFL–CIO began to promote a new "community unionism":

> The definition of community unionism is union organizing that takes place across territorial and industrial communities much larger than a single workplace. Community unionism recognizes that a worker's identities and interests are much broader than just who they work for or what they do. Workers have different identities, some that are connected to occupation or employer, some that are not – but most of which are relevant to organizing. (Fine 1999: 128)

So, not only did the AFL–CIO rediscover the language of class, which had been so prominent in the 1930s, but it also moved towards a "postmodern" conception of the worker, with multiple identities and the union as a social movement.

If there was always one area in which US unions were a byword for reaction across the world it was in relation to their international policy of acting as the labour arm of the State Department and US corporations. Now the AFL–CIO has not only turned decidedly internationalist, recognizing the overwhelming reality of globalization, but it has acknowledged its murky past and sought to build a progressive future. Barbara Shailor, ex-director of the AFL–CIO International Affairs Department, acknowledges that "too often in the past the international stage was dominated by the arguments and differences of the past" (Shailor & Kourpias 1998: 281) and goes on to declare:

> No worker in the world should be exploited by any multinational within the reach of a US-based union. [...] We need to strategically organize companies, industries and entire sectors of the global economy. For this, we must be clear that our unions are operating independently of the foreign policy considerations that so dominated the Cold War period across the world. (Shailor & Kourpias 1998: 282)

Finally there was a recognition that what is good for General Motors may not necessarily be good for US workers.

We cannot pretend that the changes outlined above are without limitations and contradictions. For example, when the AFL–CIO calls for a return to the expansionary economy, when "a rising tide lifts all boats", we should point out that "those days, to whatever extent they ever existed, may well be gone" (Mantsios 1998b: 56). By romanticizing Fordism one is incapacitated to deal with post-Fordism. In addition, leaderships come and go, and the lure of the Democratic Party can always be renewed. I can only but agree with Denis MacShane, however, when he says that it is premature to bid "[a]dieu to the trade unions" (MacShane 1996). They have shown themselves capable of regeneration and have even sought to catch up with the "information age". The rise of the union website and of the "cyber-picket" signals a new era in labour organizing. New communication methods are aiding inter-union dialogue and the ongoing struggle to organize against capital.

Across the North the trade unions began to revive after the mid-1990s. There were, for example, general strikes in France, Belgium, Greece, Italy, Spain and Canada in the second half of the 1990s, not quite but nearly matching those across the South. The trade unions were to some extent taking up the mantle of the working-class leadership abandoned by the social democratic parties now busy administering neoliberalism. Moody rightly points out that this return to working-class action "had deep roots in the previous period and was shaped by it. The changes within the working class had been disorienting, but had also made new developments possible" (Moody 1997: 14). Social recomposition can take a decade or more after an intense period of economic restructuring such as that experienced by the working classes of the North in the 1980s. The political disorientation caused by the collapse of communism and the definitive defection of social democracy to the cause of capitalist modernization took even longer to recover from. And, of course, this recovery is quite uneven, hesitant and faltering, although it nevertheless seems real.

The brief verdict on the state of the unions worldwide at the turn of the century was, according to the ILO, "battered but rising to the challenge" (ILO 1997). Basically, the proportion of union members in the labour force has declined, sometimes sharply, almost everywhere over the past two decades. But numbers alone tell only part of the story. Considerable variations exist between regions and within each one (ILO 1997: 2).

So, for example, against the general trend, Spain and the Netherlands saw a significant rise in union membership from the mid-1980s into the 1990s. The decline was most precipitous in the East (see below). The South saw considerable advances (see Chapter 5). Furthermore, the influence of trade unions in national politics has increased in many countries. And, as we saw above, there has been a new repertoire of actions and strategies developed. As in the past, periods of numerical decline have also been periods of political renewal. For the ILO, "[w]hat is involved here is militant unionism rather than weight of numbers" (ILO 1997: 2). Most workers do not have the luxury of abandoning their main means of representation. The trade unions will often fight to make themselves relevant again after a period of retreat, as the 1980s undoubtedly were.

As to the issues facing the labour movement, we could well start with a list developed by an ILO- and ICFTU-sponsored electronic conference in 1999–2000. The background document for this conference on organized labour in the twenty-first century listed the following.

- Challenges of a hostile economic environment – end of the golden era, supremacy of flexible financial capitalism.
- The international economy – globalization challenges the hitherto national regulation of the employment relations (ILO 1999: 1).

Most significant were the range and depth of responses from various trade unions to this agenda. Locating the right questions is always half the battle, and here the unions were beginning (perhaps rather late; certainly patchily) to address the major issues facing working people across the North.

Two examples of labour's responses can be given from different ends of the technological spectrum: the airline industry and the garment industry. Since the

1990s the civil aviation industry has been engaged in a paradigmatic exercise in liberalization and deregulation that has had profound effects on the industry's workforce, which has also been paramount in the companies' considerations. The intensification of labour and the decline in job security have prompted a serious reaction from this "structurally" globalized workforce. The new management strategies have forced the unions into a more internationalist approach (see Blyton *et al.* 1998). For their part, the super-exploited garment workers (often immigrants) in the North's ghettos have also responded in novel ways to conditions imposed by neoliberal globalization. Traditional trade union strategies were often beaten back by ruthless employers in the non-union sweatshops. Hence, as Andrew Ross puts it, "the leading edge of activism has shifted towards the high-end publicity stakes of targeting the image of large, well-known companies" (Ross 1997: 26). Not only have these campaigns against household names been successful, particularly in the United States, but they have helped bridge the gap (in theory and practice) between production and consumption, and between workers of the North and of the South.

As has been seen in the past, capitalist innovations in the labour process can be turned in workers' favour by worker innovation. One example of this dialectic was the wave of successful strikes in the 1990s when JIT production models were turned against the bosses. Early in the decade General Motors was forced to close a number of factories immediately when workers found a way of cutting off JIT supplies. By the mid-1990s this labour strategy was generalized, and the United Automobile Workers in the United States took action in two General Motors parts plants in Ohio, which virtually paralysed GM across the country at the cost of US$47 million per day. The shift away from large inventories, as was traditional in the motor industry, to JIT supplies, as pioneered in Japan, had left a major corporation feeling quite vulnerable to labour actions. In one spectacular action, in 1998, a plant in Michigan that supplied the lines of spark plugs and fuel injectors to all General Motors' assembly plants in the American West closed down production in what is considered the biggest company in the world.

Lest we be carried away by an "optimism of the will" regarding a labour revival, it is well to review the very serious challenges facing labour in an exercise of "pessimism of the intellect". From outside the trade unions, but from a broadly progressive stance, Castells says, "If unions carry on negotiating within the framework of the enterprise, globalization or the informationalization of the enterprise will overwhelm them" (Castells 1998: 2). From a strong trade-union-based but independent perspective, MacShane advises that, "[u]nless trade unions reinvent themselves, their role in the twenty-first century political economy will get smaller and smaller" (MacShane 1996: 16). The past may be a source of inspiration and historical experience but it cannot provide the answers. Society is today more complex and is changing at an ever faster speed. Capital is dynamic and setting the pace of change. Labour is still marked by the economic structures, political reflexes and aspirations of the past, when not totally brow-beaten by the new capitalism. Reinventing oneself is not easy.

An examination of two sectors – the state and the high-tech – demonstrates some of the major practical challenges facing unions today. The restructuring and recomposition of the state in most Northern countries have fundamentally altered the position of public sector workers. The public/private, profit-making/public service divide has largely evaporated. Even at an international level now, public services are becoming completely subordinated to market logic. The outcome, as Peter Fairbrother explains, is that "in the state sector broadly defined ... industrial relations are no longer as predictable as once was the case" (Fairbrother 1999: 1). While this may lead to novel tactics it also, predominantly in the short term, disrupts what was once a traditional trade union bastion in many countries of the North.

In terms of public services, we note that they are being increasingly "denationalized" and globalized. Since 1995 the General Agreement on Trade in Services (GATS) has been the main mechanism to extend the multilateral trading system to the service sector, complementing the General Agreement on Tariffs and Trades, which provides such a system for merchandise trade. Under the heading of services "provided on a commercial basis", public utilities such as water and electricity, as well as many health and education services, would need to be opened to competition and "liberalization". The European Public Service Union (EPSU), among others, has questioned how these public goods are becoming commodities to be "exported" as profitable businesses: "Public services are services that are underpinned by the principles of universal access, affordability, democratic control, continuity and equality ... Regulation is fundamental to prevent commercialisation leading to cherry picking and a two-tier service ... Democratic decision-making is not a trade barrier" (EPSU 2015).

Likewise, the "flexiworkers" or "networkers" of the information and communication sectors may one day be the new trade union vanguard, as dockers and miners were in their day. Today, however, these workers, many on short-term contracts, find it very difficult to unionize. At the "upmarket" end, the young high flyers of the "internet revolution" see little point in trade unions, which they see as male/manual/modernist relics. To build up their membership, relevance and capacity for action in the "new economy" and appeal to these workers, who are as vulnerable as their manual worker forebears of the industrial age, are the key tasks for the North's trade unions. The European and US trade unions are increasingly aware of this challenge. When it is put to them that they need to change, however, the response of organizers to me has been: "We represent the members we have, not those we might wish to have." Although there is a real tension between representing existing members and potential ones in terms of the scarce resources available, there is a need to counteract conservative tendencies in the unions and their membership. Historically, and even today, older male unionists often turn on women and young workers in defending their own short-term interests.

It is a truism but still worth pointing out that the main challenges facing trade unions today are ideological and political. The major international trade union body, the ICFTU, which sponsored the electronic conference on the future of trade unionism mentioned above, is indicative of that crisis. Its ideological identity for the whole postwar period up until the 1990s was shaped by the "struggle" against communism, but now with its demise there is a curious vacuum. With no one to fight against, its ideological bearings are unclear. Certainly, the "challenge" of globalization is recognized, and its main promoters, the US state and capitalism, are now regularly criticized. Yet one of the main documents for the electronic conference argues:

> Trade unions ... need to demonstrate their approach is not incompatible with the creation of successful market economies ... few trade unions have managed so far to come to terms with the new world of increasing globalization but if they hope to survive and grow again they will have to make radical accommodations.   (Taylor 1999)

It is all very well being cynical about wishful thinking but the accommodation with the dominant paradigm seems too enthusiastic and appears to leave little room for reinvention, let alone subversive thinking.

A forward-looking perspective, developed by Fairbrother, among others, is the "trade union renewal" thesis. As Fairbrother defines it, "[R]enewal is about the way unions reorganise and recompose themselves to meet the problems of work and employment ... [I]t is in the workplace that unions organise, sustain and renew themselves" (Fairbrother 1989: 3–4). This is a perspective that brings the labour process into focus and that understands that workers can be active agents. Trade unions are not just formal organizations but social movements with tensions and struggles– for example, over the issue of union democracy. Perhaps Fairbrother is somewhat idealistic in arguing that "any movement towards union renewal must and will come from the bottom up" (Fairbrother 1989: 6), but it is important to reintroduce union politics into the debate. Trade unions can (and do) become bureaucratic, as well as conservative in their methods, and they can be co-opted by the state and capital. Trade unions can (and do) go through a process of renewal – in terms of organization, strategy and methods – and combat routinization. At least some trade unions have begun to reinvent themselves to represent workers better in the era of globalization.

At a national level, many trade unions have gone through a process of "renewal" (if not reinvention) since the mid-1990s. No change is more dramatic, perhaps, than that in the US labour movement, once the paradigm of union bureaucracy and labour imperialism overseas. The AFL–CIO, under new leadership since the watershed elections of 1995, recognized the challenges it faced if it was to survive (let alone prosper) in the new era. Its new leaders asked openly: "Why did a labor movement that was so vibrant, massive and capable of bringing about fundamental change in the 1930s and 1940s become virtually moribund in the 1980s and 1990s?" (Mantsios 1998a: xv). The US unions now have half the membership they had in the middle of the twentieth century and they "represent" only one US worker in seven. The AFL–CIO now sees itself going "back to basics", asking itself about its purpose, its representativeness, its strategy and its organization. While remaining staunchly pro-market in many ways, the AFL–CIO has realized the limitations of a Washington-based lobbying approach and is rediscovering its roots as a vigorous, campaigning social movement. Whether better organization and more militancy will "renew" the US labour movement is, of course, an open question.

The point is that the process of trade union renewal can be assessed in different ways depending on one's perspective. An attitude of *plus ça change* ... is common among radical critics. Thus, Peter Meiksins writes of the 1995 change of guard at the AFL–CIO that, in the absence of a "class project", it runs the risk of falling prey to divisions "both by retreating further from the use of class as an organising principle and by relying on a variety of vague formulations which create the illusion of unity rather than its reality" (Meiksins 1997: 42). The organizing drive of the AFL–CIO was also fairly neglectful of the new workplace regimes and the need for union democracy. Yet it seems somewhat abstract to declare: "To really overcome the divisions within the working class, organised labour would have to create an alternative 'model' for the organisation of production" (Meiksins 1997: 41). It is maybe time to overcome the old critical distinction between reform and "really" revolutionary measures that this type of analysis depends on. In this regard, we could consider Roberto Unger's deceptively simple definition of "radical reform" as a species of transformative politics: "Reform is radical when it addresses and changes the basic arrangements of society: its formative structure of institutions and enacted beliefs. It is reform because it deals with one discrete part of this structure at a time" (Unger 1998: 18–19).

Back in 2000 the ICFTU engaged in a millennial review of its organization, capacities and strategy. Even its most fervent critics began to recognize that the ICFTU was changing from the Cold War, pro-imperialist, narrowly bureaucratic organization it once was. After its millennium conference, held in Durban (significant in itself), the then ICFTU general secretary, Bill Jordan, declared,

"In periods of revolutionary change, and we are in one now, we must be able to think and act outside the straightjacket of our traditions … The trade union movement, once again, needs new ideas for the needs of new workers, new occupations, new forms of work organisation, new employment relationships" (Jordan 2000: 2). The millennial review was designed to meet precisely these challenges. The policy review broke with a number of traditions, and the external face of the labour movement has begun to reflect the gender and geographical spread of its membership much more. It has, since the turn of the century, become a more inclusive and more accessible organization than it once was. Its organizational capabilities are still extremely limited in terms of finances and personnel, however, in spite of better links with the ITSs. And the limitations of a North-based movement when the centre of gravity has shifted to the global South is a permanent problem, yet to be overcome and barely recognized.

Again, how we assess the ICFTU "renewal" depends on our perspective. It is probably good all round – for critics and supporters alike – to have a more sober appraisal of the ICFTU's capabilities, rather than viewing it simply as a "slumbering giant". In terms of the politics of the ICFTU it would not, perhaps, be unkind to see it in terms of Jordan's old British TUC politics writ large. The TUC also had its phase of "new unionism" in the 1990s as it sought to come to terms with declining membership and the new "flexible" labour market conditions. We should not exaggerate the radicalism of a turn towards a more realistic and engaged trade union politics. Nevertheless, I am not convinced by the verdict of Dimitris Stevis and Terry Boswell that, "[o]n balance, the ICFTU has adopted a regulatory rather than a reformist internationalist strategy" (Stevis & Boswell 2001: 25). The "social clause" is certainly a less radical strategy than Charles Levinson's vision in the 1970s of trade unions establishing a countervailing power to that of the MNCs, with its echoes of Leninist "dual power" strategies. Yet if the international trade union movement can play a role in terms of social regulation, through the "social clause" and other means, it would still be a revolutionary reform in Unger's sense.

If we were to derive one key issue for labour renewal at a national level, it might be that of working-class unity and articulation. Solidarity starts at home, in a sense, and trade unions have always had a problem in maintaining unity across gender, racial, ethnic, religious, age and skill divides, not to mention transnational migrants. Globalization exacerbates national differences as the drive for "competitivity" reaches down into every workplace. So capitalism accentuates differences, and in its present "speeded-up" form takes this to a new pitch. Unity among workers was never a given, of course, and the myth of working-class solidarity in a past golden era was often based on an exclusivist male/manual/skilled/permanent employee. A related aspect is that of union "articulation", defined by Jeremy Waddington as "cohesive and coherent interrelationships between workplace, regional and national levels of organisation" (Waddington 1999: 3). If a labour movement does not achieve a degree of articulation it is prone to damaging internal conflict between its various levels of organization. Finally, in the era of globalization, union articulation is required at the international level also to meet the new challenges, but this adds a whole new level. At the international level the main issue in labour renewal terms is the emergence of a new sense of global solidarity. The drive for an international trade union strategy in the 1970s may have failed, but it was renewed in the 1990s in possibly more propitious circumstances. Reconsidering the earlier debate in terms of the new context of globalization, Harvie Ramsay finds that "the *incentives* for unions to pursue internationalism have grown in the last decade", even if "the *capacities* of unions to organise themselves internationally are more problematical" (Ramsay 1999: 214, emphasis in original). International economic integration and the methods of lean production push the drive towards international labour solidarity. Greater harmonization of capitalist structures and procedures (the "one right way" of neoliberalism) also presents an easier target for labour. Certainly, the obstacles to a successful international strategy still exist, and the trade unions have been severely weakened by the era of neoliberalism. It is well worth recalling, as a Ford executive once supposedly did, that employers are at a disadvantage *vis-à-vis* the unions at the international level in so far as they lack the equivalent international institutions and traditions of solidarity (Ramsay 1999: 217).

In conclusion, has the process of trade union renewal/reinvention created a new global labour movement capable of confronting the effects of globalization? I would say that the international trade union movement is, at one and the same time, a "new" transnational social movement in the making and a representative organization that is "more" than the transnational advocacy groups, promoting gender, environmental and human rights issues. By necessity the ICFTU has had to reconsider its Cold War past and, however unevenly or hesitantly, move towards a united and democratic approach to globalization. In doing so, it has learnt much from the "new" social movements and from NGOs way of working. Trade unions, as always, advocate on behalf of their members, however, and – whatever the problems with "representativeness" – they are more democratic than, say, Greenpeace. The international trade union movement certainly has the motivation to "go global" (even if it is just to survive), and it has the "technology" (internet, cheaper travel, etc.) to do so. It will, if the analysis in this book is at all soundly based, play a central and increasing role in achieving a degree of social regulation over the worldwide expansion of capitalism in the decades to come. The Northern unions have a large responsibility in terms of the reinventing of the global labour movement, not least because of their huge resources compared to Southern unions and their geographical proximity to political and corporate power. In the twenty-first century they have broken with the open alliance with imperialism they had in the past; they still have some way to go before they can become co-leaders of a new truly global labour movement alongside the rising trade union and social movement mobilizations in the Global South.

5

WORKERS SOUTH

The processes of globalization have brought previously closed (or semi-closed) economies into the global capitalist economy, but have also excluded parts of the world – such as broad swathes of Africa – from the new order. This chapter traces the fate of workers in the Global South from the transition from colonialism to the new international division of labour to the era of globalization, with particular attention paid to transformations in countries such as Brazil, South Africa and South Korea, where considerable levels of industrialization were achieved. I also examine what was once particular to the South – but is now also increasingly a Northern phenomenon – namely the high level of informal working relations and practices. There is a particular focus on women working worldwide, bringing to the fore the gendered nature of the globalization process, which has different impacts across regions and classes. The final section, on Polanyi's double movement, shows the extent to which we cannot really study workers in the North and South separately any more. The dialectic of the double movement has created new working classes and new forms of resistance in all parts of the world, which, while distinct, have similar roots in the uneven accumulation of capital on a global scale.

It is sometimes forgotten, or denied, by the critics of development that "[t]he period of 1950 to 1980 was also – and in an important sense – the Golden Era of development for the poor countries of the world" (Singh 1994: 171). This is not the wishful thinking of a modernization theorist or the preaching of a World Bank apologist but the sober verdict of the ILO. It is indeed vital to recognize the unprecedented economic development of the South since the Second World War, in spite of all its unevenness and its glaring inequalities. In fact, the industrial revolution in the South actually bettered the record of the Global North in the second half of the nineteenth century. As Ajit Singh summarizes this startling historical reality: "The South did this in half the time, at twice the growth rates, and with five times the North's population in the nineteenth century" (Singh 1994: 171–2). This dynamic transformation of the South was to lead to a new international division of labour, with profound effects on workers across the world.

A new international division of labour

The "old" international division of labour was centred on the overwhelming social, economic and political reality of colonialism. The imperialist or colonial powers began to produce manufactured goods, and the colonial world (later referred to as the Global South) was exploited for its raw materials, especially minerals. Even as industrialization proceeded in some parts of the South in the early and mid-twentieth century, this was, arguably, a "dependent" form of industrialization, with the colonial (or ex-colonial) powers retaining control over the leading sector. From around the 1970s onwards, however, a "new" international division of labour was diagnosed, most categorically by a group of German researchers, Folker Fröbel, Jürgen Heinrichs and Otto Kreye (1980). Their basic thesis was that the transformations that accumulated in the postwar period "generated a world market for production sites and for labour which embraces both the traditional industrialised and the underdeveloped countries" (Fröbel, Heinrichs & Kreye 1980: 44). This was seen to have undermined the traditional division of labour, whereby there were only two global sectors: the industrialized countries and the producers of raw materials.

On this basis, the NIDL fundamentally restructured the relations of production in the South, with the emergence of a substantial manufacturing sector oriented towards the world market. These "world market factories" often employed women workers and thus also had an impact on the gendering of work in the South. We must bear in mind the limits of this pre-globalization internationalization of production: in 1975, according to the German study cited above, there were 725,000 workers in the South engaged in the internationalized production sector, of whom 420,000 were based in Asia, 265,000 in Latin America and 40,000 in Africa (Fröbel, Heinrichs & Kreye 1980: 307). The next wave of internationalization would impact on far more workers of the South.

While the NIDL theorists did point towards some fundamental transformations, there were serious flaws in their overall paradigm. Essentially, their theory focuses on the world market, to the detriment of changes in the production process, and neglects the role of the state in the South, assuming that the world market could simply impose its policies across the globe. It also seriously underestimated the level of industrialization that existed in the South – particularly in Latin America and India, for example – prior to the 1960s. This led the NIDL theorists to isolate the "world market factories" and the so-called free trade zones as the main sites of capitalist development in the South when, in fact, their importance was relative. At a general level we can also concur with Robin Cohen, for whom "[t]he NIDL theorists use as their predominant data, aggregate trade and investment figures – i.e. they use measures of the migration of *capital* to measure changes in the division of *labour*" (Cohen 1991: 130, emphasis in original). A labour-oriented study would have to focus on the shifting contours and flows of labour rather than capital. Nor should a focus on manufacturing (as per NIDL theorists) lead us to neglect the big shifts between and within agriculture, industry as a whole and the services sector.

The NIDL not only occurred at the level of international trade but also impacted on the relations of production in the South. A form of what has been called "bloody" Taylorization was created in the super-exploitative FTZs in Sri Lanka (and elsewhere) and in the textile *maquila* plants of the Mexican border. A form of "peripheral" Fordism also emerged in the big new car plants and manufacturing factories that emerged in Brazil, Mexico, South Korea, Indonesia and South Africa in the 1960s and 1970s. Lipietz provides the classic definition of this new labour process, as

> an authentic Fordism based on intensive accumulation combined with market expansion but [which] remains peripheral to the extent that, in the world circuits of productive branches, jobs and production corresponding to skilled work processes and above all engineering remained outside these countries as a whole.   (Lipietz 1987: 78–9)

Today, thanks to rapid growth in the BRICS countries, for example, many of these processes do exist in the South, but these economies will still be peripheral to whatever is the latest technological advance of the day, be it information technology, biotechnology or something else that is monopolized by the core countries in the North, and in particular the United States.

If the 1970s were dominated by the NIDL, so the 1990s were overwhelmed by the process of "globalization" (see Chapter 3), which had been maturing in the 1980s. Although the development process of the postwar period was centred on nationally oriented industrialization, the new dominant process of "globalization" represents a break with national economic development models. By the 1980s "development" had been redefined to mean liberalization in all domains – that is, opening up the economy to the world market – doing away with the role of the state wherever possible and making private profit the *sine qua non*. Philip McMichael detects an explicit "globalization project", encapsulating the idea that this is something driven that does not occur spontaneously. For McMichael, the globalization project combines several strands: (1) an emerging consensus among policy-makers favouring market-based rather than state-managed development

117

strategies; (2) centralized management of global market rules by the G7 states; (3) the implementation of these rules by the multilateral agencies: the World Bank, the IMF, the WTO; (4) a concentration of market power in the hands of transnational corporations and financial power in the hands of transnational banks; and (5) subordination of former Second and Third World states to these global institutional forces (McMichael 2000: 177).

It would be wrong to assume that, if the NIDL brought Fordism to the South, so globalization would bring post-Fordism. Certainly, some aspects of JIT associated with post-Fordism or Toyotism were introduced, but not as a full "social model", more advantageous to workers than peripheral Fordism. One of the most interesting aspects of the labour process in the advanced technological sectors of the South is their combination with "traditional" forms of exploitation. For example, in India the consumer electronics industry is characterized by an unbroken commodity and labour chain, from the large "modern" firm, employing thousands of workers in reasonable conditions, through to the smallest of workshops, employing "technology ranging from automatic processes in con- trolled conditions to hand-operated presses of monotonous hand assembly by rooms of girls" (Hölmstrom 1984: 127). The cosy Northern image of the "elec- tronic cottage", where autonomous "teleworkers" (defined as technology-assisted work conducted outside a centrally located work space) enjoy the benefits of post-Fordism, is matched in the South by a high-tech cottage industry in which computers are put together or used in dilapidated workshops under very poor working conditions, which may equally be pointers of future labour regimes if things continue as they have been.

Only certain regions of the South, and then certain countries and certain social sectors within them, are being drawn into the accelerated pace of capitalist development in the era of globalization. While the social inclusion of millions of workers in the capitalist world economy is occurring (as we saw above), there is also an increase in social exclusion both within and between nations and regions. Castells refers, with very little exaggeration, to "the rise of the Fourth World" (Castells 1998: 70). The social regression in the former Soviet Union, the so- called "lost decade" of the 1980s in Latin America and, above all, the margin- alization of most of sub-Saharan Africa (with the exception of South Africa) from the world economy are all part and parcel of the globalization process. Economic development in some parts has economic underdevelopment in other parts of the world as its necessary counterpart; social inclusion is matched by social exclusion.

What is important to note at the general level is that globalization does not have necessary, inevitable or automatic consequences for labour in a given situ- ation. There is no better example to demonstrate this than a comparison of Chile under General Pinochet and democratic Chile in the 1990s. Much radical ink has been spent trying to show that the Christian Democrat and Socialist governments that followed Pinochet's dictatorial regime carried on with basically the "same" economic policy. The export-driven growth model under Pinochet (1973–90) was an early neoliberal experiment based on extreme labour repression. The subsequent Chilean "model" has, indeed, maintained the outward orientation of its predecessor (an alternative under globalization is hard to imagine for one country) but with a social and economic growth policy aimed at sustainability and diminishing inequalities. Political democracy, social stability and a broadening of the domestic market mark off the 1990s from the dictatorial period. For the rest of Latin America – and, indeed, for the South as a whole – the two Chilean models contradict the mantra "There is no alternative" reiterated by the gurus of globalization. The complexity and nuances of the Chilean "models" also contest simplistic leftist models that act on the basis that capitalism has only one modality and do not recognize its historical and geographical varieties.

Finally, in this section I would like to emphasize that the NIDL and the "newest" international division of labour created by "globalization" hinge around workers above all. As Castells puts it, "[T]he position in the international division of labour does not depend, fundamentally, on the characteristic of the country but on the characteristics of its labor (including embodied knowledge) and of its insertion in the global economy" (Castells 1996: 147).

The issue of "competitiveness", which dominates contemporary economic policy debates, is, in fact, something that occurs not between nations (which cannot "compete" in any meaningful sense) but between workforces, or, to be precise, labour regimes. It is an apparent paradox of the era of globalization that, while the labour movement has never been weaker, workers have never been more important to capitalism. The implementation of the new ICT and the development of a new(er) international division of labour depend on workers to implement them, in the South as much as (if not more than) in the already industrialized North. Workers are not pawns in the game of globalization but, rather, an integral element in its successful "take" in a given region or sector of the economy.

Informal work

If we were to mention just one characteristic of working life that distinguishes the South from the North, it would have to be what is called "informalization". Informal work is usually defined as any work that takes place outside the formal wage labour market, such as clandestine work and illegal work, but it also includes various forms of self-employment. This has become a global phenomenon and not just a feature of work in the South, although it occurs at a much higher

rate in the South. It is estimated that informal work in the industrialized economies involves between 2 and 15 per cent of the working population (Standing
1999: 112), whereas in the South it is considered to fluctuate between 30 and 80
per cent of the working population (ILO 1997: 175). Such a wide variation in
estimates indicates that no one really knows the extent of the informal sector,
in so far as its definition, let alone measurement, is very much contested. What
I shall stress in the pages that follow is less the informal sector (which gives it a
unity and coherence it does not possess) than the *process* of informalization –
a tendency, accentuated by globalization, for work and workers to become
informalized.

The "informal sector model" was developed in the 1970s as a theoretical device
to account for the reality of "underemployment", a category derived from the
formal labour markets of the industrialized economies of the North. It assumed
the exclusion of workers from the formal economy and their absorption into the
informal economy of small enterprises, often employing family members. It was
assumed that "barriers to entry", in terms of capital, skills or technology, were less
than in the formal capitalist economy. There was an implicit expectation in the
model that this sector would help "absorb" the growing mass of people thrown
off the land or out of urban jobs through capitalist development. As Alison Scott
writes, however, "informal sector theory has been extensively criticised on empirical, methodological and theoretical grounds" (Scott 1994: 181). Barriers to entry
were not so low, and the implicit dualism of the model (the formal/informal
divide) was dubious given the movement of workers between the "sectors". The
optimism of these theorists was also seen to be misplaced; the informal sector
was no panacea for the labouring poor of the South.

The problem of dualism was probably the most fundamental one in the
informal sector theorizing. Like all dichotomies or binary oppositions, the notion
that formal/informal employment were rigid categories was flawed. It assumed
a distinction between the two sectors that did not exist, given that the two were
completely interrelated. It ignored intermediate or mixed forms of employment.
It failed to recognize the diversity of class interests within the overall category of
the informal sector. The sector was said to embrace a whole range of occupations,
including the small manufacturing workshop, small-scale retailing and transport
units, casual building labour, domestic service and various illegal activities. The
only unifying factors across the range of work and workers are a certain general
instability of employment, an avoidance of most labour laws and a tendency to
remain outside normal capitalist rules of contract, licensing and taxation. If the
first attempt to theorize the sector was flawed, we might seek to examine this
kind of work and workers from within a class perspective.

From the "world systems" perspective pioneered by Immanuel Wallerstein
and others, which saw the world as a single unit even before globalization,

Alejandro Portes seeks to integrate the notion of informality within a class analysis of peripheral societies (Portes 1985). The urban informal sector (the petty bourgeois self-employed and the informal proletariat) is seen as a subsidy to capitalist accumulation, given its high levels of self-exploitation. In a later landmark analysis with Castells, Portes points to how the informal economy "simultaneously encompasses flexibility and exploitation, productivity and abuse, aggressive entrepreneurs and defenceless workers, libertarianism and greediness" (Castells & Portes 1989: 11). These dichotomies capture well the essentially contradictory nature of informalization, even more significant perhaps than its universal character. Its social boundaries are fluid and its politics are indeterminate. As a specific production relationship, the informal should not be read as a simple euphemism for poverty or social exclusion. This unregulated relationship of production and income generation activity is not "marginal" to capitalist development in the South today but an integral element of its dynamic.

It is important to realize that the informal sector is not some unfortunate carryover from an earlier era. What is most noticeable in Latin America is precisely the continuity with regard to the informal sector, which accounted for 30 per cent of all employment in 1980, exactly the same proportion employed in informal activities in 1950. Nor is informalization a process that governments resist on behalf of the rule of law; on the contrary, it is a rich source of patronage and a potential means to defuse social conflict. As to the dynamic of informalization, Castells and Portes are surely right to argue that "[u]ndermining organized labor's control over the work process seems to be a common objective of informalization, although it is not its sole cause" (Castells & Portes 1989: 28). Certainly, a major incentive for the managers of informalization is a weakening of the social role of labour and an atomization of the workforce. Yet informalization can also be seen as an early precursor of the wave of liberalization in the 1980s, as "entrepreneurs" sought to escape state regulation of the economy in terms of taxation, labour legislation or general rules on the conduct of capitalist business.

Women and the informal sector

A major issue to emerge in the reconstituted informal sector analysis of the 1980s was that of its gendered nature. Scott summarizes the findings of this research in terms of "a) a disproportionate concentration of women in the informal sector, compared to men, b) excessive gender segregation within both formal and informal sectors, and c) significant male–female earning differentials" (Scott 1994: 28–9). Informalization can thus be seen to proceed hand in hand with the feminization of the labour force, increased poverty and diminishing regulation. According to the ILO, women make up 80 per cent of the world's workers working from home (ILO 1997). It is the economic restructuring on a world scale that preceded and accompanied globalization (see Chapter 3) that has, according to Val Moghadam, "entailed increasing utilisation of female labour in formal and non-regular employment" (Moghadam 1995: 118). While women increasingly entered the paid labour market in the 1980s, they did so largely in a subordinate role. Women in the process of informalization also provided a crucial link with the domestic economy and the community, however, in a process that would have far-reaching effects.

In terms of the thesis that globalization is leading to an increase in informalization, along with all forms of social exclusion, the World Bank advances an optimistic view that "[t]he informal sector shrinks with development" (World Bank 1995: 35), but provides little evidence beyond aggregate statistics for a few countries. There are considerably more indications that informalization is on the increase. Consider, for example, that nine out of ten jobs created in Latin America in the 1990s were in the service sector, and, out of those, 90 per cent were in the informal services (ILO 1997: 173). So, only one in ten of these new jobs is in the "new economy", in the communications or financial markets sectors, for example. The rest are in domestic service, non-professional self-employment or in micro-enterprises – all poorly paid, unstable and precarious forms of employment, on the fringes of legality in many cases. Yet again we see the combined and uneven development of the labour market, as globalization brings high-tech sectors to the South but also reproduces the "traditional" informal activities of domestic services and other such occupations.

Informalization has distinct connotations in different regions of the South. According to the ILO, it is estimated that in Africa the urban informal sector around 2000 "employ[ed] about 61 per cent of the urban labour force and ... generate[d] some 93 per cent of all additional jobs in the region in the 1990s" (ILO 1997: 179). The ILO estimates that at the turn of the century in Asia the informal sector accounted for between 40 and 50 per cent of the urban labour force, but this figure masks a wide variation between the NICs (or "Asian Tigers"), at around 10 per cent, and Bangladesh, with a figure as high as 65 per cent. In Latin America, as already mentioned, nearly nine out of ten jobs generated in the first half of the 1990s were in the informal sector. This growth of informalization can be accounted for generally by a lack of dynamism in the formal economy, the severe contraction of public sector employment due to the structural adjustment programmes of the 1970s and the overall trend towards flexibilization of the labour market (see Chapter 3). Indeed, for the workers of the South, the much-vaunted "flexibilization" of work actually spells informalization.

We can conclude that the 1980s saw "the romanticising of the *informal sector*, as a vehicle for labour absorption and means of redistribution" (Standing 1999: 581, emphasis in original). As late as the mid-1990s a major United Nations

University study of "global employment" still felt compelled to warn that "the informal sector should not be idealised or considered a permanent panacea for unemployment and underemployment" (Simai 1995: 20). Even this framing of the issue seems to concede too much: is it even a "temporary" panacea? The whole notion of "upgrading" the informal sector, which permeates most of the literature, seems misconceived. Capitalism would not be capitalism if it was willing and able to "upgrade" the informal sector with "more stable and sustainable and skill-intensive production" (Simai 1995: 20), as the informal sector's reformers argue for. Instead, we need to recognize that informalization is a critical component of capitalist globalization today, particularly, but not exclusively, in the Global South. Its main effect is to undermine organized labour and facilitate the development of disorganized capitalism.

Trade unions and the informal sector

Informalization militates against organization: can trade unions mobilize workers in this sector? As the ILO puts it, "It would be unrealistic to expect trade unions and/or employers' organisations to cover entirely the needs and demands of such an expanding and heterogeneous sector" (ILO 1997: 193). As with the high-tech and information sector worker-employees of the North, however, a breakthrough in this sector is probably the litmus test of the continued relevance of trade unions to the world's workers of today. There is a willingness on the part of the trade unions, including the international leadership, to engage with the issue. Thus Luis Anderson, a leading ICFTU unionist in the 1990s, argued that the trade unions in Latin America had become involved with the informal sector, "assuming responsibilities that should be borne by governments, the political parties and the more powerful classes. They assume that role due to solidarity" (Anderson & Trentin 1996: 52). They engage with the informal workers, perhaps assisting them in creating a co-operative, or a "third sector" firm that, if successful, may in time lead them to distance themselves from the union.

Women's labour organizations

It is in relation to women workers that some of the most significant organizational advances in the informal sector have occurred. As the ILO noted in the mid-1990s, "The past decade has witnessed a proliferation of women's groups in the informal sector" (ILO 1997: 197). Ties of solidarity based on gender interests have been significant. Perhaps the paradigmatic case is that of the Self-Employed Women's Association in India, which evolved out of the women's wing of the

Textile Labour Association. This case shows most clearly that, while informal workers may resist, for good reasons and bad, incorporation into traditional trade union structures, they can readily find common ground with trade unions that allow space for their particular characteristics and needs. As an ILO report notes, specifically referring to SEWA, "[I]nformal workers would normally welcome any association with mainstream trade unions if this allowed them to deal with issues concerning their precarious situation and economic and social disadvantage" (ILO 1997: 204). When dealing with women-only or gender-oriented organizations we also find a much greater role being played by NGOs and other non-labour-movement bodies.

Confronting the issue of informalization has also made trade unions more aware of the community beyond the workplace, and issues beyond wages and conditions. Informal workers' organizations are often neighbourhood-based, thus breaking with one of the essential characteristics of trade unions. Less bound by the traditions of labour, if at all, and often individualist, and then communalist, in orientation, they are still recognizably labour organizations. A traditional industrial relations structure and a "free collective bargaining" orientation by the trade unions would hardly be relevant in these situations. Workers in the informal sector may well not organize around traditional "worker" issues, as, necessarily, they will need to deal with the threat of eviction, access to credit and low prices for their goods, for example. It is also important to realize, however, that many of those working under conditions of informalization may have been industrial workers before structural adjustment, back in the 1980s. While informalization, in essence, conspires against the strength and interests of organized labour, the informal workers themselves have played an important role in helping revive labour strategies in the 1990s.

Women working worldwide

It is now clear that the number and the proportion of women working (i.e. in paid as against unpaid work) worldwide has increased significantly in the era of globalization. Indeed, one of the main features of the NIDL diagnosed in the 1970s was, precisely, the increased employment of women workers in the "world market factories". This shift in the composition of gendered labour in the 1970s and 1980s was consolidated in the 1990s as globalization got into full swing. In the East (ex-Soviet Union and Eastern Europe) half the paid labour force was female still in 1990; in Southeast Asia that proportion was around 40 per cent; and, as Moghadam puts it, "even regions where cultural restrictions and economic structures inhibited female employment – the Middle East, North Africa and South Asia – saw increases in female labour force participation and in the female share of the formal sector labour force" (Moghadam 1995: 111). It was these changes, just sketched in here, that led to the development of the "global feminization" thesis in the 1990s.

In 1989 Guy Standing (of the ILO) systematized this perspective, arguing that the 1980s was the decade of labour deregulation but that it 'also marked a renewed surge of feminisation of labor activity" (Standing 1989: 1077). This entailed not only an increase in the proportion of women in the paid labour force but also the transformation/feminization of what had hitherto been considered "male" occupations. Export-led industrialization and the SAPs severely impacted on the economics of the South and in the political economy of labour. In particular, they led to the deregulation of labour standards, a "flexibilization" of work and a decomposition of jobs. What the "global feminization" argument then does is link these transformations with the growing incorporation of women into the paid labour force, which, argues Standing, has "almost certainly more to do with the feminisation of labor, a desire to have a more disposable (or 'flexible') labor force with lower fixed costs, and so on" (Standing 1989: 1086) than with changes in legislation or women's educational levels or other factors. This thesis was not without its critics, however suggestive it might seem.

First of all, there can be too quick a leap from detecting increasing participation by women in the paid labour force to conclusions about a changing gender division of labour. Elson rightly concludes that "the restructuring of labour contracts and the altering of job boundaries in the name of 'flexibility' is in fact much more likely to take place in a gender differentiated way than to be a force for overcoming the sexual division of labour" (Elson 1996: 38). Gender segregation and subordination within the world of work are not "overridden" in some way by flexibilization. In both the formal and the informal labour sectors, a gender division of labour pre-exists the processes that structure how "flexibilization" will occur, and even how it will be interpreted (e.g. its positive or negative connotations will be gendered). The second main issue is the implicitly negative connotation Standing and others put on "flexibility". It has been argued on the basis of case studies – for example, Marta Roldan's study of women in the light engineering industry in Argentina – that "it should be possible to adapt JIT systems to women workers' co-operatives and other units of the social sector" (Roldan 1996: 85).

At an empirical level we need to take note of the changes the global feminization argument draws attention to. In a follow-up analysis in 1999, Standing examines trends in male and female activity rates between 1975 and 1995 in a sample of developing countries, and finds that, in 74 per cent of cases, women's participation increased, compared to 17 per cent when men's participation increased (9 per cent showed no change) (Standing 1999: 587). The change in the gender composition is seen to be even greater when we consider the fact that, in most of the countries where male participation rates fell, total labour force participation actually increased. Although it would be wrong simply to equate flexibilization and feminization, Standing is surely right to draw attention to the possible linkages between the two processes. The point for Standing is that, while women's participation in the labour force is leading (at least potentially) to greater gender equality, the conditions under which they are working have not improved. Indeed, "the trend is towards greater insecurity and inequality" (Standing 1999: 600). Although some positive potential for "flexibility" may exist, from a labour point of view its negative connotations should not be ignored.

The global "feminization" of work thesis is intimately related to the issue of "flexibilization" supposedly characteristic of the new information economy. There is an optimistic rendering of "flexible specialization" that imagines it as a panacea for workers. Yet this benign view is imbued with a deep-rooted Northern perspective, inimical to the interests of the majority of the world's workers. Thus Michael Piore and Charles Sabel, leading proponents of the flexible specialization school, argue:

> It is conceivable that flexible specialisation and mass production could be combined in a unified *international economy*. In this system, the old mass production industries might migrate to the underdeveloped world, leaving behind in the industrialised world the high-tech industries.
> (Piore & Sabel 1984: 279, emphasis in original)

Here we find a continuity between the implicit dualism of the core/periphery model of segmented work in the North and the uncritically accepted dualism between North and South in the international division of labour. While the "new technology" cannot be seen as progressive or even neutral, it has had a significant impact in the South.

From the Fordist assembly line of the "world market factories" in the 1970s to the JIT methods of the 1990s, technology has been upgrading in the South. Although it is not linear or necessarily cumulative – because development is always uneven and combined – technological change is having a profound impact on the social and sexual division of labour. In the 1970s, as never before, female labour power became a marketable commodity in the South. A Malaysian investment brochure illustrates well how capitalism and patriarchy have a synergy in this regard, telling the potential Northern investor that "[t]he manual dexterity of the oriental female is famous the world over. Her hands are small and she works fast with extreme care. Who, therefore, could be better qualified by nature and inheritance to contribute to the efficiency of a bench-assembly production line than the oriental girl?" (cited in Elson & Pearson 1981: 149). It was not surprising to see capital, the state and patriarchal interests in society working together towards the efficient exploitation of women in these factories created by the new international division of labour.

Nonetheless, it is well to remember that the one thing worse than exploitation is not being exploited at all, as Joan Robinson is supposed to have said. Thus Kumudhini Rosa, in a broad overview of women workers in the FTZs, points out how "some recent [research] contributions have stressed the gains for women in terms of greater freedom and status from earning a wage" (Rosa 1994: 74). So, in spite of the precarious, exploitative and patriarchal nature of this employment, it could be empowering for women workers. Cooperation and different forms of solidarity – of gender, of class, of community or others – could be generated in their workplaces. Sites of exploitation can also be sites of contestation. Coincidentally, or probably not, many women workers in "world market factories" began to lose their jobs in the late 1980s in a reverse process of "remasculinization", we might say. What continued in these workplaces, and in their new "post-Fordist" successors, was a totally gendered struggle between capital accumulation strategies and strategies of labour defence and renewal.

There are two general points to be made usefully at this stage, I believe. The first is that in much of the "feminization" debate there is an implicit male norm against which transformations are measured. Yet the notion of a full-time, permanent, skilled male job is basically a myth. To measure the "flexible" job of today against a mythical norm can only lead to a debilitating binary opposition. Second, neither "flexibilization" nor "feminization" can be seen as unidirectional or permanent trends. Rather, they reflect specific capital accumulation strategies at different times in different places. They reflect also differentiated state strategies in specific conjunctures and regions. The third problem arises in relation to the "visibility" of the high-tech sectors compared to the more "irregular" (although the term is problematic when it describes what is actually the regular) forms of employment in homeworking and in the informal sector, in which the majority of women, especially in the South, actually work.

If some women have been sucked into the maelstrom of the globalized information economy, many more are working in the informal sector and are the mainstay of the homeworkers' labour economy. As Scott notes, in much of the informal sector research "the focus has been on the way women's activities complemented and replicated their domestic roles: much of women's informal work was carried out in the home (e.g. outwork, front-room shops, laundry work)" (Scott 1994: 29). Work and home intersected here in a way that was extremely profitable for capital. The role of women in terms of basic "household survival strategies" across the South was harnessed in the interests of capital accumulation. In the reproduction of that particular commodity known as labour power (people's capacity to work), women's work both in the home and in the labour market thus acts as a substantive subsidy. In terms of women working worldwide, this sector is probably the one in which most research needs to be done to understand better the relationships between class and gender, production and reproduction, domestic economy and labour markets.

What work in the informal sector mainly means for women workers is "casualization". That is to say, "[f]or women, flexible working often means greater insecurity, reduction in working hours and pay, changes in shifts, loss of national insurance benefit, loss of overtime bonuses, and loss of holidays, maternity leave, sick pay and pension" (Mitter 1994: 13). This type of worker is as much part of "flexible specialization" worldwide as is the graduate computer expert in Silicon Valley. It is an integral part of the way the big MNCs operate on a worldwide basis. International subcontracting out into the informal sector has become normal practice, including, significantly, for the big brand names. The advantage, as Swasti Mitter explains, is that "the workers employed by the local sub-contractors remain flexible and invisible" (Mitter 1994: 21). Of course, as we shall see later, this growing connectivity between capital and labour, in all its myriad forms worldwide, also exposes it to various new forms of campaigning, for example from the consumption end.

Homeworking, as a specific form of waged employment, has since the mid-1980s been recognized by the international trade union movement as a priority for organizing. Previously there would have been an attitude that this was not "proper" work or that it "undercut" work done by established trade union members in the formal sector. In 1990 the ICFTU issued a substantial and influential report, entitled *On Organising Workers in the Informal Sector* (ICFTU 1990), which was helpful in pushing the ILO towards new legislation for homeworkers across the globe. Although it was subsumed under the slightly anomalous label of "atypical" work, homeworking was now placed firmly on the labour movement agenda. It is significant that the issue of homeworking also broadened out the way trade unions operated. Inevitably, women's organizations internationally played a major role in the networking, researching and organizing involved, and thus, to some extent, influenced the way trade unions operated. In many ways these activities were precursory and exemplary of what later became known as social movement unionism.

> In conclusion, while in the era of globalization (and the period leading up to it) women entered the labour market in greater numbers than ever before, they did so in a situation dominated by the watchwords of liberalization, privatization and flexibilization. In short, women working worldwide entered what can only be called a "casualized" labor market. Even the World Bank acknowledges that women [workers] are often more vulnerable than men, disproportionately concentrated in

low-wage sectors or occupations and often segregated into the informal sector. Not surprisingly, their relative position has often deteriorated during structural adjustment.   (World Bank 1995: 1071)

Women are often among the last to be drawn into the labour market when an economic upturn occurs, and among the first to be expelled from it during cyclical downturns. From a long-term perspective, however, it can be said that women workers are no longer a "reserve army" of labour, having been fully integrated into the capitalist labour market on a worldwide scale.

Labour movement and gender

It would be hard to overestimate the importance of a gender lens in a critical study of work and the labour movement. From the start of industrialization to most trade unions today, the world of work and its representative organizations has been predominantly (often exclusively) male and masculinist in discourse and practice. The artificial separation of the worlds of production and reproduction lie at the basis of this continued analytical failure to grasp the world of work in all its complexity. Recent work extending the "global value chains" has sought to bridge this divide. Whereas the first has a purely economic focus, the latter shows how domestic workers, for example, are part of a change linking households in the global service economy. As Nicola Yeates puts it, the global care chain concept "attends to the distributive dimensions and outcomes of international migration", often neglected, and also "expands the realm of social inequalities ... to include emotional as well as social (labour) geographies" (Yeates 2009: 46–7). This is but one theoretical advance for labour studies generated from a gender perspective.

The dialectic of production and reproduction, which is at the heart of any gendered analysis of work, has its roots in an earlier debate around subsistence and the household. Rosa Luxemburg had, in 1913, contested Marx's view that capitalism did not need colonies or extra-economic forms of coercion to maintain the mode of production. Reproduction or subsistence did not enter into the debate in any explicit way. For Luxemburg, "capitalism in its full maturity depends in all respects on non-capitalist strata and social organizations existing side by side with it" (Luxemburg 1951 [1913]: 280). She also emphasizes the ongoing structural role of violence in that process. Although it was not written from a gender perspective, this insight fed into an analysis of women in the 1970s as "the last colony" or "the housewification of work" (Mies 1986). Thus Luxemburg's analysis can be extended to women's work, generally seen as invisible, and to homework in particular as a modality of the substance economy. Clearly, a traditional trade union strategy based on male workers in a factory setting would be inadequate to organize against this form of exploitation.

Today there is a growing attention to the "global feminization" of work and its relationship to flexible labour (and also to the informal sector). Most of us are familiar with the gendered nature of work in the "new world factories" of Southeast Asia and the *maquilas* in Mexico from the 1980s onwards. Although many of these jobs went from women to men in the 1990s as they became better paid, the overall tendency of feminization of the global labour force continued. From data collected by Standing we find that, from 1970 to 2000, the global trend has been for female labour force participation to rise while male participation rates have been falling (Standing 1999: 588). This is in the context of considerable gender biases in labour statistics, as many countries leave out unpaid or own account workers. Nonetheless, it would seem, as Standing argues, that "it is the spread of more flexible and informal employment that accounts for much of the upward trend in the female share of the labour force" (Standing 1999: 588). The tendency for the gender gap to close overall has been reversed since the 2007–9 global financial crisis, as we saw above.

Feminized and casualized work has led to new forms of labour organizing and has sometimes transformed labour organizations. SEWA became an international model of best practice. Homeworking has also gone through a transformation thanks to agitation by feminist and labour activists. While once homeworking was seen as a threat by the organized labour movement, today 300 million homeworkers across the world – from informal small-scale production to highly skilled IT workers – are recognized by the ILO as a labour category with rights. Whereas once organization among poor women workers was restricted to the "weapons of the weak" (Scott 1985), now we see a development of a whole range of collective strategies of resistance and struggle (Kabeer, Sudarshan & Milward 2013). Organization, mobilization and action have cut across the intersecting inequality of gender, class, race, ethnicity and caste to produce vibrant new models of labour mobilization.

The labour movement's response

If in the golden era it seemed that the workers of the North were the undisputed pioneers of organizational methods and ideological innovation, in the era of globalization this role has in many ways passed to the workers of the South. It is symptomatic that US labour analyst Kim Moody heads one of his chapters on labour's response to globalization "Looking South" (Moody 1997: 201). The labour leaders of Europe and North America have been forced to leave behind their paternalism towards the labour movements of the South. Globalization integrated production on an unprecedented scale and (as seen in Chapter 2) brought together the fates of workers across the globe to a much greater extent. If US labour leaders were "looking South" with other than a "trade union imperialist" perspective, it was because the workers of the South now counted in the global political economy of labour. One area in particular in which a breakthrough occurred was in the semi-industrialized or semi-periphery countries, such as Brazil, South Africa and then South Korea, where vibrant labour movements had crystallized in the 1980s.

As part of the NIDL, countries such as Brazil and South Africa went through a process of forced industrialization from the 1970s onwards. This was a state-led industrialization under conditions of severe political repression – in short, what at the time was dubbed a "savage capitalism". As Gay Seidman explains, in a powerful analysis, "From the perspective of both states, economic growth required high profits to attract foreign and domestic investors to new industrial sectors; and it required closure of political space to protect the stable business climate required to compete with other potential investment sites" (Seidman 1994: 259). In these pressurized hothouse conditions capital accumulation flourished, but so too did a new industrial working class. In practically "classical" capitalist growth conditions, a proletariat was generated that began to take cognizance of its situation, to organize and to act on behalf of its social needs, thus confirming Polanyi's thesis of a double movement whereby society protected itself from an unregulated market. We need only note that in South Africa there were 30,000 black trade unionists in 1973 and 550,000 by 1983. In Brazil the "new unionism" shot to prominence after strikes at the end of the 1970s and played a key role in the later transition to democracy.

In South Africa, the best organized of the first independent labour federations, the Federation of South African Trade Unions, was operating by 1983 in over 500 factories, with a commitment to:

- democratic factory floor organization;
- a united labour force irrespective of race, gender or creed; and
- social justice, a decent standard of living and fair working conditions for the whole working class (MacShane, Plaut & Ward 1984: 38).

FOSATU and its affiliates were key players in a number of successful consumer boycotts against recalcitrant employers, and in campaigns around housing issues and for cheaper transport. Although FOSATU was dubbed "workerist" in the inter-trade-union debates, it was increasingly drawn into community-based as well as factory floor struggles, and began to take positions on the key political issues of the day. By 1985 a united labour federation, the Congress of South

African Trade Unions, had been formed, which went on to play a crucial organ-izational, mobilizing and political role in the struggle against apartheid rule and in the new democratic South Africa.

In Brazil, strikes in the metallurgical plants in São Paulo's industrial belt in 1978–9 spread to other professions and to the remotest provinces of the country. An important feature of these strikes was the advanced level of organization, in the form of a general strike committee, with struggles frequently cutting across occupational lines and massive street demonstrations being arranged. Struggles in the working-class districts occurred around a whole series of day-to-day issues, such as healthcare, running water and, above all, housing. When the strike wave began, the dense social networks built up in these communities played a crucial role in generating solidarity for the factory workers. Churches often provided shelter and cover for the organizing of the then clandestine trade unions. In the words of Zé Pedro, one of the São Paulo metalworkers' leaders, workers started "by demanding a share of what they produce", after which they wanted "better wages, better living conditions, and then start[ed] viewing polit-ical parties in a different light" (cited in Antunes 1980: 33). After the formation of the united Unified Workers' Central, in 1983, unions, and others, effectively went on to form the Workers' Party in 1989, which was to play a key role in the struggle for democratization and beyond.

Practically a decade later a new unionism was generated in South Korea, one of the much-vaunted "Asian Tigers", under fierce authoritarian rule. An even more intensely forced capitalist growth – by the mid-1990s 80 per cent of the population of this once rural economy lived in the cities – created the conditions for a verit-able explosion of labour activism from the late 1980s onwards. Women workers accounted for 40 per cent of the workforce and, as one South Korean study puts it, it is they who "have really been the driving force, not only to bestow on the nascent labor movement a dynamic character, but also to actually lead it at the grassroots level" (cited in Moody 1997: 214). With the formation of the Korean Confederation of Trade Unions in 1995 the labour movement had come of age. The 1996 gen-eral strike, an unprecedented confrontation by labour with capital and the state, established the labour movement on the political scene and within civil society. In the 2000s these trends repeated themselves in Indonesia, in Mexico and elsewhere.

China

The rise of the Chinese working class since 1990 is one of the most remark-able labour phenomena since the Industrial Revolution. In the late 1980s, as China began the turn towards marketization under Communist Party lead-ership – "market Leninism", perhaps – migration from the rural areas to the coastal regions began in earnest. By 2005 migrant workers accounted for 60 per cent of the total industrial workforce and only slightly less in the services sector. What began as migrant labour in construction and domestic work was soon generalized across both the formal and informal sectors, the latter characterized by poor labour standards. These workers, who have made China the industrial power it now is, are hugely exploited: "The vast majority of them have no written employment contract, little training, few rest days, no social security and little health and safety protection. They work extensively long hours [and] live in poor conditions" (Blecher 2010: 58). Their ability to organize will undoubtedly determine the future of China, and, to some extent, of the global labour movement.

There has been much debate around whether the Chinese working class is really a slumbering giant held back only by the state-run trade union movement. This "glass half full" versus "glass half empty" debate around labour's ability to act is somewhat limited. There are, in practice, very distinct patterns of capital accumulation and labour exploitation across China. It is difficult to discern one single pattern, or even trend. Marc Blecher has usefully distinguished between the distinct capital/wage labour relations of the highly globalized Southeast "sunbelt", characterized by "globalised despotism"; the relatively less reformed, barely globalized decaying Manchurian sunbelt, characterized by defensive action; and the rest of the reformed but hardly globalized economy, oriented towards the domestic market (Blecher 2010). We must thus clearly distinguish between different regions, and cannot generalize. Nor can we conflate the role of the All-China Federation of Trade Unions with that of Western state-run unions. The socialist discourse of the ACFTU has an impact on workers and their expectations, and there is a complex interplay between the Chinese developmental state, the unions and the various fractions of the working class that cannot be reduced to simple exploitation.

We can discern a turning point around 2010, with a wave of significant and high-profile strikes in foreign investment plants such as Honda, Hyundai, Toyota, Panasonic and Carlsberg. In the aftermath of the 2007–9 global crisis there was a dramatic knock-on impact on the Chinese working class. At that point between 15 and 20 million migrant workers lost their jobs as a result of the downturn in the West. Nevertheless, as Beverly Silver and Şahan Karataşli note, "The movement of capital into China had created a new and increasingly militant working class – the outcome of the 'creative' side of the creative-destructive process" (Silver & Karataşli 2015: 51), which is capitalist development. Basically, where capital goes, labour must follow, and then we have a capital/wage labour relation that is always antagonistic and often conflictual. While capital may relocate – and it has done so, from China to Vietnam and Cambodia, and even Bangladesh – that relationship is re-formed, and what once seemed like a cheap and compliant labour force may begin to seem not so amendable to exploitation.

Chinese labour developments are hugely significant within global labour, but we cannot conflate them with existing Western patterns. Conducted under the aegis of a traditional communist party, China's entry into global capitalism cannot be equated to any other experience, either in the originally industrializing countries or in the postcolonial world. It is a globally oriented national developmental state quite distinct from the Western neoliberal state of the 1990s. State strategy is central to any subsequent unravelling of the capital/wage labour relation. In terms of labour strategy, Chris Chan, Pun Ngai and Jenny Chan are quite correct to point out that "the complexity of state–trade union–NGO relationships in contemporary China diffuses the optimistic elaboration of the new social movement unionism thesis" (Chan, Ngai & Chan 2010: 133). International NGOs and the international trade union movement have very little understanding of this complexity, and both in very different ways miss out on basics by focusing on a mythical civil society and a sclerotic trade union central respectively.

Emergence of social movement unionism

Over and beyond the particular cases cited above and their specific national histories, there seem to be certain general conclusions to be drawn. The particular conditions of late industrialization generated not only a new working class but also a new form of trade unionism, which we can call social movement unionism, as against the economism of "free collective bargaining" and the tradition of "political bargaining". These workers turned increasingly to those beyond the factory gate, including to the informal sector, and took up issues other than production ones, such as the consumption and transport concerns of the broader working population. Their trade unions also turned to organizations and movements beyond the traditional confines of the labour movement, including community groups, women's organizations, human rights movements and radical church groups and networks. The social movement unionism that emerged also turned naturally to the political arena, articulating a clear workers' voice in the struggle to impose democracy on the repressive political order that had prevailed as it took shape.

Another area already mentioned, that of workers in the South pioneering labour strategies of renewal and resistance, was in relation to the informal sector. Although we must be wary of elevating the case study into a trend, SEWA in India remains exemplary. Renana Jhabvala, analyst and member of SEWA, describes how this movement cut across occupational categories in its organization and combined trade union and co-operative methodologies: "When the co-operatives become part of the trade union it changes the image of the union and helps it win allies, sometimes even with the 'enemy'" (Jhabvala 1994: 133). Thus SEWA could combine aggressive trade union demands with "softer" action in health- and childcare co-operatives for workers in conjunction with the district administration: "[E]ven the employers were shamed into supporting the childcare centres" (Jhabvala 1994: 133–4). What SEWA has created, in its imaginative and forceful discourse and activity, is a vision of a new society. It has shown how an organization of the labouring poor can be grounded in the day-to-day reality of its "non-pure proletarian" members and articulate a general alternative to dependent capitalist development.

What SEWA and other similar organizations across the South have actually done is to break with the formal/informal labour sector dichotomy. SEWA members include many sectors of the self-employed ("casualized labour" being rejected as a derogatory term), from small-scale vendors and traders to home-based producers such as weavers and *bidi* (cigarette) makers, as well as agricultural and other labourers. This array of occupations is unified only (if at all) by gender. In the same way that it cuts across work categories, SEWA conflates political categories, combining distinct forms of organization and synthesizing different oppositional ideologies. Unsurprisingly, from the perspective of "contradictory class locations" (Wright 1985), or fluid identities, it organizes and defends the interests of labourers and the co-operative self-employed in a given industry at the same time. The context in which SEWA and similar organizations operate is, of course, always that of underdevelopment and the overarching need for social and economic development. In this sense, they represent not just the "particular" interests of their members but the general interests of society as well.

Trade unions, labour movements, social movements and the labouring poor in the South were severely affected by so-called "structural adjustments" to meet the requirements of liberalizing globalization. Trade union "density" (i.e. union membership as a percentage of all wage and salary earners) declined overall between 1985 and 1995, but not everywhere. An ILO report finds that, in 1995, roughly 164 million of the world's united workforce belonged to trade unions (ILO 1997). In all but 20 countries membership levels had declined in the previous decade, although, overall, the ILO found that this had not translated into a decline of union influence. Even this complex and uneven picture is only part of the story and masks the qualitative picture on the ground in developing countries. It tells us very little about developments in the broader social movement of labouring people or of political transformations. Our conclusion can only be a cautious one. Some notable "success stories" have been mentioned, when trade unions responded imaginatively to the forces unleashed by globalization. This picture must be tempered, though, with an acknowledgement of the fundamental social weakening of labour during this period.

Global labour rights

The "social clause" campaign was another form taken by the "double movement", whereby there was an attempt "from above", as it were, to protect workers from the effects of the unregulated market. The social clause is at once the most divisive issue separating workers in the South from their counterparts in the North, and, arguably, the strategy best placed to unify the world's workers. I examine here arguments for, arguments against and a credible way forward for a global labour rights strategy. The current round of interest in a "social" or "workers' rights" clause in international trade agreements became marked during the Uruguay Round of the GATT negotiations in the early 1990s. The concept goes back at least to the period after the Second World War, however. Although in the heyday of the neoliberal drive, in the early to mid-1990s, this initiative was presented as some form of protectionist nightmare, the issue of "labour standards" was taken up by the WTO, which succeeded GATT in 1995. What was at one time a fairly marginal (even token) concern of the international trade union movement (the ICFTU, to be precise) now became a key debated point in the world's powerful multilateral trade regulator.

The basic argument for the "social clause" is that trade liberalization, promoted by GATT and the WTO, would undermine workers' rights without such a clause, as investment would inevitably move to where workers' rights were weakest. This would create pressure on all countries to weaken labour regulation to make their products competitive and their territory an attractive investment location. What the "social clause" to be incorporated into multilateral trade agreements would include are, basically, the main ILO "core conventions", as they are known. These included no. 87 (1948) on freedom of association, no. 98 (1949) on the right to organize and engage in collective bargaining, nos. 29 (1930) and 105 (1957) on the abolition of forced labour, no. 138 (1957) on the abolition of child labour and nos. 100 (1951) and 111 (1918) on discrimination in employment. These were deemed "core" conventions because governments, employers and trade unions (part of the ILO's tripartite structure) across the globe freely subscribed to them as applying to *all* who work, including those in the informal sector and in the FTZs. In 1998 the International Labour Conference adopted an ILO declaration that obliged all member states to implement the "core" conventions, even if they had not ratified them previously.

At first glance there is little here that any worker anywhere could object to. It is also fairly easy to dispose of the arguments against core labour rights from a neoliberal perspective, which sees them conspiring against the hegemony of market principles. First, "it is neither conceptually nor empirically clear that higher labour standards mean higher labour costs" (Freeman 1994: 108). Thus, in terms of international competitiveness, there would be no undue burden on particular nations or companies if basic labour rights were to be respected worldwide (starting with the United States, where ILO core conventions remain unratified). To harmonize labour standards worldwide would prevent a "race to the bottom", which would not be beneficial to capital. There is also a view that adhering to international labour standards would be detrimental to the prospects of developing countries. In a lengthy study of this issue, however, the OECD concludes that "any fear on the part of developing countries that better core standards would negatively affect either their economic performance or their competitive position in world markets has no economic rationale" (OECD 1996: 105). So, labour standards are not necessarily bad for business.

The governments of the South have good reason to see Northern enthusiasm for social and environmental clauses in trade agreements as somewhat suspect. They would almost certainly operate in a protectionist way in denying market access in the North to developing country exports. For Vandana Shiva, the social clause does not empower civil society in the South but, rather, business and governments in the North (Shiva 1996: 108). Furthermore, she argues that the social clause "does not challenge the logic of free trade and the globalization of every aspect of local and national economies"; nor does it "stop the processes that cause Third World poverty" (Shiva 1996: 108). On the level at which it is posed, this argument is incontestable. Certainly, as in the ICFTU campaign for the social clause, there are huge concessions to the logic of globalizing neo-liberalism. It is akin to telling trade unions not to pursue higher wages for their members, however, as this does not tackle the roots of oppression in the capital/wage labour relation. Indeed, there is now an argument being made that all the anti-globalization protests need to be unified under an anti-capitalist banner to tackle the "real" roots of all their complaints.

There are more specific and grounded criticisms of the "social clause" campaign made by organizations such as Women Working Worldwide. Thus, we can critically unpack what a social clause would mean for women workers in the South. We have already seen above how the ICFTU campaign of the early 2000s explicitly excluded the informal sector from the child labour campaign and, indeed, most children working in the countryside. In relation to women workers, Angela Hale makes the apparently simple but far-reaching point that the social clause "is mainly raised in high-level international forums where there are few women, and workers are referred to without reference to gender. Yet women's work situations are not the same as men's" (Hale 1999: 28). Much of women's work is in the informal and domestic economies, far from local, let alone international, regulation. Women workers may also have other demands arising from their strategic gender interests. From this perspective, the social clause campaign as it exists appears somewhat over-general, rather top-down and not thought through as to how it might benefit the workers, who are also gendered, who are also citizens of the various regions of the South.

It is probably not fruitful to debate the "social clause" as a for-or-against issue. To pose a North/South, male/female, formal/informal, industrialist/environ-mentalist, globalizer/localist set of binary oppositions will simply not advance the debate. Nevertheless, it is worth posing, briefly, an alternative perspective to the binary oppositions. We could pose Amartya Sen's politico-philosophical position that "the increasingly globalised world economy calls for a similarly globalised approach to basic ethics and political and social procedures" (Sen 2000: 127). Not only does this approach mean going beyond an international approach to a truly global one; it also entails viewing labour in a holistic manner. Work is situated within its broad social, economic, political and cultural context. For Sen, in specific terms, this means that "[t]he universality and comprehensive conception of goals is a well-chosen alternative to acting only in the interests of *some* groups of workers, such as those of the organised sector; or those already in employment or those already covered by explicit rules and regulations" (Sen 2000: 120, emphasis in original).

What we are taking away from this chapter is that the world – and the world of work and workers – is increasingly integrated in terms of how the powerful view it and the rest of us must respond. We note that the World Bank in the draft 2019 edition of its flagship *World Development Report*, on "the changing nature of work", states that there is a pressing need for fewer regulations protecting workers and that much deeper "reforms" to deregulate the labour market are necessary (World Bank 2018). The minimum wage needs to be lowered, the Bank argues, and employers should be granted much greater "hire and fire" powers. Although these recommendations are aimed mainly at the Global South (as the main frontier of capitalist expansion today), they will clearly impact workers everywhere. The Bank finds that the prevailing "strict contract forms" and "bur-densome regulations" are the main problem in setting countries up for a high-tech future. They are essentially saying that the informal unregulated labour market of the Global South should become the new global norm, with flexibility extended across the board. The ILO and the global unions soon showed alarm in reacting to this draft report, not least its acceptance of the Uber *et al.* argu-ment that the gig economy workers were emerging as a separate labour category. It would seem that the world of capital has few new tunes to play. It is now to be seen whether the world of labour can develop its own alternatives beyond rejecting these dangerous "more of the same" remedies to global capitalism's ills.

6

A GLOBAL PRECARIAT

The massive expansion and acceleration of capital accumulation and the almost universal real subsumption of labour in the one-time non-capitalist and radical nationalist areas of the globe are generating a new global working class, coming under the sway of capital on a global scale for the first time and subject to similar pressures and reacting in similar ways. In the North the precarious and insecure nature of most work, especially in the wake of the 2007–9 global capitalist recession, has increased dramatically. Some have suggested that a new social subject has emerged: a "precariat", which now constitutes a "dangerous class" akin to the urban poor in Victorian Britain (Standing 2011). For the millions of workers and urban poor in the global South, precariousness has always been a characteristic of work. What we see now, however, is the emergence of a truly global precariat with different forms and degrees of exploitation but sharing features and, above all, a common interest in the democratization of the global economy and the establishment of social control over the rule of blind market forces.

In recent years there has been an intense debate around the concept of the "precariat". We saw, for example, *The Economist*, on the 200th anniversary of Marx's birth, telling its readership among the international financial elite:

> Yet once again Marx's argument is gaining urgency. The gig economy is assembling a reserve force of atomised labourers who wait to be summoned, via electronic foremen, to deliver people's food, clean their houses or act as their chauffeurs ... Marx's proletariat is being reborn as the precariat. (*The Economist* 2018)

Undoubtedly, this has been beneficial in focusing attention on the workers of the world and how their condition has been impacted by globalization. The term has been questioned by many experienced researchers and analysts (e.g. Breman 2013; Palmer 2013) and has even generated a special issue of the *Global*

Labour Journal (May 2016, entitled "Politics of Precarity – Critical Engagements with Guy Standing"). The issues addressed in the precariat debates are not new. The term's popularity as shorthand for the changes in the experience of work for the Global North brought by new technology and new flexible working has grown, but I would argue that it does not herald the arrival of a new social class so much as a change in the experiences of existing classes, particular the middle classes and their children (the millennials), that has intensified since the GFC and the austerity politics that has prevailed subsequently. By bringing precarity to the North, what globalization has done is to bring the workers North and workers South into a global working class. The implication of this for the labour movement are explored in the pages to come.

When the term "precariat" burst onto the mainstream scene some years ago (with the publication of Standing's book *The Precariat: The New Dangerous Class* in 2011), it seemed to herald the dawn of a new sociological phenomenon. The term has a long genealogy, however, and it is necessary to examine it in relation to earlier notions of marginality, informality and social exclusion in order to situate it and to understand its possible conceptual benefits, but also its potential weaknesses.

The theory of "marginality" emerged in Latin America in the 1960s to account for the vast number of underemployed internal migrants who surrounded the main cities with their makeshift dwellings, and who appeared to be, in all senses, "marginal" to the capitalist system. In the 1970s, this time in Africa, another term arose, namely that of "informality" or the informal sector, to describe workers outside the formal capitalist system. Its means and techniques of production are non-capital-intensive, the means of production are owned by those who operate them and the division of labour is rudimentary. For Keith Hart (1973), who did much to popularize the term, the masses who were surplus to the requirements for wage labour in African cities were not "unemployed" but, rather, were positively employed, even if often for erratic and low returns. He proposed that these activities be contrasted with the "formal" economy of government and organized capitalism as "informal income opportunities".

Marginality

Latin America's particular theoretical contribution to the study of precarity was the "marginality" debate of the 1970s. The origins of the term "marginality" lie in the US sociology of the 1930s referring to the psychological disorientation supposedly felt by individuals at the interface of two cultures, for example after migration. In Latin America it was taken up by the early modernization theorists (see Germani 1964) to refer to the consequences of the postwar urbanization process referred to above. Various names were used to describe the informal settlements that arose around the big cities because of rural–urban migration – *villas misérias, barriadas, favelas, callampas, ranchos, campamentos*, etc. – but in all cases they were physically on the periphery of the city and they lacked even the basics of communal services. Thus, marginality could refer to the social condition of these new urban dwellers or, more often, it was the people who were deemed "marginal", in terms of their access to decent jobs, housing or living standards. There is some common ground here with the much later European concept of "social exclusion" (see Munck 2005).

By the late 1960s the modernization approach was losing traction, not least because its overblown promises of development and democracy had not been delivered. Into this vacuum came various approaches, from those that stressed external dependence from the mainstream structuralism of the Economic Commission for Latin America to revolutionary positions that argued that only socialism could provide a break with dependency. The focus on the new urban dwellers led to the marginality theory, which also had its reformist and revolutionary variants. The first variant, associated with the research group DESAL (Centre for Latin American and Social Development), focused on the self-employed and casualized unskilled workers living in the shanty towns. Most often marginality was seen as being equivalent to poverty. Politically, this group was associated with Chilean Christian democrats, and they were explicitly seeking forms of integration for the poor that would remove them as possible recruits for the various leftist groups vying for hegemony among the masses through a series of land occupation and urban settlements.

The most systematic Marxist study of "marginality" was that of José Nun (1969), but see also the work of Aníbal Quijano (1966). What Nun was essentially doing was creating a new category – a "marginal mass" – to distinguish the Latin American situation from Marx's classic categories of "industrial reserve army" and "relative surplus labour". As with their modernization theory counterparts, Nun and Quijano were addressing the issue of why the postwar industrialization drive had failed to absorb the rapidly increasing labour force. Marginalization is designed to address the proportion of the working population not utilized by monopoly capital in particular, which had become (or was becoming) dominant from the 1960s onwards. Thus we see a category of the poor not envisaged by Marx, a relative surplus population that is not functional (or maybe is even dysfunctional) for the monopoly sector. The reason that it is not deemed to be functional is that it has no influence on the wages of the monopoly sector, whereas the classic reserve army of labour helped depress wages.

The positions of Nun and Quijano were vigorously contested by a Brazilian think tank (Centro Brasileiro de Análise e Planejamento), with positions led by Fernando Henrique Cardoso (1971) and Francisco de Oliveira (1972) in particular. For Cardoso, the phenomenon of combined and uneven development could explain the emergence of the marginal urban population, and there was no need to go beyond Marx's original theory of relative surplus population and a reserve army of labour. Oliveira's "critique of dualist reason" focused on the underlying dualism Nun and Quijano shared with the modernization theorists. The activities of the so-called "marginal sector" were both profitable and linked into the overall pattern of capital accumulation. Small-scale commerce could facilitate the distribution of industrial goods, and the construction of informal settlements saved capital considerable costs. The dialectic of capital accumulation required the provision of labour and raw materials from the "backward" geographical areas and economic sectors. Above all, the relationship between marginality and dependence was questioned: "[A]lthough there are significant causal relations between dependence and marginality, these relations can be better studied and analysed at a more concrete level" (Singer 1973: 72).

In a broad overview of the Latin American "informality" debates in the 1970s and early 1980s, Caroline Moser concludes that "identifying with accuracy the social relations of production in a specific context was deemed critical to understand the diversity of exploitation within the informal sector" (Moser 1994: 28). It also became evident in the research of this period that definitions of employment and unemployment were often quite arbitrary and that the main issue was employment rather than unemployment. In the late 1980s and early 1990s the debate shifted, according to Cathy Rakowski, to a more policy-oriented agenda around key questions such as (a) which informal activities generate economic growth and employment, (b) which serve as a buffer against unemployment and (c) which policies promote informal activities? (Rakowski 1994: 6). There was a move away from the broad question of whether development models had managed to generate employment or not to a more individual-based approach around how to promote micro-enterprise.

We should also note a decisive critique of both informality and marginality perspectives for their alleged dualism, whereby they continued to mirror the modernization theory in a belief in a binary opposition between traditional and modern sectors. Quijano and Nun – not to mention the more culturalist views of the modernization theorists – tended to have an over-optimistic view of the pre-monopoly capital era and its ability to absorb labour. The critique of the "external" dependency approach focused on the "internal" development of capitalism in Latin America and rejected the dualist notions of a traditional versus a modern sector. Best exemplified by Oliveira in his "critique of dualist reason" (Oliveira 1972), it showed how the activities of the so-called "marginal sector" were in fact quite profitable for the broader economic system. Small-scale commerce, or the petty commodity mode of production, could facilitate the distribution of industrial goods, and, for example, the self-constructed dwellings of the informal settlements saved capital the costs of building workers' houses. The dialectic of capital accumulation actually required the provision of labour and raw material inputs from the "backward" sector. Marginality/informality discourses were also criticized for being residual categories, not integrated into a broader political economy of development.

The debate around marginality has continued sporadically, and its original protagonists came back to it at the end of the century (Nun 1999). It was clear that the original polemic had been addressed to the 1960s Left, which saw the shanty town dwellers as a new revolutionary vanguard. The underlying and continued mission was to distinguish what was happening in Latin America from the wage labour society, theorized by Robert Castel (1995), in which most workers are salaried, there is full employment and wage workers enjoy status, dignity and social protection. Latin America never followed this model, and even under ISI (and those countries in which some form of welfarism was adopted) vast layers of the population fell outside the capital/wage labour relation. The 1990s indeed saw a massive shift towards informal employment, which, to some degree, confirmed the original underlying meaning of the marginality thesis. The impact of structural heterogeneity, poverty and social inequality in Latin America cannot be blamed on its victims (as the World Bank and the whole "poverty industry" still does) but requires objective and specific analysis – something the marginality writers at least tried to provide.

We are clearly not dealing with a debate of relevance to the 1960s only. The *Latin American Research Review* ran a symposium some 40 years later entitled "From the Marginality of the 1960s to the 'New Poverty' of Today" (de la Rocha *et al.* 2004), arguing, in its editorial introduction, that

> there is now increasing evidence that although classical marginality may have lacked empirical veracity in its earliest iteration, changing economic conditions born out of the structural adjustment and austerity of the 1980s, together with the neoliberal restructuring of the 1990s, have in the 2000s been creating the very conditions and cultural constructions conceived and predicted by Nun, Quijano and Lewis in the 1960s.
>
> (de la Rocha *et al.* 2004: 186)

Certainly, rising unemployment, the generalized precarity of employment, privatization and declining opportunities, even in the informal sector, have accentuated the phenomenon of marginality. What is different is a much more interventionist state in terms of social policies and a much greater degree of political participation than was possible in the conditions of the 1960s.

Marginality has returned to mainstream discourse in Latin America in one particularly negative variant. The term had fallen into disuse by the 1980s, with terms such as "social exclusion" and "spatial exclusion" taking prominence, congruent with the new language of rights and citizenship. Then in the 1990s, particularly in Brazil, the term "marginal" returned to favour to denote the drug dealers and gangs of the *favelas*. While the original dwellers of the *favelas* were no longer seen as marginal, the criminal gangs were categorized as "marginal", and a whole subculture has grown up around them. Interestingly, Loïc Wacquant has taken up the term "new marginality" as a way to describe the new poverty in the post-industrial North (Wacquant 1994). Thus the Chicago ghetto and the French *banlieue* were seen to be characterized by a form of marginality based on territorial separation, dependency on the welfare state and a generalized stigma attached to its (sometimes immigrant) inhabitants.

In Latin America, Bryan Roberts has most consistently examined the shifts inherent between 1960s "marginality" and post-2000 "social exclusion" (Roberts 2004). For him, a key issue "in analysing the 'new' poverty is whether the change in concepts that we use reflects a change in reality, a shift in intellectual fashions, or a combination of both" (Roberts 2004: 195), with his conclusion being that it is a bit of both. While the peripheral urban settlements are today much more consolidated than they were in the 1960s – and some of the physical problems are less – deregulation has opened up this land to speculators. Furthermore, the free trade regimes of the 1990s exposed even the petty commodity mode of production to a degree of competition that was not present in the ISI period. Above all, for Roberts, "the 'informal economy' grows, but incomes drop within it" (Roberts 2004: 196). The notion that, in the informal economy, people could create their own opportunities, as it were – as articulated by Peruvian neoliberal informality guru Hernando de Soto (1986) – has proved quite illusory.

The concept of "marginality" – along with that of "dependency", which also emerged in Latin America during the late 1960s and early 1970s – has both theoretical and empirical shortcomings. It is still remarkable that the debate on informality or the informal sector that began in the early 1970s rarely, if ever, made any references to it. As Cristóbal Kay writes, "[T]he analysis of marginality undoubtedly opened up a useful debate on an important issue for Third World countries and for the world economy as a whole, as Third World labour can be considered as the industrial reserve army of the world" (Kay 1989: 123). Certainly, it has contributed to current attempts to (re)construct a political economy of development and of labour fit for the global era. Unlike the informality debates, the one on marginality was not co-opted by the international financial institutions, and it retained a certain critical edge. Dependency, as a particular variant of capitalist development, and marginality, as a labour condition in that process, are still very relevant in the era of globalization, which has not superseded uneven development or overcome the structural divide between powerful and dominated countries.

Northern precarity

What is most noticeable in the broader literature around precarity, and the precariat, is that it is almost totally Northern-centric in its theoretical frames and its empirical reference points. There is a Northern sensibility at play here, it seems, focusing largely on Britain in the 1950s as the model of economic and political development to whose social settlement the precariat aspires to regain. In fact, Fordism and the welfare state are the exception to the rule from a global perspective. Decent work has never been the norm in the postcolonial world. Rather, super-exploitation, accumulation through dispossession and what might be called "permanent primitive accumulation" have, by and large, prevailed. From a Southern perspective, work has always been precarious, a basic fact that unsettles the notion that something new has been discovered. Although the precariat discourse exudes nostalgia for something that has passed (the Keynesian/Fordist/welfare state), it does not speak to a South that never experienced welfare state capitalism. The Southern experience of precarity is marked by the nature of the postcolonial state and, later, by the developmental state where this has emerged. The changing nature of work as a result of the erosion of the welfare state does much to popularize the notion of informality, "the distinction between formal and informal income opportunities is based essentially on that between wage-earning and self-employment" (Hart 1973). Significantly, this conception was also picked up and developed around the same time by the International Labour Organization (ILO 1972). The informal sector – or "informal economy", as it became known – embraces a whole range of occupations, from small-scale manufacturing and retail to domestic service and various illegal activities, united only in terms of being beyond the reach of labour law, labour contracts, licensing and taxation laws.

Informality

In a similar way to the debate around marginality, that around informality began in reaction to the unfounded optimism of orthodox modernization theory. The latter had posited, since the 1950s, that capitalist modernization would surpass and transform the "traditional" economy and work practices then characteristic of the developing world. Some Marxists also shared in this optimistic view of capitalism's revolutionary and transformative capacity. In fact, not only did so-called informal work persist but it also spread to the North in the 1970s, as the long-term crisis of Fordism and Keynesianism came to a head. Alejandro Portes and collaborators wrote influentially about the informal economy in "advanced and less developed countries" (Portes, Castells & Benton 1989), while Saskia

Sassen (1994) argued, against the wisdom of the time, that the informal sector was, in fact, the driver and most entrepreneurial sector of advanced capitalism.

In the post-Fordist era it seemed that informality was becoming generalized and was no longer an unfortunate hangover from the past. In the North it was used to describe the work of creative professionals such as architects, artists and software developers. In the South, de Soto published his influential *El otro sendero* (de Soto 1986), using the terminology of the Peruvian Maoist group Sendero Luminoso, but referring here to the dynamic informal path to economic development. This anti-statist manifesto blamed state interference in Peru (and more generally) for stifling the entrepreneurialism that would lead to economic development. The informal economy, in its brave defiance of the state (and the law), acted as a champion for development and thus also served to vindicate the free market policies of triumphant neoliberalism. The informal economy was no longer a problem; rather, it embodied the promise of an unregulated market system.

Social exclusion

In the 1980s a new concept emerged, in Europe this time, namely that of "social exclusion". This would emerge as an overarching paradigm to analyse the "new poverty" of the era of globalization, especially in the context of the need to produce a social "safety net" alongside the unregulated expansion of finance and capitalist development more broadly. It was multidimensional, embracing exclusion not just from employment but also from the political process and shared cultural worlds. In some variants – in France, for example, but also in the United States – the social exclusion paradigm focused on the need for social order and moral integration. This discourse detected the emergence of an urban underclass that supposedly suffered from a "culture of dependence" it would have to be weaned off. From this perspective, it was the social behaviour and social values of the poor that needed to be addressed, rather than the social and economic structures that themselves generated poverty. This discourse was reminiscent of how, in the 1960s, the spectre of "marginality" had generated a moral panic in Latin America that was shared by Left and Right, to some extent.

The social exclusion paradigm, I would argue, cannot be reduced to the moral agenda of the underclass theory, nor to its Eurocentric origins and deployment. The ILO, for example, carried out a major research project on social exclusion in the 1990s (ILO 2004), deploying it as an overarching framework for understanding (and combating) the growing social inequality caused by globalization. As a research paradigm, social exclusion did break with economistic and individualistic traditional parameters of poverty. It was multidisciplinary and multidimensional in its approach. It was not static in its analysis but emphasized, rather, the dynamic and ongoing transformation of social exclusion. It was, above all, relational, in that it showed how poverty and exclusion had as their counterpart the wealth and power of a few. Ultimately, however, promoting "social inclusion" as policy and practice to counter exclusion was weak as a social policy and certainly not robust enough politically for an era in which a brash neoliberalism defined the horizon of possibilities.

To be "marginal", "informal" or "socially excluded" is to be beyond the parameters of the capitalist development process – if that is seen as a harmonious process, of course. It is about being shut out from the social, economic, political and cultural mechanisms of social integration. Policy-makers might thus design programmes to address marginality and exclusion, much as capitalism has always sought to address poverty in one way or another. But the prospects for social engineering would be limited if poverty and exclusion are structural and inherent features of an unequal system based on power differentials. The recent emergence of the term "precariat" needs to be situated in the context of these earlier attempts to theorize a form of work (and living) that does not appear to conform either to liberal notions of harmonious development or to Marxist theories of capitalism generating a proletariat that would be its own gravedigger.

Reconstructing the precariat

New concepts to explain social processes need to be both analytically rigorous and empirically robust. I argue that the term "precariat" should be reconstructed as a clear acknowledgement of precarity as a key feature of the condition of the global working class today.

Before it was popularized in its English-language incarnation, *précarité* had already been deployed in the French socio-economic literature around the changing patterns of work since the 1980s, often in close association with the processes of *exclusion sociale* (Barbier 2002). It was seen as part of the process of decline of the centrality of the wage relationship in structuring society. Precarious forms of work and precarious modalities of employment were on the rise as the Fordist social regime of accumulation was losing its hegemony. Employment norms were being eroded from within, as it were, and various forms of non-standard working relations were coming to the fore. Precarity was probably more of a descriptive category and was not deemed a totally new phenomenon or a self-sufficient one. Most often it was taken in association with social exclusion or as part of a broader analysis of the shifting patterns of employment and the sociology of work. Perhaps the most influential writer in this tradition was Robert Castel, whose *Les métamorphoses de la question sociale* (1995) defined the analysis of the shifts in the wage relationship consequent on the emergence of the neoliberal social regime of accumulation. His emphasis was on *travail précaire*, which he saw as central in defining the new social question, namely the erosion of traditional work relationships and the centrality of the wage relationship.

Current definitions of the precariat claim the emergence of a new class or "class in the making". The precariat is defined more or less by what it is not – a mythical, stable working class with full social and political rights – and by its vague feelings of anomie and distance from the orthodox labour movement.

Class locations are determined by their role in the relation of production and reproduction. Social classes are also relational: they do not emerge on their own, and we need to specify the antagonistic relations of production they are based on. In brief, I would argue for the concept of a global precariat (encompassing migrants) as a current manifestation of the working class that is moving towards a global working class.

If we take the current interest in the precariat and precarity as a symptom of conceptual dissatisfaction with orthodox thinking, and a desire for more original critical thinking, then we might try to reconstruct its object of analysis. If precarity is to be more than a Euro-May-Day slogan, we need to situate it more carefully. A transformative perspective on labour needs to recognize the dialectic of proletarianization and dispossession that is framing the remaking of the global working class. If we focus only on precarity (in the North), we miss out on the massive expansion of the global working class in classic Marxist forms. We can perhaps pose the current dynamics of social transformation in terms of Marx-style proletarianization processes, conjoined with Polanyi-style accumulation by dispossession (Polanyi 2001 [1944]). It is important to remember that every "unmaking" of the working class (for example, through increased precarity) always inevitably leads to its remaking. This sort of dialectical thinking is quite absent from much of the teleological reasoning of the precarity discourse, which sees it as a one-way street to social disintegration and the rise of authoritarianism.

The accumulation of capital on a global scale begets a global working class in the sense of an accelerated process of proletarianization. Globalization over the past 35 years has also deepened the shift from the formal to the real subsumption of labour, in the sense that formal subsumption allows for the continuation of the pre-capitalist labour process, while the "real" subsumption of labour implies that the social relations and modes of labour use are really subsumed under capital. Put simply, only capital can create the conditions for capitalist production. If capital is understood as a social relation, its dramatic global expansion will expand the working classes. The basic fact is that the numbers of workers worldwide doubled between 1975 and 1995 as part of what we called globalization, but which really should be seen as an expanded reproduction of capital on a global scale and the dramatically increased subsumption of non-capitalist forms of production. This continuing expansion of the global working class was accompanied by the full incorporation of the state socialist East and the national development South into the expanded circuit of capital accumulation. Against the theorists of new/networked/virtual capitalism, David Coates has put it neatly: "Globalization in the modern form is a process based less on the proliferation of computers than on the proliferation of proletarians" (Coates 2000: 511).

From a capitalist perspective, "the globalization of labour is inevitable", and there is a clear priority placed by global managers on human resource management (Johnston 1991: 115). Perhaps the most salient feature in the qualitative composition of the great quantitative leap forward of the global labour force is its concentration in the South, or what economists still call "developing regions". Whereas the number of workers in the OECD countries increased only from 372 million in 1985 to 400 million in 2000, the number of workers in the South increased from 1,595 million to 2,137 million. The gender composition of the global labour force also changed dramatically over the same period, with female labour force participation surpassing 50 per cent by the mid-1980s. The expansion, feminization and what we might call "Southernization" of the working class went hand in hand and changed utterly the composition of the global working class.

The massive extension of proletarianization does not mean that the working class remains as is, with the same leading sectors as in the 1950s or 1960s. Indeed, the working class has always been in flux, being continuously made, unmade and remade. If we take manufacturing and mining workers as an example, we can see how their vanguard role in one phase of capitalist expansion may now have come to an end. We know how, in the North, trade unions are increasingly based on the services sector rather than manufacturing. In the South, miners (such as in Bolivia) and other traditional worker sectors have ceased to play a leading role as the working class has become more complex in composition. Traditional relations of representation and hegemony construction have been thrown into disarray and trade unions are no longer the undisputed articulators of mass discontent. As Michael Hardt and Antonio Negri put it: "This shift, however, signals no farewell to the working class or even a decline of worker struggles but rather an increasing multiplicity of the proletariat and a new physiognomy of struggles" (2009: 110). We must also note that proletarianization is not incompatible with informalization. As Mike Davis has shown, "the global informal working class (overlapping with but non-identical to the slum population) is about one billion strong, making it the fastest growing, and most unprecedented, social class on earth" (2006: 178).

Since the structural adjustment crises of the 1980s the informal sector has grown three to four times more rapidly than formal sector employment.

Multinational corporations have taken advantage, of course, of this phenomenon through their subcontracting networks, now central to commodity production change. It is also an integral element of China's blossoming industrial economy, which is underpinned by a traditional informal sector playing nothing like a traditional role. There is not, to be sure, a dichotomy between the formal and informal economies but, rather, a continuum, based on considerable synergies and grey overlapping areas.

The informal economy might be growing but it is still based on a lack of formal employment contracts or any respect for labour rights. Furthermore, there is no indirect social welfare wage in this sector, something the Northern precariat still has a recent memory of. No longer deemed "marginal" in Latin America, informal workers are now more likely to be seen as part of an urban and rural semi-proletariat, thoroughly integrated into the modern, internationalized economic system. Interestingly, it is the continuing differences between North and South in terms of the informal proletariat that emerge as a key differentiator. While the total proportions of informal workers in Latin America in 1950 and the United States in 1900 are roughly comparable (40 to 50 per cent), we see that the proportion of self-employed in the US manufacturing sector had dropped to 3 per cent by 1930, while it was still around 20 per cent in Latin America in 1990 (Portes & Hoffman 2003).

Taking a global perspective on labour today entails a clear refusal of a Eurocentric (or North Atlantic) perspective that centres on the history of the former metropolitan territories. Informalization and precariousness did not emerge with the 2007–9 crisis. It might not be too fruitful, however, to draw a clear dividing line between North and South in terms of the characteristics of capital/labour relations. We should perhaps think more in terms of a radical global heterogeneity as the dominant characteristic of labour relations. A postcolonial perspective would thus not emphasize either Southern uniqueness or Northern exceptionalism. Sandro Mezzadra argues in this regard that global capitalism is increasingly infused by heterogeneity: "[B]y the contemporaneous and structurally related existence of the 'new economy' and sweatshops, corporatisation of capital and accumulation in 'primitive' forms, processes of financialisation and forced labour" (2012). As always, global development is uneven but combined in the way it advances and in its impact on the world of work.

Increasingly, labour studies are taking a global turn, first in sociology and international political economy but now also in terms of a global labour history. There is a growing recognition that Marx and Engels could only have had a very partial and time-limited understanding of what wage labour meant. Although "free" wage labour lies at the heart of the Marxist class theory and political project, it was unpaid subsistence labour that was, and remains, the dominant form from a global perspective. Domestic labour, while crucial to the reproduction of the working class, has always been unpaid labour. Van der Linden proposes a greater focus on the way in which labour power is commodified by capitalism in different forms, and suggests that the concept of "subaltern labour" should be extended to also embrace self-employment, sharecropping, indentured labour and chattel slavery (van der Linden 2008: 331). Finally, we might propose an overall dynamic of working-class deconstruction and reconstruction on a global scale, based on a Marx–Polanyi dialectic. Marx's focus on proletarianization, based on the separation of workers from the means of production, can be supplemented by Polanyi's emphasis on the commodification of labour along with land and money. This provides us with a more nuanced understanding of how neoliberal globalization has subjected the world's workers, through classic capital accumulation mechanisms but also through what is becoming known as "accumulation through dispossession", which essentially amounts to a modern and permanent version of Luxemburg's extension of Marx's theory of primitive accumulation (Harvey 2006). There are clear limits to accumulation through dispossession and the "race to the bottom", or apartheid-era South Africa on a global scale would not have been sustainable (Arrighi, Aschoff & Scully 2010).

What this might mean, as a perspective for examining the global dynamics of labour contestation, is suggested by Beverly Silver. While an emphasis on "Marx-type labour unrest" leads us to focus on "the struggles of newly emerging working classes" (such as China), a complementary emphasis on "Polanyi-type labour unrest" turns our attention to "the backlash resistances to the spread of a global self-regulating market" (Silver 2003). A Marx optic engages us with the new emerging working classes of the South, but a Polanyi approach shows us how other working classes are being "unmade" and precaritized in the North, and separated from the means of subsistence in the South, as, for example, through the privatization of water. I would argue that neither approach is sufficient on its own but that their close interplay and interweaving go a long way to unravelling some of the contemporary processes affecting labour.

A perspective from the Global South would seek to understand precarity as part of the broader process of dispossession and the generation of new "surplus populations". The dominant development paradigm seems oblivious to this dimension, as in the way the World Bank (2008) analyses the "transforming countries" and their transition beyond agriculture without visualizing the massive impact it is having across Asia in terms of dispossession, food insecurity and unemployment. As Tania Li notes, "[W]elfare provisions to keep the dispossessed alive" do not figure in the World Bank account, which simply "assumes hundreds of millions of deeply impoverished rural people will find their way onto the transition path" (Li 2010: 69). In the face of global turmoil and the massive wrenching up of traditional working relations and work practices, some token "safety nets" will not prevent a huge human catastrophe. As in other earlier debates around marginality, reserve armies of labour and various categories of surplus population, it would be rather complacent to believe that losses in one sector of the global workforce will be automatically compensated for elsewhere. Certainly, some forms of dispossession, such as that of the South African Bantustans under apartheid, may have been consciously designed to produce a "reserve" pool of labour, but at the moment the churning of labour under global capitalist development is simply producing collateral damage in society. As Li notes, however, "[T]he dispossessed do not go quietly," with under-reported mass protests in China being but one example of this resistance (Li 2010: 72).

As Kate Manzo puts it in relation to development theories:

> Even the most radically critical discourse easily slips into the form, the logic, and the implicit postulations of precisely what it seeks to contest, for it can never step completely outside of a heritage from which it must borrow its tools – its history, its language – in its attempt to destroy that heritage itself. (Manzo 1991: 8)

The ILO has now enthusiastically taken up the notion of the precariat and the problem of insecure work, as it already has the answer: a rather backward-looking, utopian and impossible-to-implement "Decent work" campaign.

The "Decent work" agenda of the ILO picks up where its focus on "social inclusion" in the 1990s left off, but with a similar political dynamic. How could globalization be given a "human face"? How could capital be persuaded that workers were vital to its reproduction? Decent work is defined by the ILO as employment in conditions of freedom, equity, human security and dignity. The "Decent work" agenda, for the ILO, has, "in a relatively short period of time, forged an international consensus among governments, employers, workers and civil society". Its ambition is to provide a key element "to achieving a fair globalization, reducing poverty and achieving equitable, inclusive and sustain-able development". Whatever its aspirations, this agenda never translated into effective measures, and its credibility finally crashed in the wake of the 2007–9 Great Recession (ILO 2012).

The ILO has now seemingly adopted the term "precarious work", in a reprise of the dualism implicit in the earlier formal/informal and inclusion/exclusion categories it had deployed in relation to the world of work. While accepting that the definition of precarious work "remains vague and multifaceted", it argues that it is a useful term "to describe non-standard employment which is poorly paid, insecure, unprotected, and cannot support a household". Precarious work is characterized by uncertainty and insecurity. The ILO and the international labour federations understand that "in Africa precarious work is the norm", but argue that "the phenomenon has now reached the heartlands of industrialised countries with the spread of temporary forms of employment" (ILO 2011: 30). This is perhaps a similar analysis to the "Brazilianization" thesis referred to above. "Decent work" is, I would argue, not an innocent term when considered from a Southern or postcolonial perspective. Throughout the colonial world the subaltern classes struggled against the imposition of wage labour by the colonialists. There was nothing liberatory about being torn from traditional communal modes of production to become a "wage slave". Even the early Western labour movement railed against wage slavery in its campaign for the eight-hour day, for example. In South Africa the process was particularly dramatic. There, as Barchiesi puts it, we did not have to wait for the recent financial crisis "to see precarisation emerge as a mode of appropriation by capital of the social cooperation of living labour" (Barchiesi 2012: 243). Indeed, the whole narrative of modernization hinged around the civilizing influence of capitalism and the way in which waged work could tame the recalcitrant multitudes. Work and decency were twinned in the colonial imaginary, and that is why the "Decent work" agenda can be seen as less than liberatory from a Southern perspective.

The "precariat", I would argue, plays a similarly discursive role today to that played by the terms "underclass" and "marginal" in earlier debates. In Marx's work there was a similar term, namely that of the "lumpenproletariat", deployed in a similar manner. For Marx, this was a "class fraction" that was not an integral part of the class structure nor defined by the relation of production, consisting of, inter alia,

> roués with dubious means of subsistence ... vagabonds ... swindlers, mountebanks, lazzaroni, pickpockets ... maquereaux [pimps], brothel keepers ... organ-grinders, knife grinders, beggars – in short, the whole infinite, disintegrated mass, thrown hither and thither.
>
> (Marx 1976 [1867])

In the Marxist theory of history social, classes develop through their role in the relations of production. Thus the lumpenproletariat, defined precisely outside these relations (like the "non-historic" nation), cannot become a historical actor. If history is the history of production, and society is structured by relations of production, then the lumpenproletariat undermines the whole edifice. Similar problems emerge with the precariat, as we saw above, especially if it is placed in a Marxist – or, indeed, any recognizable – sociological framework.

The politics of a "dangerous class" discourse is, I would argue, quite simply incompatible with any form of progressive social transformation politics. It is a politics of social pathology that has no place in a progressive view of history and human potential. Victor Hugo in *Les Misérables* had already answered the *classes dangereuses* prophets of his time, showing that the working poor were victims of an exploitative system and not all potential murderers and extortionists. Thus, as a political strategy for the twenty-first century, to even pose an emerging precariat as a new dangerous class is politically irresponsible, to say the very least. Nor is it even impressionistically accurate to pose recruitment of the "precariat" by the new racist right as an imminent danger. In fact, the European and other emerging racist and fascist formations are appealing more to the "old" working class, displaced by the ongoing economic crisis and fearful of becoming precarious and disposable.

The notion of a "dangerous class" has a long history in the racist construction of the Southern "other". The dismantling of communal modes of production and the production of a disenfranchised urban underclass were an integral element of "modernization". The degradation of the living conditions of those who were no longer peasants, and not yet urban workers, inspired fear and revulsion among the classes that benefited from their exploitation. As James Ferguson (2007) puts it: "Urban black South Africans have long been understood as dangerous in Mary Douglas's sense – matter out of place – betwixt and between those 'proper' social categories which their very existence seems to threaten" (Ferguson 2007: 74). This racialized discourse of exclusion and construction of the "other" as dangerous was replicated in Latin America, where slum dwellers were once called *cabecitas negras* ("black heads") by the decent burghers of the city.

The new precariat discourse ultimately operates within the "labourist" framework it criticizes rhetorically. "Labourism" is sometimes taken to mean labour unions but, more often, it is a shorthand for the social democratic state, full employment and the whole corporatist bargaining apparatus. This is set up as a traditional labourism, against which to contrast the precariat and its organizations, or lack thereof. Yet this ill-defined "labourism" did not even prevail in pure form in the 1950s Britain that is seen as the "golden era". It certainly has had no bearing whatsoever across Asia, Africa and Latin America.

The main political weakness of the precariat concept is the complete lack of understanding of contemporary labour or of the labour movement's organizations and strategies. The organizations of the broad working class – national and transnational trade unions, social movement and grass-roots organizations, etc. – have also begun to revive after the long neoliberal night, and can no longer be so easily dismissed as relics of "old labour". Bringing labour back in is now crucial to an understanding of the world of work and workers in the era of globalization, especially after the crisis of 2007–9 and the clear signs since that neoliberalism has lost its hegemonic position as a global development ideology.

The organized labour movement simply cannot be written off in a few lines. By way of example, in mid-2012 a new global union, IndustriALL (www. industriall-union.org), brought together affiliates of three former global union federations, namely the International Metalworkers' Federation, the International Federation of Chemical, Energy, Mine and General Workers' Unions and the International Textile, Garment and Leather Workers' Federation. It covers 140 countries and has 50 million members across a wide range of sectors, including the extraction of oil and gas, mining, the generation and distribution of electric power, the manufacturing of metals and metal products, ship building, automotive, aerospace, mechanical engineering, electronics, chemicals, rubber, pulp and paper, building materials, textiles, garments, leather and footwear, and environmental services. That might be seen to be akin to a corporate merger, but among its few founding principles we find a commitment to "Fight against precarious work". This was not just a ritual incantation, and, shortly after forming, IndustriALL signed a temporary work charter with Volkswagen, a major transnational corporation operating in the North and the South, limiting temporary work to a maximum of 5 per cent of the workforce, along with the principle of equal pay and access to training for contract and agency workers – something that represents a significant blow against *précarité*. As Elizabeth Cotton (2013) notes: "[I]t's no revolution but it commits one of the largest multinational companies in the world to putting a limit on insecure work." Organized labour is clearly part of the solution, as well as being a problem at times – I would be the first to acknowledge. But, even if we are pessimistic about the prospects that trade unions might restructure and re-energize to face the new challenges to labour, we need to acknowledge that they do make a difference for those in a precarious position in the labour market and that agency really does count in terms of shaping the future. Certainly, radical interventions in the broad labour movement, seeking the revival of social movement unionism, for example, seem to be more likely to render a positive outcome for social transformation in the era of globalization than does trying to frighten the ruling order and liberal professionals with the spectre of a monster precariat.

The debate around precarity on a global scale continues to pick up pace, and the term seems to have captured something about the nature of work in a contemporary capitalism that does not appear to have a major dynamic, innovative phase ahead. There is no real basis for discerning a "precariat" outside, or opposed to, the "proletariat" (see Wright 2015), just as the "marginal mass" in Latin America was shown to be part of the working poor. What is correct is that "precarity" is probably the dominant form of labour exploitation, comparable to "flexibility" in the early days of neoliberalism, when the constraints on the working of the market (e.g. trade unions) were criticized by its ideologues. From our understanding of the continuous making, deconstruction and remaking of the working class we need to consider how the decisive efforts to create precariousness over the last 20 years is to be reversed.

Contrary to some of the advocates of the precariat thesis, there is no reason to believe that trade unions are defunct as a means to defend precarious workers. Indeed, trade unions are now forced to "organize the unorganized", even from the point of view of the established workforce, which could see its pay and conditions undermined otherwise. Although new forms of organizing, especially at grass-roots level, have been taking place, it is only trade unions that have the organizational capacity to translate that effort into sustainable and organic growth on the part of a renewed labour movement. The strong precariat thesis (as in a new class), in its bid to find a new leading or vanguard class (educated youth, in this case), dismisses too casually the organizing experience of migrant workers (see Chapter 7), often a key issue in the North but also in the South, albeit sometimes created by internal migration. Different forms of social movement or community unionism have shown the ability of the labour movement to organize in new ways and, in doing so, to revitalize itself.

What this chapter argues is that we have seen the emergence of a new facet of the global working class that can be called a global precariat. It is not separate or opposed to the working class, but a new facet of its ever-evolving nature. Labour conditions once characteristic of the colonial and postcolonial world have now become generalized across the globe. The very particular historical and geographic settings of the golden era in the North Atlantic are now seen as an anomaly and not the norm others could aspire to. This emerging global precariat is a precursor, I would argue, of a truly global working class that is the eventual corollary of global capitalist development and its now nearly universal reach. It is not without its contradictions, between old and new working classes, women and men, North and South, but it is being unified by capitalism and by its own innate capacity to organize and resist. The global trade unions are very well aware of this emerging class of workers, and are by no means irrelevant today – at least potentially, if they rediscover their roots as a social movement. Their own future depends on it, but so does also that of the global precariat, which is a "dangerous class" only for capital and not for other workers.

PART III

NEW CHALLENGES FOR GLOBAL LABOUR

Global labour faces key challenges that could, paradoxically, present opportunities for the organization of labour and social change. Labour migration dominates political discourse across the North, as workers seek better conditions in a globalized economy and are willing to take big risks to move to jobs and new lives in foreign countries. Although they are traditionally opposed to the importation of workers, in terms of the making of a global working class trade unions may play a unifying and democratic role in integrating international migrants socially.

I also turn to the story of labour and its "others" – that is, those social movements that have sometimes been in competition with it, such as the environmental movement, but that would make up together a powerful force for sustainable democratic development. Too often opposed to the workers' movements, the "new" social movements based on identity politics may well play an invigorating role in terms of reviving and reinventing trade unions. Finally, I examine the little-known story of workers and labour internationalism, which is, at one and the same time, an old story and part of the making of the working class but which, today, is a key issue if labour is to offer a global alternative to global capitalism. If we are moving towards a globalized setting for workers' struggles, the need for a new internationalism is a pressing task, not only for trade unions but also for social movements more generally.

7

MIGRANT LABOUR

A spectre haunts the world and it is the spectre of migration. All the powers of the old world are allied in a merciless operation against it, but the movement is irresistible.   (Hardt & Negri 2000: 213)

The global precariat is on the move, with what Hardt and Negri call its "irrepressible desire for free movement" (Hardt & Negri 2000: 213). While exodus can indeed be seen as a powerful form of class struggle against the new imperial order, it is still a manifestly spontaneous, even unintentional, form of struggle. Mobility and migration are seen as a disruption of the disciplinary constraints under which workers labour. Certainly, labour is in movement in many diverse ways, and its management is seemingly beyond even the most stringent border controls of most capitalist states.

At a more prosaic level, migration can be seen as an integral part of labour market regulation in the era of globalization. Clearly, the economies of the once affluent North still depend critically on the availability of migrant labour. These workers are most often vulnerable, and many basic labour rights do not apply to them. As Harald Bauder points out, "[I]nternational migration is a regulatory labor market tool" (Bauder 2006: 4), allowing employers to drive down wages and lower labour standards through the introduction of a "cheap and flexible" migrant labour force. Is it that we are seeing the emergence of what Pierre Bourdieu has referred to as a "global reserve army of labour" (Bourdieu 2003 [1998]: 40)? If that is the case, it should be incumbent on trade union movements to respond with an inclusive policy towards migrant workers, and not through national protectionism, as has happened quite often in the past (Penninx & Roosblad 2000), even though this is sometimes forgotten.

This chapter does not seek to provide an overall analysis of migration in the current era. My focus here is simply on the interaction between labour migrants and the labour movements in the receiving countries. I begin with a unified theoretical and historical reconstruction of migration and the making of the working class that breaks with the traditional approach of considering migration and labour studies as separate domains. The labour movement was born through the migration of workers from the land to cities in the Industrial Revolution, and migrants are (by and large) workers. These are not separate problematics. Migration – within countries and transnationally alike – has played a major role in the making of the working class and has increasingly become a major global issue and one in which the labour movement has a crucial role to play. Migration plays a major role in the development process both North and South, and, as I show, it is as much gendered as it is racialized in its structuring and impacts.

Finally, I argue that migrant labour is both a challenge and an opportunity for organized labour and trade unions. Migrants may often be introduced into a settled labour force with the intention of undercutting wages and conditions, which trade unions have naturally opposed. Recent examples point to the positive role that trade unions can have, however, in terms of migrant integration, and to the possible impact of migrant workers on trade union revitalization by giving them a strong democratic and organizational boost. Economic migration poses social and political challenges but it also has the power to transform the future of societies in the North beset by declining birth rates and an ageing population. The current "migration crisis" in Europe shows it is an issue that can dramatically divide, not least across the working classes, and give rise to massive political crises directly or indirectly.

Migration and the working class

"The story of nineteenth-century labour is one of movement and migration," as Hobsbawm once put it (Hobsbawm 1951: 299). The "tramping artisan" was symbolic of work and workers in the transition to industrialism. In the early British trade unions, the rule books and constitutions provided facilities and mutual support for the artisan who went from town to town in search of work, sometimes on a seasonal basis. The system was common across Europe and traced its origins back to the eighteenth century. The itinerant worker could thus deal with seasonal or irregular unemployment by travelling to another town, knowing that labour solidarity mechanisms existed. Indeed, down to the twentieth century, this was the only form of unemployment benefit for builders, for example. The lesson here is a simple one: the origins of the labour movement are inseparable from labour migration.

This is also true at a global level, with the making of the working class being inextricable from the movement of workers within countries and across borders. From the plantations through to the assembly lines, as Ferruccio Gambino and

Devi Sacchetto show, capitalism has depended on the shifting maelstrom of labour migration (Gambino & Sacchetto 2014). For colonialism, the search to enslave able person-power was a crucial driver and motivation. Labour markets were segregated by race, ethnicity and national origin, as well as age and gender, and thus the formation of class solidarity was often constrained by these divisions. The mobilization and displacement of labour power has taken different forms – from the open brutality of the slave trade to the state acting as the direct agent for the export of workers to other countries, as in the Philippines today – but it is always at the behest of capital. As Gambino and Sacchetto put it, "[A]s long as capital has not succeeded in eliminating alternative, non-capitalist ways of life within a given territory it is forced to go in search of labour-power" (Gambino & Sacchetto 2014: 118).

From a critical labour studies perspective, it is crucial to understand the historical and ongoing role of migration in terms of labour market regulation. While labour markets are usually seen as the drivers of migration flows, another perspective is that labour markets are shaped by and regulated by migration. Bauder argues that international migrants may be seen as a welcome addition to the labour force if they are "cheap and flexible" and thus may have a large impact on the labour market: "They facilitate the reduction of overall wage levels, help to lower labour standards, and assist in introducing more flexible employment practices" (Bauder 2006: 4). Although workers around the world may, in general terms, be suffering under the same overall aegis of capitalism, competition between migrant and non-migrant factions of the working class can be divisive and detrimental to their living conditions. It is hard to escape the conclusion that labour market analysis and labour movement strategy cannot proceed without foregrounding labour migration.

We may now assume, in the era of late globalization, that mass migration has become essential for the sustainability of capitalism and is, indeed, a structural necessity. It has become a key element in the regulation of labour markets. Labour is not, of course, a mere commodity that is reproduced straightforwardly in the economic and social domains. When labour becomes mobile, the linkages between production and social reproduction become more complex. This process is both socially and spatially contingent. A facile view of migration would just see it as deregulating the labour market – that is, through diminishing labour standards and weakening the bargaining position of established/local workers. But, as Bauder articulates this question, the international migration of labour actually facilitates the regulation of labour in new ways; in part, it does this by strategically dividing the global labour force through citizenship categories (Bauder 2006: 29), which can thus be disciplined and managed by the state.

We also need to highlight how, today, labour migration is, along with labour arbitrage, a key element in the restructuring of contemporary capitalism. "Capital flight" from the North to lower-wage regions and labour migration are usually treated as separate phenomena, with discrete logics, but it would make more sense to see them as two sides of the same global capital development crisis. As Jeff Henderson and Robin Cohen put it,

> While some sections of metropolitan capital have taken flight to low-wage areas, partly in response to the class struggles of metropolitan workers, less mobile sections of Western capital have enormously increased their reliance on imported migrant labour to cheapen the labour process and lower the costs of reproduction of labour in the advanced countries. (Henderson & Cohen 1982: 130)

Capitalism as a global system of capital accumulation and labour exploitation will, quite obviously, take up every opportunity to expand its reach. It might take the form of capital export to low-wage locations, but also, logically, it might include the import of cheap labour. Both forms are part and parcel of the same global capitalist labour system.

The globalization of production – which really took off in the 1990s – created an integrated system in which the flow of capital, finance and labour played an equal part. Outsourcing allowed capitalists in the North to overcome troublesome traditional barriers at home, such as labour unions and cohesive communities. And, despite all the anti-immigrant or nativist discourses and ideologies, they were also free to import cheap labour from the same locations "abroad". Certainly, the process of capital accumulation on a global scale is complex and contradictory, not least with regard to migration. But Smith is correct to point out how

> capitalists increasingly lean on and utilize imperialist divisions to practice divide and rule, to force workers in imperialist countries into increasingly direct competition with workers in low-wage countries, while using the cheap imports produced by super-exploited Southern labour to encourage selfishness and consumerism and to undermine solidarity. (Smith 2016: 46)

In their influential book *Empire*, Hardt and Negri describe migration as an act of refusal, of insecurity, violence, starvation, and a desire for peace, freedom and prosperity. Migrants can be seen as both the product of globalization and its expression, in so far as they treat the globe as a common space. There is a definite streak of romanticism in Hardt and Negri's rendering of migration, and we should beware of translating the necessity to move directly into a desire for freedom. Nor should we mirror the irrationality of the actually existing "empire", which views every traveller to its homeland as a potential, if not actual, terrorist. There is a great deal of truth, however, in Hardt and Negri's later uncovering of the great irony (or should it be contradiction?) whereby "the great global centres of wealth that call on migrants to fill a lack in their economies get more than they bargained for, since the immigrants invest the entire society with their subversive desires" (Hardt & Negri 2000: 133).

As a subject, writes Sassen, "the immigrant filters a much larger array of political dynamics than its status in law might suggest" (Sassen 1999: 294). Immigration can be used as a sharply focused lens to understand the contradictions of contemporary nation states in the era of globalization. Denied the rights of citizenship that are accorded to the national subject, the immigrant becomes an alien in law, or a "non-national". This highlights the tension in the behaviour of nation states, which partake willingly of globalization in all its glory, but seek to maintain or even reinforce the rigid control of their boundaries *vis-à-vis* the mobile person. That is, unless they are clearly part of the new transnational managing or information classes, who are truly global citizens today, beyond the major and petty indignities of border control. Migration also has a major influence on global development, although not in a simplistic way. It is a challenge for global governance because there are no simple solutions to the human cost it entails. But, above all, migration policy tells us a lot about the quality of democracy in a given territory: for which other sections of the population do basic equality and justice principles not apply so shamelessly? No other social group in society is so stigmatized, exploited and deemed a threat to national security just by its very existence.

I now focus directly on the issue of migrants as workers, for several interrelated reasons. It is an issue that causes discomfort for the promoters of the free market. This is understandable, because there appears to be no logical reason why capital, investment and ideas should flow freely across national frontiers, but not labour. At present international mobility is granted to a small elite of professional workers with skills required in affluent countries. For the many of the world's workers, national borders are, if anything, less permeable in the so-called era of globalization than in the past. Migration is securitized and the full panoply of state surveillance and repression falls on those who want to migrate to improve their situation. Despite some tentative international discussions about the need for a World Migration Organization on a par with the WTO to regulate migration, it is most likely to remain a messy and fuzzy issue for the managers of global capitalism. Could it be an opportunity for the social counter-movements now challenging the undisputed role of the unregulated market?

Trade unions and labour migration

Historically, the trade union movement has also had severe difficulties in dealing with migration in a manner that accorded with its basic principles. Too often labour activists and analysts imbued with the spirit of labour internationalism forget how often workers themselves draw on non-class forms of identity to protect themselves from the maelstrom of capitalist restructuring. While capital may well treat labour as an undifferentiated commodity, workers invariably find bonds of gender, place and race to create solidarity around their struggle to keep some kind of advantage in the chaos caused by modernization/globalization. For Arrighi, "[a]s a consequence, patriarchalism, racism and national-chauvinism have been integral to the making of the world labour movement" (Arrighi 1990: 33). This is a history often overlooked in the annals of the official trade union movement (and by its critics, for that matter), which tend to airbrush out the sexism, racism and xenophobia that form an integral element of most labour movements. To recognize it is, perhaps, the first step to dealing with it, rather than relying on anodyne stories of labour solidarity and internationalism.

"Labour rights are human rights" is an engagingly resonant slogan. It would seem to raise a sectoral right to the global and universal level. What could be portrayed as narrow economic or class-based demands can now be presented in terms of the globally recognized and universally valid rights of the human being. At a tactical level, it could also be seen as a "scaling up" of sectional or economic demands. With the end of the Cold War the liberal human rights regime became hegemonic, and the UN Summit on Social Development of 1995 saw core labour rights, including freedom of association and the right to organize, reaffirmed as human rights. Particularly in North America there have been moves by labour scholars and activists to reorient trade union strategy so as to focus on making labour legislation and policy compliant with international human rights norms (Adams 2008). This is posed as a new strategy, to overcome the economism and sectionalism of traditional labour organizations but also to broaden the appeal of labour to the liberal middle classes.

Although, on the surface, this is an attractive option for trade unions that have been weakened by 30 years of neoliberal policies, there are serious drawbacks to the human rights approach for the labour movement. As Larry Savage argues, it "threatens to undermine class-based responses to neoliberal globalization by contributing to the depoliticization of the labour movement" (Savage 2008: 68). Class power does not flow from human rights and nor does the liberal human rights regime really address the glaring inequalities of wealth and power that characterize neoliberal globalization. Nor are human rights truly global, being in practice very much Western in orientation, and not always having that much relevance in the Global South. In tactical terms also, if trade unions commit to a human rights approach – as they have done with the "Decent work" agenda, for example – they are clearly making a choice in terms of time and resources that could, arguably, be more productively deployed in other ways, such as better organizing, although in practice this need not be a zero-sum game. Trade unions exist in a strategic and conflictual decision-making situation, and not in the ideology-free zone implicit in a human rights view of the world. The international human rights movement does not have as its main aim the democratic reordering of social and economic relations, nor does it focus on workplace democracy as a goal. In terms of its methods, it focuses on changing the law and influencing policy-makers, rather than on solidarity, mobilization and direct action. It is based on the rights of the individual, whereas the trade union movement consists of, by definition, "combinations" of workers pursuing collective rights.

We can thus pose an alternative perspective on labour migration, namely a trade union organizing or mobilizing one, given that most migrants are workers and thus potential trade union members. To date, as Patrick McGovern notes, "[i]f immigration is in important respects a matter of labour, then it is extraordinary that the literatures on immigration and trade unionism come together so rarely" (McGovern 2007: 231). The discipline of industrial relations tends to focus on the technical aspects of the employment relationship, and then treats migrants as purely economic agents. The dominant economic theory assumption in terms of the immobility of labour as a factor of production, compared to capital, has also probably coloured the dominant approach to labour migration, which is seen as something of an anomaly. In addition, for many trade union leaders, migration is just one issue among many, frequently classed as a "diversity" issue, perhaps. This is a flawed perspective, however, if we accept, even to a limited extent, the verdict of Branko Milanovic that location has replaced class as the main global source of inequality:

> This is the basis on which a new global political issue of migration has emerged because income differences between countries make individual gains from migration large. The key coming issue will be how to deal with this challenge while acknowledging that migration is probably the most powerful tool for reducing global poverty.
>
> (Milanovic 2011: 1)

Labour migration today

As far back as 2000 Stephen Castles put it: "Never before has international migration been so high on the political agenda" (Castles 2000: 14). A token of this importance was the establishment in 2003 of the Global Commission on

International Migration, to place international migration on the global governance agenda. Much of the recent state attention on migration has been negative, especially after recent terror attacks across Europe and North America. The International Organization for Migration, for its part, argues: "Despite the prominence of migration on international agendas for more than a decade now, efforts to achieve global consensus on its governance have proven elusive" (IOM 2005: 368).

To refer to a "Southern" perspective on migration and development might seem perverse when we have been stating that such binary divisions have supposedly been overcome. At best, it might seem to appeal to a geographical Third-Worldism long since forgotten in a global order in which flows and hybridity prevail. Yet most current debates on migration and development are determined by the perspectives and the interests of the rich Northern countries. As Raúl Delgado Wise and Humberto Covarrubias put it succinctly, "There is as yet no theoretical-conceptual framework that takes into account the point of view and particular interest of the underdeveloped countries, which, at this point, are seasoned exporters of cheap qualified and unqualified workforce" (Delgado Wise & Covarrubias 2009: 90). What is, indeed, a global issue is invariably studied from the perspective of the receiving countries, with little or no understanding of the political economy of development/underdevelopment that caused the migratory flows in the first instance. The dominant paradigm thus studies migration in a somewhat decontextualized manner, with a sometimes heavy tinge of ethnocentrism as well as methodological nationalism.

We could argue that adopting a Southern perspective is in fact a first step towards a holistic global approach to the interlinked processes of migration and development. It is not really a question of reversing the receiving country perspective, to adopting a sending country outlook. Rather, it is a question of developing a paradigm through which a specific process – or set of processes – can be properly contextualized, and, for that matter, placed in a historical perspective. The North/South divide continues as an overarching feature of the global system and is the inescapable context within which international migration today needs to be set. The uneven development of global capitalism sets the parameters of both migration processes and development prospects in the South, or Third World. Unidirectional and undialectical treatments of the migration/development nexus – seen not least in the burgeoning literature on economic remittances by migrant workers – will not provide us with the analytical tools to understand (let alone change) the world around us. Migration studies need to be embedded within the broader debates around the political economy of globalization and its implication for development. The globalization of migration is usually taken to refer to "the tendency for more and more countries to be crucially affected by migratory movements at the same time". International migration must, in brief, be seen as part of a revolutionary globalization process that is reshaping economics, political systems and our whole cultural parameters. There is also a common belief that the current flows of migrant labour are now fundamentally different from earlier forms of mass migration. Such is the complexity of current population movement that existing explanatory frameworks are seen as inadequate. John Urry, in theorizing the new "global complexity", refers to "massive, hard-to-categorise, contemporary migration, often with oscillatory flows between unexpected locations", which can be seen as "a series of turbulent waves, with a hierarchy of eddies and vortices, with globalism a virus that stimulates resistance" (Urry 2003: 156). The migrant – from this "globalization as revolution" perspective – becomes more or less a symbol of the fluidity, impermanence and complexity of a new era of time–space compression.

The actual increase in the numbers and, more importantly, the proportions of those migrating has not actually expanded that dramatically overall – that is, from a broad historical sweep that excludes the peaks caused by the crisis in Syria, for example. The IOM points out that all 190 or so sovereign states in the world are either migrant-sending, -receiving or transit points and that there are some 190 million people living outside their country of birth at the start of the twenty-first century. That figure is double what it was as recently as 1980 and equivalent to the population of Brazil, the world's fifth most populous country. This is still less than 3 per cent of the world's population, however, and up only slightly from the 2.5 per cent of the total world population who in 1960 were classified as international migrants. What this means is that we need to see international migration in context, as just one element in the global process of capital accumulation and labour exploitation, and not that all migrants are workers, of course. Migration theories perhaps need to examine more closely not only why people move but why (preponderantly) they do not, the factors inducing immobility as well as mobility and centripetal socioeconomic factors in addition to centrifugal ones.

What is particularly interesting is to examine the broad flows of migrants, in terms of the North/South divide, in so far as international migration is often just assumed to be a flow from the South to the North. With due regard to the limitations of the data, current global migration flows can be presented as in Table 7.1.

It is immediately apparent from this table that only a quarter of international migrants go from the Global South (non-OECD countries) to the Global North (OECD countries), while not quite two-thirds of migrants move within the Global South. This reflects the reality of globalization as an uneven process, with poles of development within the South promoting migration. Certainly, media attention is focused almost entirely on the 16 per cent of migrants who move across the South/North divide, creating an imbalance in the resultant

Table 7.1 International migration by region, millions and percentage (2000)

	From OECD countries	From rest of the world	Total
To OECD countries	22.2 (16.2)	34.1 (24.9)	56.3 (41.1)
To rest of the world	2.5 (1.8)	77.9 (57.0)	80.4 (58.8)
Total	24.7 (18.0)	112.0 (81.9)	136.7 (100.0)

Source: Harrison, Britton and Swanson (2004: 4).

understanding of migration as a global process. But we must remember that most migration is internal as well as international. So, while there are probably 200 million or so transnational migrants today (that is, people living outside their country of birth), there are probably 100 million internal migrants in China and a massive 300 million (some 30 per cent of the population) in India. We should thus be wary of placing a conceptual and analytical barrier between national and international migrants. The "age of migration" is also, quite clearly, an age of massive population movements within countries, particularly in the Global South, which is becoming the locus of the next phase of global capital accumulation.

Migrants are not, of course, an undifferentiated human flow, and, at the very least, we need to unpack migration's gender, race and class differentials (see Milkman 2006). Today almost a half of international migrants are women, and yet the gendered dynamics of migration are barely understood. There is something of a dual labour market situation for migrant women. As the GCIM notes, "Migration can be an empowering experience for women ... Regrettably, however, migration can have the opposite effect" (GCIM 2005: 49). Some women get to earn more money and gain decision-making power through migration. Many more, however, migrate into domestic labour or the sex industries, where they suffer isolation and extreme forms of exploitation, whether it be in the legal or illegal sectors. It is also clear – given the prevailing gender division of labour – that migrant women are more likely to remain outside the formal labour market and will have difficulty gaining the language skills and accessing the social networks necessary to achieve social inclusion in their new homes.

Migration processes are clearly patterned along gender lines, in the same way that national labour markets are segmented along gender lines. In the sending countries the encroachment of free-market-driven impoverishment of the household economy has driven many women out of employment. Thus, there are considerably more women migrants than men in both Latin America and Russia, where the neoliberal onslaught was most severe. These women are most likely to be working in the labour-intensive manufacturing sectors and the lower end of the services sector. As Spike Peterson remarks, "The shift to an informational and service economy generates jobs that are polarised in terms of skills and work conditions, especially in big cities" (Peterson 2003: 67). Women enter both the top end of this spectrum – accentuating the so-called "brain drain" – but also the devalorized bottom end, which is both racialized and gendered in terms of which migrants enter the sector and how they do so. Migration, in and of itself, shifts and restructures traditional gender divisions of labour and the nature of the household and of the community. Shifting places can lead to shifting identities and new, complex forms of gender, race/ethnicity and communal belongings, forms of identity and repertoires of struggle.

With regard to race, as Philip Marfleet puts it simply and clearly, "Immigration control, racism and exclusion are inseparable" (Marfleet 2006: 289). Globalization theories have, by and large, neglected race and ethnicity in their accounts of the making of the new global order. While racism and anti-immigrant sentiment are certainly not synonymous by any means, the racialization of migration debates has to be noted, analysed and acted upon. Racist and (the sometimes quite distinct) xenophobic discourses are not atavistic and timeless notions of difference and simply motives for exclusion. We need, rather, to explore the particular processes of the making and unmaking of racisms in an era of flux and insecurity. In the specific area of immigration control, at the national borders where the writ of human rights barely applies, race, ethnicity and national categories are explicitly deployed to filter out the undesirable, the unclean and the unworthy. Today the most clearly differentiated is the Muslim "Other", seen as the bearer of the most retrograde social customs, cultural norms and terrorist impulses.

The racial geography of globalization is, clearly, closely related to the history of colonialism and imperialism, even if this is not usually made explicit in the dominant, and even critical, globalization theory. Likewise, the ways in which race and ethnicity are key elements in global migration are not always made explicit. Certainly, these divides do not map onto migration patterns as clearly, or as visibly, as do wealth and poverty differentials. If we accept that there is no such thing yet as a truly global labour market for all the workers of the world, then it is bound to be segmented, even segregated, along race/ethnicity lines, among others. If the history of empire was the story of race, so the unfolding history of globalization and its discontents (and resistance to them) must be written in the grammar of race and ethnicity. The dominant labour market model of migration does not really assist us in critically deconstructing this process, however. As Knowles argues, "Mapping the trajectories of human mobility and the conditions in which they are produced is an urgent task in the analysis of globalization's racial and ethnic grammar and the race making that produced it" (Knowles 2003: 124). This is a complex task that cannot be substituted by facile criticisms of "the racist state" as though that was sufficient as critique and alternative to the status quo.

Where social class is concerned, it is very easy from a globalization theory perspective to become beguiled by the mobility of the new transnational capitalist and professional classes. For the business class traveller, for whom global travel is a norm, there is a genuine global market for executive labour emerging. As the International Labour Organisation and others have pointed out, however, the era of globalization has also been marked by a return of coerced labour that, for some analysts, is tantamount to a new slavery. In its *Stopping Forced Labour* report of 2001 the tripartite ILO has declared that, "[a]lthough universally condemned, forced labour is revealing ugly new faces alongside the old" (ILO 2001: 1).

People trafficking and modern slavery

Traditional types of forced labour, such as chattel slavery and bonded labour, are still with us in some areas, and past practices of this type haunt us to this day. In new economic contexts, "disturbing forms such as forced labour in connection with trafficking for human beings are now emerging *almost everywhere*" (ILO 2001: 1, emphasis added). Leaving aside the somewhat problematic past/present binary division, the ILO is clearly and correctly locating the issue of unfree labour as a major characteristic of the new global labour market. Forced labour is defined in the IOM convention as "all work or service that is exacted from any person under the menace of any penalty and for which the said person has not offered himself [sic] voluntarily", and then, using this broad definition, it is estimated that there are 12.3 million people submitted to forced labour worldwide, of whom 2.45 million are trafficked (ILO 2008: 24).

Growing in importance as a form of unfree labour today is trafficking for forced labour (TFL), increasingly the subject of legislation – national, European and international – and of research and policy development. It is estimated that nearly a half of these cross-border flows of unfree labour are for commercial sexual exploitation, one third are for labour exploitation and the rest can be seen as mixed-mode exploitation. Trafficking for forced labour is now classified as a criminal activity in its own right, this classification only recently having moved beyond the prohibition of the sex trade traffic. Trafficking involves transportation; its means include force, coercion, fraud and deception and its purpose will be for exploitation. The United Nations' protocol on trafficking defines exploitation as, "at a minimum, the exploitation or the prostitution of others for forced labour or services, slavery or practices similar to slavery", but it does not clearly define these terms. Clearly, these migrant labour markets see a blurred line between the legal and the extra-legal, and we must also consider them part of the new criminal economy around drugs, arms and people smuggling, which have been incentivized by free market globalization and the forced retreat of the state.

The dominant interpretation of trafficking for forced labour and other coerced migration modalities is that it represents an unfortunate anomaly, part of the "dark" side of globalization. In reality, forms of unfree labour not only survive but are reproduced and even expanded when the capitalist mode of production (and thus free wage labour) becomes dominant. The capitalist relations of production have never been universal and they certainly do not emerge automatically through textbook economics mechanisms. Unfree labour has played, and continues to play, a role in the development of global capitalism. Harvey (2003) has argued in this regard that we are living through a new "primitive accumulation" (which gave rise to capitalism), which he calls "accumulation by dispossession". Agriculturalists are driven off the land by agri-business, corporate fraud dispossesses small savers, bio-piracy has become rampant and the manipulation of foreign debt has left whole populations in debt bondage. Unfree labour emerges when "normal" wage labour relations break down (as a result of indebtedness, for example) or they exist alongside free labour in a symbiotic relationship. In these circumstances, which may coexist in varying combinations, we can agree with Robert Miles, who says that "unfree labour is an anomalous necessity" (Miles 1987: 222).

In terms of the overall "costs and benefits" of migration, this cannot be read as a zero-sum game. In principle, migrants may create openings in the sending economy, contribute to development through economic remittances and bring back capital, skills and social networks when they return. Nevertheless, they also represent a drain on the educational services that trained them, remittances may diminish and most migrants do not return; rather, they create a "culture" of migration. The verdict of the policy-makers is that sending and receiving countries alike can benefit from migration, but the actual data to support the verdict is still patchy. Thus, a study conducted for the IOM has concluded inter alia that data on the impact of remittances on growth, poverty and inequality remain vague, and that, while the potential benefits of diasporas is clear, the precise way their transnational networks and capital flows operate is less so (IOM 2005: 353). Overall, there is also little evidence of the prevalence of return migration and its impact, and, finally, there are still very few sustained accounts on the direct and indirect impacts of migration on poverty and inequality in the so-called developing countries.

Recent Western governmental concern with the development potential (positive and negative) of migrants is often a thinly disguised move against migrants in their own countries. Thus there has been EU-level concern recently to stimulate the "development potential" of migration through the encouragement of circular or temporary migration, somewhat conflating these two distinct categories. This is presented as a win-win situation, with the sender country not being hit through the "brain drain" and the receiving country having a more flexible labour supply at its disposal. The Western political audience is reassured that the tap of migration can be turned off if necessary. Not only is this argument dubious in its own terms, however, because revolving-door policies rarely work in practice, but, as Hein de Haas points out, "[T]his is somehow reminiscent of the failed attempts in the 1970s and 1980s to stimulate the return of European 'guest workers'" (de Haas 2007: 820). These *Gastarbeiter* are a constant reminder of the probably apocryphal tale of the Western employer who said, in relation to migrants, "We asked for hands and we got people".

Migration and trade union revitalization

The recruitment of foreign labour creates a significant challenge to trade unions, embedded as they are in their particular national contexts and charged, as they see it, with representing the interests of their national membership. Moreover, trade unions have generally seen their interests as being best served by restrictions on immigrant labour, largely because, as Stephen Castles and Godula Kosack (1973) have pointed out, a surplus of workers on which employers can draw tends to weaken the position of trade unions and concomitantly have a depressing effect on wages. Rinus Penninx and Judith Roosblad have identified what they consider to be the three main dilemmas that, historically, unions had to face when confronted with the issue of migrant labour. The first was the question of whether to cooperate with employers and the state in the employment of migrant labour or to resist. Second, once migrant workers had arrived, whether to include them fully or exclude them. Third, if following a line of inclusion, whether to adopt a policy of equal treatment or one of special measures for this new category of union member (Penninx & Roosblad 2000). When they revisited this issue in a broad European study in 2015, in the context of the rise of populism and anti-immigrant sentiment, they found that now "trade unions are called upon to face a complex of problems, well beyond labour claims and labour equality to also, increasingly, involve social and legal status" (Marino, Penninx & Roosblad 2015: 9). Today's more flexible and less homogeneous workforce places even greater strains on trade union solidarity while, at the same time, making it more essential for the very survival of the trade unions as a democratic social movement.

Overall, I believe that a more holistic trade union approach can be derived from current debates around the need for trade union revitalization. The decline in membership of unions, and even in their relevance, can be addressed through engaging and organizing new hitherto unorganized constituencies, and, here, migrant workers are obvious candidates. Recruiting, organizing and mobilizing migrant workers can have an impact in terms of integrating the migrants in society, but such approaches also serve to revitalize the trade unions. They become more open to other perspectives and it takes them beyond an "economic" or corporate role. Another aspect of revitalization involves the unions recreating themselves in terms of how they operate. There are signs, in many countries, that the unions are rediscovering their original social movement characteristics. This shift is particularly apparent in campaigns to organize migrant workers in which trade unions have worked with various civil society organizations, from migrant workers' centres to faith-based organizations (Frege & Kelly 2004). This is social movement unionism in practice, not only building solidarity but also revitalizing the trade unions themselves.

Social transformation

If the human rights perspective suffers from a certain legalism and traditional trade unionism from an excessive economism, perhaps a social transformation approach might prove to be a possible alternative. Castles has, for some time, argued for a social transformation approach to migration. It is simply not plausible to take migration in isolation, as though it were not impacted by globalization and development, social and political struggles – or the recurring crisis of capitalism, for that matter. A social transformation approach, for Castles, would be holistic (conscious of the complexity of social relations), interdisciplinary and comparative, always set in the broader context and historically grounded (Castles 2000). This approach was also paralleled in the study of globalization that moved from the original "supportive versus sceptical" binary opposition to a transformationalist approach (Held *et al*. 1999). This allows us to focus on the ongoing transformation of social relations, resulting from shifting patterns of capital accumulation and changes in the balance of political forces, as part of the continuous contestation and renegotiation of global capitalism by diverse social, political and cultural interest groups.

What I would add here is the need for closer attention to the emerging social transformation approach for trade unions, allowing us to view them as social movements and not just corporatist entities. For most of their history, particularly in Europe, trade unions have pursued an "economic" trade unionism focused on "selling" labour power. Famously, a longstanding US labour leader, George Meany, once stated that his labour strategy was simply "More". In Latin America, the dominant modality of trade unionism has been a "political", or political bargaining, approach in which the state is seen as the privileged interlocutor that can deliver advances for workers. This approach was also typical of social democratic trade unionism in Europe at some stages, and one should not dismiss its gains, for example in relation to the welfare state. Finally, a social transformation approach promotes a "social" or social movement unionism, which takes labour not as an economic unit or political actor solely but, rather, in its full social complexity and as part of communal, household, gender and cultural relations. This approach prospered during democratic challenges to authoritarian regimes in the South but it is now seeing a revival of sorts in parts of the North that have been devastated by the impact of neoliberalism. Thus, we might bridge the migration/development and migration/democracy theoretical and practical divides in articulating a new form of migrant-oriented social unionism. This approach would bring back human agency into what are sometimes rather technical debates on migrant remittances and migrant political networks.

There is perhaps a compelling argument that "solidarity with migrant workers is helping trade unions to get back to the basic principles of the labour movement" (David 2002: 71). On the one hand, trade unions have been facing a crisis of declining membership and influence over the last two decades. On the other hand, many social and political organizations find themselves bereft of leadership on the question of migration. From either side of the argument trade unions have now an opportunity as well as a challenge. Across the world trade unions are organizing with, and on behalf of, migrant workers (see Kahmann 2002; Gray 2008; Wrench 2004). They have made common cause with migrant-led associations and with NGOs supporting migrant workers and they have also sought to directly organize migrants ("Workers are workers are workers" is a common slogan). Of course, one effect of this drive is to minimize the ability of employers to use migrant workers to undercut pay and conditions for indigenous workers. Nevertheless, its net impact, as Natacha David puts it, is that, "[i]n response to economic globalization, trade unions are organizing the globalization of solidarity in defence of migrants" (David 2002: 74).

There are many practical examples emerging in Europe, in particular where trade unions are addressing, in novel ways, the needs of migrant workers. In Spain, for example, the Comisiones Obreras (Workers' Committees), of Communist Party origins, have set up a nationwide network of Overseas Workers Information Centres (Centros de Información para los Trabajadores Extranjeros – CITE), which act as clearing houses for migrant issues ranging from visas to health, language and workplace issues. In 2001 the Spanish state passed a law making it a crime to assist undocumented migrant workers. Given that there are over three quarters of a million workers without permits, this law is explicitly ignored by the unions. One Comisiones Obreras spokesperson makes the case for immigration: "We need immigration. The union must change and become a multicultural union. The illegals must obtain their papers ... That is our vision" (Sahlström 2008). It is in such statements that we can see how the issues posed by migration, such as in relation to legality or in terms of what solidarity means, can disrupt old and stale trade union practices. The Comisiones Obreras have undoubtedly become a more agile and politically inventive labour organization since their engagement with migration issues. In Italy, the Christian Democrat trade union confederation Confederazione Italiana Sindicati dei Lavoratori has set up a similar broadly based, migrant-oriented organization called the National Association for Those Beyond the Frontiers (Associazione Nazionale Oltre le Frontiere – ANOLF), which has branches in Morocco and Senegal. ANOLF aims to organize migrants to defend their civil rights, but it also self-consciously seeks to act as a "bridge" (Sahlström 2008) between the unions and other social organizations. For trade unions to support the self-organization of migrants in such a way is a clear step in the direction of social movement unionism.

In Britain, there also have been extremely interesting moves towards what the unions call "community unionism". The emphasis was placed on securing new members and using new organizational methods. Reaching beyond the workplace and the traditional collective bargaining mechanisms, some unions, particularly in London, began to reach out to migrant unorganized workers, in particular. The London minimum wage campaign, launched in 2001, saw intense work at grass-roots level and within trade unions to create a "community unionism", supportive of the mainly migrant low-paid workers in the capital. Trade unions were slow to join what have been described as "ad hoc, spontaneous, localised or geographic-based organisations with local partners" (Holgate 2009: 66), but bureaucratic inertia was overcome and, in the process, the glimmer of a new unionism could be discovered. As Jane Wills puts it, this new community unionism in the United Kingdom is for now incipient, but it is allowing unions to find common cause with groups cemented around, religious, ethnic, or other affiliations, effectively "linking the struggle for redistribution with that of recognition, the universal with the particular, the economic with the cultural" (Wills 2001: 469).

One of the most spectacular forms of union revitalization has occurred in the United States, once the epitome of business unionism. The 1995 victory of the New Voice slate of John Sweeney marked a decisive turning point in US labour politics and opened up the doors for new thinking. It was in relation to community unionism – focused on migrant workers in particular – that the revival of the US labour movement found many of its clearest expressions (see Ness 2005). Community unions in the US context seem to be small in scale, bridging or mediating institutions based in specific communities rather than the workplace. They are, thus, not trade unions in the traditional sense but spring from solidarity movements, faith-based movements and legal or social services groups. Mindful of the overwhelming importance of legal status for migrant workers, they are, as Janice Fine puts it, "likely to focus as much attention on organizing to change immigration policy as they are on labor market issues" (Fine 2006: 154). There is also clear evidence in the United States that poor people are unionizing and that trade unions have learnt lessons from the local movements of women, African-Americans, Mexican farm workers, and so on. As Vanessa Tait puts it, "[P]oor workers' unions … value direct action, flexibility and collaboration … over the bureaucratic and legalistic methods on which traditional unions have often relied" (Tait 2005: 310). Since the 2007–9 crisis huge pressure has been placed on social alliances, and protectionism by the secure has been a standard reaction. There are signs, however, that the fusion of labour and the new social movements will continue, and that "the next upsurge", as Dan Clawson calls it, will see "a combination of trade unions' commitment and democratic representativity with the imagination and energy of the new social movements" (Clawson 2003: 196). If this materializes then the South's social movement unionism of the 1980s would have found a worthy Northern successor. Labour would have moved "beyond North and South" as much as globalizing capital has done, thus effectively creating a social counter-movement to the unregulated market.

Generally speaking, trade unions have been slow to embrace a more social movement approach to labour organizing. Thus, in 1995 it was found that 97 per cent of AFL–CIO union locals in the United States simply did not have an organizing or community outreach programme (Tait 2005: 92). The continued relevance of trade unions for a multi-ethnic, multi-status workforce was clearly in question. Yet, at the same time, there was a concerted drive by many in the trade union movement to organize migrant workers in particular. Immigrant-driven campaigns to organize, unionize and agitate for better conditions became more widespread. Often a campaign that began in one particular ethnic community expanded to embrace all migrant workers. In many cases it was not standard trade unions doing the organizing but, rather, a plethora of hybrid community organizations, workers' centres, faith-based groups and nationality-based organizations. The dominant organizational form was, more often than not, based on these varied networks with their members working within but also without the organized labour movement. What these campaigns had in common, suggests Tait, "was an aggressive organizing outlook that relied on community-based, social movement-style tactics" (Tait 2005: 191). It is too early to determine whether the renaissance over the last decade or so has changed the verdict of 1995 that trade unions in the United States existed to serve a basically white male clientele, but certainly there is a counter-tendency emerging. At a global level we see increasing signs of innovative trade union and labour movement thinking whereby migration comes to the fore as both a challenge and an opportunity for labour (see Kloosterboer 2007).

In the years to come international labour migration is bound to become more important, in both quantitative and qualitative terms, and it may well emerge as a defining issue for the trade union movement. One such "tipping point" was the Irish Ferries dispute in Ireland in 2005 (see Krings 2007). A well-unionized cross-channel seafaring group was faced with a cost-cutting employer who decided that Latvian agency workers, who could be paid half the legal minimum wage, made good economic sense. The Irish trade union movement was shaken to its very foundations, and rumours abounded about the imminent displacement of native workers by cheaper foreign imports. Quickly this dispute became a test case, not least because it involved Ireland's largest trade union, the Services, Industrial, Professional and Technical Union (SIPTU). Mass mobilization occurred and the employer was forced to negotiate by a government committed to social partnership. Nevertheless, the nativist reaction was just under the surface: in one mass mobilization by the trade unions seeking broader support for the Irish Ferries workers, official banners proclaiming "No slave ships in the Irish Sea" jostled with other more rudimentary ones on the fringes declaring "Irish jobs for Irish workers". In the end the Irish labour movement made the improvement of conditions for migrant workers a "deal breaker" in the next round of partnership talks with government and employers, in 2006. Equalizing the conditions of labour upwards received greater support within the workers' movement, as a forward-looking labour strategy, winning out over the temptation to blame the "non-national" workers brought in by cost-cutting employers.

The years after 2015 will probably go down as the years of the "migration crisis", certainly in Europe. All the contradictions of globalization – free movement of capital but not free movement of people – were coming to a head. The "blowback" from all the Western interventions in the Maghreb and in the Levant were bringing the consequences of imperialism back home. Europe was seemingly overwhelmed, and, after a brave stance by Germany and Sweden at the outset of the current "migration crisis", things were back to razor wire barriers and better "security" quite quickly. Not to be left out, the US president, Donald Trump, called for a bigger and better wall between the United States and Mexico (to be paid for by the latter), even though the US economy depended on Mexican and Central American workers. Rational discussion was left behind as panic, xenophobia, racism and irrationalism came to the fore, Brexit being just one example of such a syndrome. This is now the main issue of the day, probably across the world, as the contradictions of globalization – free movement of capital but not of labour – come openly to dominate the political agenda.

The other issue that society is driven increasingly to address is the degradation of work and workers' lives. What began 20 years ago with the term "Brazilianization" – the Global North becoming more like the Global South – has now been surpassed by the notion of the global precariat, as discussed in Chapter 6. Working and living, for most people today in most of the world, are losing any notion of security, protection and predictability. In terms of a globally fragmented and disposable labour force, it is migrant workers, caught in the quagmire of so-called circular migration, who come top of the list. They are subject to long hours of dangerous, demanding and demeaning work and live in permanent fear of dismissal and, potentially, deportation. Fortress Europe – most notably in the East – is erecting barriers forcing refugees underground as another part of a growing informal European precariat. To face up to the interlocking crisis of migration and precarity, we can pose the need for transnational frameworks of governance to the creation of enhanced human, social and labour rights. At the start of the twenty-first century there was considerable confidence that stable and efficient global governance mechanisms could be put in place. Thus, in 2007, the UN-sponsored Global Forum on Migration and Development was set up to create such a consensus in the area of migration in relation to the North/South development divide. It soon became clear that there was a wide gulf between this high-level rhetoric and the politics and practices of national governments. The whole notion of a "rights-based" approach to migration and/or precarious work becomes rather academic in the face of the events of 2015 and subsequently. A formidable transnational movement of uprooted victims of Western-generated conflicts is represented in terms of a "refugee crisis" coming as an inexplicable problem inflicted on the West. In place of addressing the economic, political and social root causes of the current crisis, the shattering of the institutions of one of the world's most powerful regional organizations is rationalized with reference to this self-inflicted humanitarian calamity. In conjunction with the eventual collapse of the WTO's Doha trade talks, which began in 2001, it spells the end of global governance as an enlightened development project.

An alternative to governance "from above" – in which it is hard to have much confidence in the current climate of moral panic and paralysis of institutional capacity – we might counterpose a governance "from below", as it were. If we look back across Europe since 2015 we see that, in relation to the plight of the refugees, it is most often groups within civil society that have responded positively to the humanitarian crisis. Trade unions have a particular responsibility in terms of integrating those workers who come from beyond their national boundaries. One instinct for these representatives of national labour forces is to join with others in a protectionist and exclusionary rhetoric and practice. We have seen over the last two decades a number of trade union movements responding very positively towards migrant and precarious workers on the basis of the old trade union principle "An injury to one is an injury to all". The stakes are high today, and the construction of a democratic alternative to the emerging Fortress Europe is an urgent task. Trade unions, based on the analysis in this chapter, can play a positive role in this quest, replacing nativist instincts by those of a solidarity in which common cause is found in pursuit of decent work for all.

8

LABOUR AND ITS OTHERS

The organized labour movement – that is, workers and trade unions – has always related to "other" societal issues deemed outside its boundaries. Diverse issues – such as war and peace, environmental sustainability and gender equity – have made their mark in both discursive and practical ways on the labour movement. Perhaps the main strategic challenge (and opportunity) facing the labour movement today is how a progressive articulation with these other issues might be forged. If the labour movement is not the sole, or even the main, agent of social transformation, this task is a crucial one.

This chapter opens with a consideration of labour as a social movement. Labour has not always and everywhere been part of industrial relations machinery nor been linked to politics through social democratic parties. The tensions pitting "struggle versus structures" is explored, as is the way unions may be moving beyond managing decline to organizing for the future. Mainstream and radical critics of the labour movement alike often lack nuance and do not see how labour is constantly evolving and can, when conditions are ripe, act as a social movement.

The environmental challenge is the overarching issue in terms of sustainability and one that poses acute difficulties (although arguably also opportunities) for organized labour. How do we move beyond the "jobs versus the environment" dilemma towards some form of labour/environmental movement alliance or articulation? Labour is no longer – if it ever was – totally tied to the industrial mode of production, and needs to grasp the critical challenge of climate change. It is not easy, as it does not fit easily into traditional collective bargaining ways of thinking, but, from a global perspective, we do see change occurring.

Finally, I turn to the issue of trade unions and global justice. Ever since the 1999 anti-globalization protests in Seattle saw "Teamsters and Turtles" (labour and environment movements) unite and fight, a new form of global justice unionism has been posed. What is the potential for this articulation at global and local levels today? For the young activists of the global justice movements, labour is often seen as irredeemably compromised by established power structures. Trade unionists, for their part, often see these campaigns as unstructured and not sustainable. But the debate to bridge this gap is now on.

Labour as a social movement

In the industrial relations and industrial sociology literature, labour is mostly treated as a corporate entity, fully integrated into the capitalist system, albeit oppositional at times towards individual managements or particular governments. This orthodoxy completely obliterates the origins of labour as a social movement. Granted, labour can become integrated and be seen as a social partner under corporatism or a tame company union, but labour can also act as a social movement again: the working-class movement has always been conscious of its opposition to capitalism and has always believed in an alternative social order. Polanyi saw this movement as society's drive to protect itself from the unfettered power of markets.

This Polanyian stress on labour as social counter-movement and non-market forms of social integration is also highly relevant for the current period of anti-neoliberalism mobilizations. In the 1980s, in relation to Latin America, for example, we saw how "the dominated masses are generating new social practices founded on reciprocity, equality and collective solidarity" (Quijano 2006: 438). Across the Global South we saw a range of "Polanyian" counter-movements based on notions of reciprocity that were at odds with the prevailing market mentality. Although they were, in part, a mode of survival – for example, in the so-called informal economy – these non-market forms of solidarity were clearly embedded in dense social networks whose logic was at odds with that of the non-self-regulated market promoted by the neoliberal ideologies. While decommodification may be a symptom of social disintegration, it is also part of labour's long historical quest to create a society based on social need rather than individual profit.

In practice, as the labour movement grew, it was both nationalized and bureaucratized. Its early phase as a transnational and social movement was rapidly overtaken by historical events. In the first instance, from the middle of the nineteenth century onwards, we note the clear "nationalization" of labour. As van der Linden puts it, "[B]y the process of state formation and the progressive growth of national infrastructures, the nascent labour movements were increasingly forced to transform into national organizations" (van der Linden 2015). The British Trades Union Congress was formed in 1868 and led the way in this gestation of national (as against transnational) labour movements. This national belonging became national chauvinism in 1914 as the inter-imperialist First

World War lined up once proud internationalist labour movements against one another. For very different reasons, the labour movements taking shape around the turn of century – for example, in Latin America – were already national in so far as the shaping of the labour movement was an integral element in the making of the new nation states.

At the same time as the early movements were "nationalized" they were also "bureaucratized" and converted into pillars of stability rather than contestation. The key analyst of this process is still Robert Michels, who, in 1911, published a book, *Political Parties*, that advanced the notion of an "iron law of oligarchy" in relation to socialist parties and trade unions (Michels 1962 [1911]). Stated at its simplest, "[O]rganisation says oligarchy" (Michels 1962 [1911]: 56). The chasm that he saw between rank-and-file members of oppositional movements and the leaders of these movements would inevitably push towards the concentration of power at the top and a political moderation of demands against the system. The period since the early twentieth century has amply confirmed this general analysis of a tendency towards bureaucratization, which is often explained by the need for professionalization, even if we must always bear in mind that there are counter-tendencies towards democratization as rank-and-file members assert their interests and leaders respond, even when it is out of self-interest.

We could argue that, taking a long view of trade union history, periods of bureaucratization are followed by ones of rank-and-file insurgency. This might be seen as labour's own "double movement", to borrow Polanyi's term describing capitalist development. Moments of mass mobilization lead to gains but, most often, they dissipate. A state of permanent mobilization is simply not possible. So, when mobilizations subside, it is then that the full-time officials and organization take over. There is a longstanding debate, often fiercely waged, around whether it is organizational pressure or disruptive protesting that yields results. For Frances Fox Piven and Richard Cloward, in *Poor People's Movements: Why They Succeed, How They Fail* (Piven & Cloward 1977), the verdict is clear:

> [I]t was not formal organizations but mass defiance that won what was won in the 1930s and 1960s [in the United States]: industrial workers, for example, forced concessions from industry and government as a result of the disruptive effects of large-scale strikes; defiant blacks forced concessions as a result of the disruptive effects of mass civil disobedience. (Piven & Cloward 1977: xv)

Essentially, what we see in these debates is a tension between structure and spontaneity. As the early labour movement organized and created structures to maintain continuity, so it tended to dampen the social mobilization perspective. Analysts such as Piven and Cloward would argue that only social mobilization leads to social gains, and these are always neutered by organization. Another perspective would probably focus on the dialectical relationship between structure and social mobilization. The latter can never be continuous – permanent mobilization is not sustainable– and so, at some point, structures need to be created to carry campaigns forward. Nor can we say that the rank and file are always militant and that organization leaders are always the ones to compromise, or worse. The new social movement debate of the 1960s brought these early tensions back into play, with emphasis placed clearly on mobilization and a fierce opposition to most forms of organization.

The "European" identity-focused theoretical approach to social movements is inseparable from the "new" social movements of the 1970s. In the cultural and political ferment following the events of May 1968 (in its French, Italian, US and Argentinian variants) the whole of past history was reassessed. It was as if it was Year Zero of a new revolutionary movement. One of the main targets of the new generation was the "old" trade union movement and its Communist Party political articulation. It was seen as bureaucratic, integrated into bourgeois society and basically senile. What revolutionary potential it might once have had was long since lost to the discrete charm of the bourgeois order. Workers in the West were seen as a "labour aristocracy" living off the exploitation of the Third World, where a vigorous anti-colonial revolution was under way. These workers had been seduced and "bought off" by Western consumerism, whereas the new generation rejected consumerism and conformity alike. The new social movements would start anew and create a new society that rejected both consumer capitalism and bureaucratic socialism.

The new social movements were seen as an expression of the new capitalism that had become consolidated in the long postwar boom in the West. Advanced capitalist societies had been subject to a process of "commodification", as social life became dominated by the market, and by "bureaucratization", as the state intervened more and more at all levels of society. The "new" mass media had also led to a cultural "massification", creating conformity and repressing creativity. The new social movements thus reflected the new social antagonisms: the youth rebellion, the ecological movement and the rising of women against patriarchy. These movements were anti-institutional and anti-hierarchical and expressed a reaffirmation of individuality as against collectivism. They were all based on social antagonisms, other than those of social class, and the conflict between the worker and the capitalist in the factory, in particular. All forms of subordination were rejected, the imagination was in power and the future would be nothing like the past.

The new social movements rejected the "totalizing" vision of the old movements, such as the labour and nationalist movements. There was no single conflict to be resolved to reach the Promised Land, in so far as there was a multiplicity of conflicts, all equally valid. The main thrust of these movements was the quest for autonomous identity against the "totalizing" or tutelary aspirations of the traditional social movements. Tilman Evers has offered four main theses that account for what was specific about these new social movements:

- the transformatory potential within new social movements is not political, but socio-cultural;
- the direction of this counter-cultural remodelling of social patterns is open;
- central to this counter-cultural distinction is the dichotomy of alienation versus identity; and
- in creating an alternative cultural project the new social movements also create the germs of a new subject (Evers 1985: 49–59).

This framework seems a utopian project in the true sense of the word, based on the classic Marxist libertarian and egalitarian call for "an association in which the free development of each one is the condition for the free development for all", as *The Communist Manifesto* declared so boldly in its day (Marx & Engels 1976 [1848]).

It is relatively easy to show, in hindsight, that there was, in fact, no hard and fast dividing line between the "old" and the "new" social movements. The labour movement in its origins was very much like the "new" social movements today and only gradually and unevenly became institutionalized. It has also had to reinvent itself periodically, and today it is rediscovering its vocation as a social movement to deal with the decline of traditional trade unionism. Labour movements were also a key component in the democratic challenge to authoritarian regimes in the "developing" world in the 1970s and 1980s. It would be quite premature to accept the verdict of Castells (1998), for example, that the workers' movement is no longer an agent of progressive social change. Movements, by definition, can change and adapt to new circumstances through renewal and regeneration.

We thus need to consider carefully whether we can operate a decisive cut between the labour movement and the "new" social movements, something we see in the literature, and also the social divide that is sometimes apparent between the two types of social movement. We have already established that the labour movement has been, and can become again, a social movement, for example in relation to the British Labour Party, which has been revived and democratized by movements such as Momentum. We also know, on the other hand, that, since they were created in the late 1960s, many of the "new" social movements have become bureaucratized. We need only think of the big NGOs: once campaigning organizations now more akin to personalized corporations in the way they operate. The main issue, for now, is to contest the notion that the "old" class movements and the "new" identity movements are intrinsically opposed to one another. The latter, as Verity Burgmann notes, "should be understood, not as a negation of working-class struggle, but as its blossoming: an enormous exfoliation, diversification and multiplication of demands, created by the revolt of previously subordinated and super-exploited factors of labour" (Burgmann 2016: 142). Both "old" and "new" social movements are unified through their antagonism to capital, and that insight needs to be central to any analysis of "labour and its others".

So, finally, we can think critically about the basis on which labour is, or could be, a social movement. In its origins, labour took on the wide range of issues affecting workers, including health, housing, education, consumption and cultural issues. This was a holistic approach and one oriented towards social transformation. Since that period – although punctuated by explosions of mobilization – the dominant trend has been one of bureaucratization. Whether labour can now be reinvented and reconstructed as a transformative social movement is clearly an open question. Even many of those within the structures – including many transnational, national and local leaderships – recognize that managing decline can lead only to obsolescence and, eventually, disappearance. We can argue, however (as shown in other chapters), that the tide has changed since around 2000 and that we are moving towards a phase of reimagining what a labour movement fit for purpose in the twenty-first century might be.

Much of the debate now on "labour as a social movement" centres around whether the trade unions can shift from "managing decline" to organizing for the future. Around the mid-1990s there was a growing realization across trade union movements internationally that they could not continue as they were if they wanted to survive as a credible force. A turn towards organizing and recruiting new members, often among those hitherto neglected, such as young workers and migrant workers, was the chosen strategy for many. This was designed to increase their power (or halt their decline), and also to enhance their legitimacy by taking on a broader democratic mantle. This process often involved the top leadership leading, as much as the rank and file, even if there were many different objectives at play. Overall, as Melanie Simms, Jane Holgate and Edmund Heery argue, however, "organizing is about more than simply building union representation – its objective is to revitalize trade unionism at workplace level and beyond" (Simms, Holgate & Heery 2012: 33). The strategic objective of trade union revitalization pushes unions towards more proactive, organizing and struggle-oriented positions, out of necessity as much as out of conviction.

The environmental challenge

Socialism bequeathed to the trade union movement a particular attitude towards the environment that lies behind current "jobs versus the environment" dilemmas. For Marx, "nature builds no machines, no locomotives, railways, electric telegraphs, self-acting mules, etc. These are products of human industry; natural material transformed into organs of the human will over nature" (Marx 1976 [1867]: 706). Elsewhere, Marx was able to sound more "ecological", but, overall, he bequeathed a Promethean view of humanity as against its other, nature. If nature is, for Marx, an object to be mastered, he did, however, recognize limits to this process. These natural limits are not purely "natural", for Marx, but result from humanity's interaction with its natural environment. Perhaps inevitably, Marx was immersed in a nineteenth-century conception of progress through scientific advance and industrial control over nature. His polemic with Thomas Malthus over the way population growth limited economic growth made Marx wary of all natural limits arguments.

One hundred years later, when the environment had risen to the top of humanity's concerns from the 1960s onwards, this early socialist position has had grave repercussions. As the new social movements formed, they tended to attract many social layers but potently not the traditional manual working class. For a range of social theorists (André Gorz, Alain Touraine, Manuel Castells, etc.), this was because the working class was part of an increasingly obsolescent industrial capitalist era. They were committed to a mode of production, a political system and an industrial relations order that was inimical to what the post-1968 social movements were about. Although some unions did pose ecological questions, overall the trade union movement did not question the nature of production and growth, or the meaning of work, to the same extent that the ecological movement did. The latter, for its part, maintained a sometimes hostile (at best indifferent) attitude towards the traditional working class and the labour movement as a whole.

Today "jobs versus environment" is still the dominant way to frame the issue both for trade unions and for environmental movements. It is easy to see why this is the case, when the labour and green movements are so separate and even opposed to one another. Historically, for the environmental movement, "nature needs to be defended against uncontrolled and thoughtless industrialisation and the productivism of capital and labour alike" (Räthzel & Uzzell 2012: 82). Trade unionists in petrochemical, nuclear or armaments industries have, for their part, often defended their jobs against the claims of environmental or peace movements. Historically, there would also have been a sociological divide in terms of the social composition of the labour and environmental movements, which fed into this divide. As Nora Räthzel and David Uzzell put it, "Neither labour movements nor environmental movements see labour and nature as allies, needing each other to produce the material resources necessary for human survival" (Räthzel & Uzzell 2012: 83).

Another massive structural divide, in relation to ecology, is that between the affluent industrialized rural North and the poor industrializing South. North/South differentials – a product of colonialism and subsequent structural power imbalances – mean that ecological issues, such as a reduction in industrialization and consumption, will be viewed very differently. Developing common international environmental policies to deal with climate change would require dealing with the North/South divide and its impact on the workers of the world. There is even a marked imbalance within the trade union movement between the powerful and well-funded Northern unions and their Southern counterparts. This relationship is changing, with much relocation of production to the South and outsourcing, but that may not help find a unified labour position on climate change. Many Southern workers and their trade unions sometimes see climate change measures as a Northern imposition on a South now finally industrializing and achieving a measure of mass consumption.

Increasingly, though, there is a realization from both sides of the labour/environmentalist divide that a binary opposition is not the most productive way to pose things if what we seek is a sustainable labour-oriented future. The labour movement, in its formative stage, was quite conscious of the environment. As one international trade unionist recounts:

> If you look back in history, trade unions were some of the first environmentalists. We were the first ones that made the link between the workplace and the local community. So when you look back on the industrial revolution it was the trade unions that were saying, "Hang on a minute, these rivers are polluted, and our families are getting sick."
> (cited in Räthzel & Uzzell 2013: 8)

Trade unionists – like every other citizen – are well able to appreciate the urgency of climate change and the challenge it poses. A progressive labour approach would offer an alternative economic strategy to the current model and, in that sense, would have a greater structural effect than just changing industrial consumption patterns in the affluent North.

From the environmental side, there is a growing recognition that the labour movement is a potential ally and not the dreaded opponent once feared. Particularly since the 2007–9 global financial crisis, analysts have recognized the global ecological limits of capitalism as a mode of production. The bulk of scientific opinion is now very clear on the imminent and extreme dangers posed by global warming. At the same time, it is clear that global capitalism has produced a social crisis based on untold wealth for the top "1 percent", while devaluing whole regions in the Global South and many cities in the North. These twin disasters – social and ecological – are clearly caused by the same unsustainable model of capitalist development. While the socialist/trade union movement in the past has tended to set aside long-term ecological concerns, so also the ecological movement has tended not to focus on the social impact of ecology and the need to imagine an alternative economic order, rather than just "cleaning up" the present one.

To go beyond the binary opposition of jobs versus environment one might start with some concrete actions when workers have taken up environmental issues. To take just one emblematic case among many, we can consider the life and activism of Chico Mendes, the Brazilian rubber tapper, trade union leader and environmentalist, assassinated by a big rancher in 1988. The rubber tappers' union was created in 1970, with Mendes as its first general secretary, who then went on to play an important role in creating the trade-union-based Workers' Party in 1980. Their livelihood issues included the impact of big ranching and, above all, deforestation. The trade unionist gradually (and naturally) became an environmentalist, and was assassinated as much for that reason as for his trade union organizing. In Brazil the national trade union movement has continued to place environmentalism at the very core of its concerns, with the creation of a dedicated environmental portfolio. One reason for this synergy between the labour and environmental movements in Brazil was that the latter in Brazil never disconnected environmental degradation from the struggle against poverty and decent work.

In the advanced industrial societies there has also been a growing concern among trade unionists with environmental concerns, no longer seen as just part of a residual "health and safety" set of issues at the workplace. The environment does not find a ready-made place in the traditional bargaining agenda, but over the last decade it has made its presence felt. One rare national survey of unions in the United Kingdom found that, with regard to environmentalism, "although [it is] not yet a 'core' union activity, most unions anticipate increasing their activity" (Farnhill 2016: 18). There is little opposition and considerable enthusiasm for the green agenda among union members. The problem, according to this survey, was that there was no discernible "product" like those generated by the "equity and diversity" agenda. Employers seem quite willing to engage with unions on environmental issues, and, even though that may only be because it does not impact on the "bottom line", it does point to a fluid situation for the advancement of labour–environmental partnerships.

It is also important to note that in recent years many trade unions, at both national and international levels, have taken up environmental issues. There have always been exceptions to labour's historical indifference to, if not hostility towards, environmental issues. One such example was the so-called Green Bans in the Queensland region of Australia in the 1960s. Local construction was booming, with the rise of the Brisbane business sectors and the high-rise buildings of the Gold Coast. The boom was fed by the emerging coal projects and mineral resource extraction in northern Queensland. This boom, and the role of construction, placed the Queensland Building Trades Group in a powerful position. It was also part of a leftist tendency that supported indigenous rights and the movement against the Vietnam War. Its Green Bans throughout the 1960s were extremely effective in protecting historically significant sites, often in association with local residents' groups or against expressways cutting across working-class areas. The Green Ban movement had a major impact on urban planning in Australia, and also internationally, as it symbolized an early successful cross-sectoral labour–environmental alliance.

Today the spirit of the Green Bans in Australia is alive in the international trade union movement. In 2007 the UN Environment Programme, supported by the ILO and the ITUC, published a study entitled *Labour and the Environment: A Natural Synergy* (UNEP 2007), which symbolizes this new rapprochement. It begins on the simple basis that "employees at the lowest end of the wage scale do the dirtiest jobs, have the least job security and are too often the most vulnerable to environmental risks" (UNEP 2007: iii). The struggle for sustainable development is now seen as an integral part of the struggle against exploitation and precarious work. Not only are workers among the first victims of environmental damage, but their pivotal role in production positions them well to promote an alternative production model and not just alter individual consumption patterns, as is the case with many environmental movements. Protecting the environment may yet become a new way to protect employment and combat poverty.

So, if there is some breakdown of the divisions between labour and environmental movements, what might a viable transformation strategy look like? If we take a systemic approach – accepting the interrelationship between economic and environmental crises, as argued above – then our focus will necessarily be around power, rather than this or that environmental measure taken in isolation. Clearly, across the trade union and labour movements, there is an uneven understanding of the climate crisis. It is also easy to see how groups of workers – in transport, for example – might find it hard to immediately embrace a green politics. Why would I support a measure that will probably put me out of a job? For Asbjørn Wahl, a former official of the International Transport Workers' Federation, the answer lies in "systematic work, education and debate [, which] could go far in developing both knowledge and an ambitious and radical politics in the climate policy areas within the trade union movement, including in areas where major adaptation is executed" (Wahl 2016: 3).

So, just taking transport workers as a case study, we can see the "jobs versus environment" contradiction at play, but also a way in which it can be overcome. The international transport industry is a major producer of greenhouse gases and a dynamic economic sector. To reduce greenhouse gas emissions a reduction in transportation is essential. But, as the 2010 ITF congress stressed, such a reorientation would require much stronger political control of the economy than exists as present. In brief, there is no market-based solution to the climate change crisis. Rather, what is needed is a much broader Polanyian style re-embedding of the economy within society through which social needs could dictate much stronger environmental measures within a planned transition to a new sustainable economic order.

The relationship between trade unions – as representatives of the workers of the world – and the environment, in particular over the challenge of climate change, is crucial for humanity. There is a strong case for understanding the social and ecological crises we now face as equally based on the unsustainable nature of capitalism. If we discount the possibility that a "clean capitalism" could develop (and the history of carbon credits and green tech must be taken into account) then these twin contradictions make a new global order necessary. If the ecological and social crises we face have a common cause – how could they not? – then a common riposte is called for. This would necessarily take us beyond the historical tensions between the trade unions and the ecological movements. The stakes are high, because, as Polanyi stated over 50 years ago,

> to allow the market mechanism to be the sole director of the fate of human beings and their natural environment ... would result in the demolition of society and nature would be reduced to its elements, neighbourhoods and landscapes defiled, rivers polluted ... the power to produce food and raw material destroyed.
>
> (Polanyi 2001 [1944]: 73)

Trade unions and global justice

The "new" social movements emerging from the political ferment of the late 1960s and early 1970s were an expression of the new capitalism, which had become consolidated in the long postwar boom in the North. Advanced capitalist societies had been subject to a process of "commodification" as social life became dominated by the market, and by "bureaucratization" as the state intervened more and more at all levels of society. The new social movements thus reflected the new social antagonism emerging in the North: the youth rebellion, the ecological movement and the rising of the women's movement.

These movements were anti-institutional and anti-hierarchical and represented a reaffirmation of individualism against collectivism. They were all based on antagonisms other than social class – or the conflict between workers and capitalists in the factory, to be specific. All forms of subordination were rejected, the imagination was in power and the future would be nothing like the past.

Although the problematic of the "new social movements" was not necessarily novel, it might, however, direct our attention to an alternative vision of social movements more generally. Alberto Melucci, while strenuously rejecting the "new social movements" label, nevertheless starts from the premise that "in complex societies fundamental aspects of human experience are presently undergoing profound changes, and that new needs, together with new powers and new risks, are being born" (Melucci 1988: 330). Whether we call the new order "post-industrial", "postmodern", a "knowledge society" or a "network society", it is clear that some fairly fundamental social transformations were afoot. We can therefore expect social reactions to this order to become more network-based, more pluralist, less focused on institutions and more daring and innovative. In the era of "disorganized capitalism", as a new dominant order is forged, social movements might well be more focused on identity questions, less confident in their bold meta-narratives and more sensitive to the contingency of structures and events.

The collapse of communism as an alternative social order and of the national development state as agent of modernization does not ensure the sustainability of the dominant order. Indeed, global capitalism can be seen to carry many "new" contradictions, as well as those inherent in any exploitative and divisive social order. The new global capitalism has successfully co-opted much of the spirit of 1968. Mass consumption is out and individual choice is in, bureaucratic organizations and methods are out, with flexibility the new watchword. Above all, democracy is sacrosanct across the world; very few today defend authoritarian regimes openly, as was the case in the 1970s. This means that the democratic discourse that runs throughout most social movements today is not necessarily a challenge to legitimate authority, as was the case in 1968. Grass-roots democracy, bottom-up development, popular empowerment, gender-proofing, anti-racism – all these are largely accepted (although arguably co-opted) terms and concepts in the dominant order. It was the "new" social movements that put them there maybe, but that is another story.

Perhaps the most enduring legacy of the new social movement analytical and political tradition is its emphasis on cultural politics. As Sonia Alvarez, Evelina Dagnino and Arturo Escobar note in relation to Latin America, the cultural politics enacted by these new social movements "in challenging and re-signifying what counts as political ... can be crucial ... to fostering alternative political cultures and, potentially, to extending and deepening democracy" (Alvarez, Dagnino & Escobar 1998: 12). The rules of the political game, and even what now counts as politics, are openly in question. Social movements have subverted the traditional nostrums of the dominant political order. The legitimacy of what was once considered normal and natural is now in question. The women's movement has probably been the most successful in turning traditional politics inside out. The human rights movements of Latin America and Eastern Europe in the 1980s also played a fundamental role in exposing the shallowness of established liberal human rights discourses, and placed on the agenda current concerns with a substantive global human rights agenda.

In the era of the global social movement the lessons of "new" versus "old" social movements may also be apposite. The "old" labour movement was, in its origins and in its very essence, global. The early women's movement addressed women everywhere and not just in particular countries: sisterhood is global too. Even the much-maligned nationalist movements most often saw themselves as part of the "fraternity of nations"; their values were global even though their territorial expression was bounded. The universal claims of religions such as Catholicism or Islam have always transcended national boundaries and have, indeed, pre-dated the modern nation state. Faiths recognize only their universal transcendental gods and not the man-made paraphernalia of politics and narrow self-interest. Thus religious, social and national movements all have a universal or global significance, as does, of course, the human rights movement, with its origins in the European Enlightenment period.

The Battle of Seattle

The great wave of global popular protest that began in the 1990s became increasingly more coordinated and organized, with much clearer political targets emerging. This was also a period of democratization across the greater part of the world, and the post-authoritarian governments then emerging allowed greater space for the social counter-movements to organize. The development of a transnational militant Islamic movement was one particular facet of this period's mobilization. The human rights, environmental and women's movements also began to develop a much more transnational agenda. The annual World Bank and IMF meetings began to act as a focus for an emerging anti-globalization movement. In 1995, the 50th anniversary of the Bretton Woods agreement that had set up the World Bank/IMF system, was marked by an active "Fifty Years Is Enough" campaign. As Jackie Smith recounts: "Many of the older activists in Seattle ... traced their opposition back to the 1980s mobilization around Third World debt and its relationship to conflict and economic justice in Central America and other developing regions" (Smith 2001: 12). The background to Seattle was thus a global one, and a rather "traditional" anti-imperialism was certainly a powerful motivating factor.

So there is a broad historical context that needs to be provided to make sense of the Battle of Seattle in November/December 1999, but there is also a very local labour history that plays a key context-setting role. Contrary to the media images of the incongruity of anarchists smashing windows in the genteel home city of Boeing, Amazon.com and Starbucks, "Seattle is a city with a long past of militant labor and anarchist actions" (Levi & Olson 2000: 309). This stretches back to the militant Seattle General Strike of 1919 and the 1934 West Coast dockers' strikes. This region was a strong organizing base for the IWW, the anarcho-syndicalist and internationalist "one big union" of the early twentieth century. When the US labour federation, the AFL–CIO, organized a big unionization drive in the mid-1990s Seattle was to become one of the first "union cities". There have been major strikes at Seattle's Boeing plants, and the unions have managed to break in to unionize at Microsoft and other software companies.

One of the apparent ironies of the Battle of Seattle, write Margaret Levi and David Olson, "was the presence of the longshore workers who thrive on international trade, at the forefront of actions directed at regulating international trade' (Levi & Olson 2000: 316). Yet, if we take a long view of Seattle's labour history, it is not odd at all to see a group of workers struggling in a militantly particularistic manner over their own conditions, while also seeking to forward a broad social and environmental progressive agenda. Dockers have frequently been seen as a traditional male/manual/militant occupational group but they have often, even naturally, taken up internationalism. There is no need to romanticize the labour struggles of the longshore workers to understand that they were well able to move from local to national to transnational forms of labour solidarity. The threats they faced in the mid-1990s could lead to a protectionist response but also to an internationalist strategy. That they became part of the labour contingent that formed the backbone of the mass events of Seattle shows that political agency still counts and can alter the course of political events. The Battle of Seattle did not, of course, simply happen; it was organized by clearly identifiable social and political organizations. One of the key organizations was the People for Fair Trade (PFT) network of labour, trade and environmental groups that had previously mobilized around NAFTA. Symptomatic of the fluid globalization politics emerging, the PFT mobilized in tandem with the Network Opposed to the WTO (NO! WTO), even though the latter aimed to "shut down" the WTO while the PFT was seeking, rather, the incorporation of labour and environmental standards into the WTO agreements. As Gillian Murphy puts it:

By framing the issue as a critique of neoliberal trade policies rather than an opposition to globalization per se, and by celebrating the diversity of participants rather than pressing for conformity, the group advocated creating an environment in Seattle that would enable it to attract the maximum number of participants. (Murphy 2004: 32)

Organized labour was also to the fore in the mainstream political arena, and, as Ron Judd, one of the organizers, recounts: "What happened in Seattle was not an accident. For months labour led an effort to educate and inform the community about the devastating impact of the WTO and its policies" (cited in Murphy 2004: 33).

Alongside the big battalions of labour and the mainstream environmental groups, such as the Sierra Club, a very different alternative mobilizing model was being implemented by fringe groups such as Direct Action Network (DAN). This was a young movement, influenced by anarchism and committed to direct action. Its aim was not to find "a seat at the WTO table", as the AFL–CIO wished to achieve, but, rather, to mount a festival of resistance to the forces of global capitalism. DAN invested in massive non-violent resistance training and the creation of self-reliant "affinity groups" of around a dozen members, not unlike the old communist traditional cells but without the secrecy. From this milieu came the "shock troops", who were committed to "Shut down Seattle". Although they were shunned by the majority of trade unionists and mainstream environmentalists, it was the innovative and energetic direct action tactics of these sectors that, in the streets of Seattle, made the difference between symbolic protesting and actually influencing the management of globalization.

While Seattle 1999 was, indeed, a turning point in the struggle between the architects of globalization and the great counter-movement against it, we should also be clear about its limitations. The first one surrounds the popular image of Seattle 1999 in terms of the "Teamsters and Turtles unite" slogan, signifying a new labour–environmentalist alliance. The reality was more prosaic, as Kenneth Gould, Tammy Lewis and J. Timmons Roberts recount: "At no time in Seattle did a unified rhetoric connecting labor and environment emerge from either camp. That unifying rhetoric was provided by the organizations focused specifically on corporate globalization such as Public Interest Trade Watch and Global Exchange' (Gould, Lewis & Roberts 2004: 94). The social movements representing labour and the environment did not naturally coalesce, and, in fact, the ideological or discursive bonding element was provided by third parties that were seeking to build a common platform against neoliberal globalization. The "blue–green" alliance, in brief, has still to be built.

The World Economic Forum for its part had become, in the 1990s, the leading "think tank" for the leaders of the globalization process. In January 1999, however, its Davos meeting met a counter-demonstration involving, among others, a French organization, ATTAC, and the MST (Movimiento Sêm Terra), the landless people's movement in Brazil. This was the start of the movement to create a "parallel summit" to the hidden, elitist and technocratic managers of globalization symbolized by Davos, where they got together with their own "organic intellectuals". The Seattle events of 1999 showed that the power of the supranational decision-making bodies was not omnipotent. Parallel summits could confront directly, and in a very visible manner, the architects of the new globalization and articulate the programme or project of the emerging "global civil society".

The French political monthly *Le monde diplomatique* was the seemingly unlikely progenitor of ATTAC. Its driving force, Bernard Cassen, describes how the *Diplo* (as it was known) had published an editorial in 1997, entitled "Disarming the Markets", that ended with a call for action to control the tyranny of the financial markets: "The appeal was launched like a bottle into the sea, without any idea of what the reaction might be" (Cassen 2003: 41). In the event, ATTAC was formed, and grew to 30,000 members, as well as having semi-autonomous branches in Scandinavia, Germany, Italy and elsewhere, which all saw themselves as loosely part of a "No-globo" movement. ATTAC is probably known best for its meticulously researched analysis of globalization and neoliberalism, shifting public opinion firmly away from *la pensée unique* ("one way of thinking") on eco-nomic policy. In France it effectively "mainstreamed" the critique of neoliberal globalization and, in international terms, it played an important role in gener-ating the World Social Forum. The other proximate cause of the WSF experience lay in Brazil as part of, and following, the redemocratization of that country in the second half of the 1980s. The social revolt against state authoritarianism was led by the workers' movement, but it also created the conditions for a flourishing of the NGOs, many influenced by the radical sections of the Catholic Church. In organizational terms, this movement coalesced in the formation of the Workers' Party (Partido dos Trabalhadores – PT) in 1980, which soon began to make significant gains in elections, not least in the southern city of Porto Alegre. The Porto Alegre "participative budget", developed under a PT governorship, became known worldwide (see Bruce 2004) and thus made the city a logical choice for hosting the WSF when the Brazilian NGOs – along with the MST, the landless peasants' movement – met with Cassen and ATTAC and agreed to organize a counter-summit to that in Davos.

The First World Social Forum took place in Porto Alegre in 2001 as an explicit counter to the World Economic Forum taking place at the same time in Davos. Although this event had had vague precursors in Bandung 1955 and the 1968 counter-movement, it was new in many ways. The Workers' Party in Porto Alegre was understandably nervous that it might be outflanked on the Left by this gathering. Many of the more traditional labour organizations were also reti-cent about supporting a movement with such a strong counter-cultural flavour. But the event was a huge success and symbolically put an end to the international retreat of the Left, already slowed down in Seattle in 1999. As Cassen describes WSF 1, "[I]n purely geographical terms its range was limited. But in media terms, its impact was enormous, because it coincided with the meeting of global elites in Davos" (Cassen 2003: 49). In the globalized media-dominated times of the new century, this media visibility of the counter-movement was crucial.

The Second World Social Forum was held in 2002, again in Porto Alegre but now focused on giving meaning to the emergent slogan of "Another world is possible". The WSF concept was beginning to "internationalize", at least in part because of the initiatives of the large Italian contingent that attended WSF 1. The Genoa counter-summit to the G8 in 2001 was thus dubbed a "social forum". In Durban, in protest against the limits of the World Conference against Racism, also in 2001, another "social forum" was created. In Latin America there were a series of regional "social forums", most noticeably in Argentina, then in the midst of a cataclysmic crisis arising from the mechanical application of neoliberal eco-nomics for over a decade. Some 60,000 people attended the WSF 2 conference, compared with the 20,000 who had been attracted to the first event. The social forum concept, principles and particular mode of organization began to spread to most parts of the world, with the exception of Asia.

The Third World Social Forum, in 2003, took up the theme of how the WSF might itself actually embody the principles of "Another world". The 100,000, or more, participants who attended the forum this time included many "main-stream" political and social leaders attracted by the WSF "brand". The US anti-globalization movement, quite insignificant at the previous events, was also now making its presence felt. Some of the more radical anti-globalization participants began to feel somewhat isolated. Was the WSF moving from the "alternative" end of the political spectrum towards becoming the "mainstream"? Certainly, there was a noticeable re-emergence of the "old" new Left of 1968 in leadership positions and in the WSF general discourse. Peter Waterman, at the event from a critical pro-labour stance, argued that "there is a danger that the Forum will be overwhelmed by the past of social movements and internationalism" (Waterman 2003: 7). Nationalist reactions to globalization were much in evidence, and many components of WSF were quite state-oriented. A new model of internationalism was certainly not going to be born fully formed overnight.

Addressing the relative lack of the WSF phenomenon in Africa (except for South Africa) and in the vast expanse of Asia, the fourth WSF was held in Mumbai (India) in 2004. According to one observer: "Beyond the success of the Indian organizational process, Mumbai demonstrated the flexibility of the WSF's iden-tity, which enables it to adapt to local social and political contexts without losing its energy" (Caruso 2005). This might be a slightly self-congratulatory view, in so far as Mumbai was often dominated by the large organizations, whether of civil society or of the politics of an older, more traditional Left. One of the organizers of the Mumbai event, Jai Sen, had already warned of the dangers of "giganticism", or what might be called the problems of success (Sen 2004: 74). The WSF as a "big event" was beginning to look like the 1969 Woodstock Festival, with most of the audience being fairly passive "hearers" or "observers" of the "big names", who now felt compelled to attend the forum.

Following the Mumbai WSF a decision was made to return to Porto Alegre in 2005 but then to make the 2006 WSF a decentralized affair, with events in Africa, Asia and Latin America. The issue of "giganticism" and the dominance of "big names" had already been tackled by reducing the number of plenaries at Mumbai. After that event, as Hilary Wainwright explains, "the International Committee of the WSF took the risky decision to eliminate the official programme altogether" (Wainwright 2005). Henceforth, a *consulta* (consultation) with past WSF attendees would lead to a choice of themes that would constitute the clusters, or "terrains", for debates. This radical experiment was (at least partially) successful at the 2005 WSF event in Porto Alegre, articulating a more purposeful and self-conscious movement for social transformation. The problems of growing size were still present, however, and it was significant that Venezuela's president, Hugo Chávez, proved the biggest draw for audiences.

At a certain point, around 2013–14, the World Social Forum began to enter a crisis of perspectives. Many were dissatisfied by what they saw as bureaucratic leadership, a turn towards the institutions and a Northern focus for what had originated as a Southern perspective. The WSF was held in Tunis in 2015, reflecting the importance of the "Arab Spring", but there was some surprise when the WSF moved to North America for 2016. There was also a growing realization that the semi-spontaneous revolts of the "multitude" had their limits and that power could reconstitute itself after serious shocks to the system. Without a convergence with more organized segments of the contestatory movement, revolts would eventually dissipate. The WSF had moved from a "happy" phase to an "anxious" phase (Beandet 2016) and was now at a real crossroads. Seemingly, it had not escaped from the long-term dilemmas of institutionalization or decline, and it also showed the clear limits of any politics of transformation based purely on spontaneity.

Global justice is not, to be clear, something that happens only at the global level. It is at a local level that issues around social justice most often emerge, for example in the way in which trade unions approach the issue of migration (see Chapter 7). By 2010 we were seeing many examples of what we might call "social justice unionism". These are unions that, according to Tait, "exhibit a melding of social movement and workplace union characteristics" (Tait 2005: 219). Whereas mainstream unions most often moved away from the social movement tradition, some engaged with communities and included the fight against sexism, racism and anti-migrant discrimination as part of their mission. Poor workers' unions – active in the 1960s, for example, and now reviving – have operated on an inclusive social justice principle of what workers' organization is about. Rank-and-file activists have, not surprisingly, been extremely active in these movements, although they can – as in the current period – also be promoted by the leadership as part of a trade union revitalization strategy.

Trade unions and the labour movement

The future of the trade unions as part of democratic transformation will depend, I would argue, on the extent to which they can find common ground with other social movements and articulate a viable politics of social transformation. This fusion could combine the organizational strength of the trade unions and the imagination and energy of the global justice movements. Of course, combining two weak movements – declining trade unions and ephemeral protest movements – will not create a strong and viable new mass movement. But we can start with Clawson, for whom "even run-of-the-mill unions include thousands of dedicated labour activists, and no force in our society has more democratic potential (or radical possibility) than the labour movement" (Clawson 2003: 196). When precarious workers seek to organize, or when migrant workers seek representation, it is still trade unions they turn to. Trade unions – themselves transformed by working outside their comfort zone – will continue to be key players in the politics of social transformation, needed more urgently today than ever before.

An underlying issue in the interaction between the global justice movement, broadly understood, and the trade unions is the progressive potential, if any, of the latter. While the radical case against trade unions as agents of liberation is often heard in both opposition and mainstream circles, what is less clearly articulated is why they might yet have a role with regard to social transformation. Yet we can take, almost at random, any technical study of trade unions today and find that they recognize their potential role as social movements. Thus Andrew Lawrence, in a study of "workers' collective action" in Germany, South Africa and the United States, concludes that "unions are the only organizations that combine workplace representation with a political voice beyond the workplace, usually with a national reach" (Lawrence 2014: 10). Furthermore, given that most urban households the world over depend on wages for their survival, and these are being earned in the workplace, "unions have great potential to improve the lives of their members and broader communities" (Lawrence 2014: 10). This is basic, but it is still a key factor to bear in mind when seeking to write off unions as agents of change.

The "political voice" of the trade unions centres around the question of democracy, whether in the workplace, the community or at a national state level. We can argue, based on the historical record, that trade unions have always had a democratic mission with regard to the workplace and the wider society. They have many times fallen by the wayside in this mission and compromised with anti-democratic forces, and their own internal life has often been far from democratic. But, for a radical democracy to flourish in the twenty-first century, the traditional modes of contestation of the trade unions – strikes, go-slows, boycotts and electoral interventions – will be a necessary element. We need to look back at the early labour movement, with its communal and solidaristic forms, and also to the newer social movements, as Gerald Friedman argues, to deploy the tools of "mass public demonstrations and direct challenges to private property through sit-downs and the occupation of workplaces" (Friedman 2008: 162). Everywhere, democracy and solidarity must come to the fore if any broad process of social transformation is to have a chance of success. Labour and its "others" have a far better chance of achieving these shared objectives together than if they allow divisions to fester and continue.

9

LABOUR INTERNATIONALISM

At its inception the labour movement was almost instinctively internation-alist in its outlook. In the twentieth century, however, there was a steady drift towards a more "nation-statist" perspective by most Northern unions and labour movements, examined in the section on the national era below. Conventionally, the First World War is seen as the point at which labour internationalism died. Following the Second World War the international labour movement was split by the Cold War between the West and "communism". This gave rise to the nefarious practice of "trade union imperialism", through which Western unions sought to influence their counterparts in the South. The international trade unions also began to counter the multinationals in the 1970s, however, in what we can call a transition period, by trying to build countervailing power on the labour side of the capital/wage labour relation. There is now, across the political spectrum and across the world, a feeling that we are entering a new period of labour internationalism. The global era demands a global labour response now that the divisions of the Cold War are a distant memory. In a way, this "new" inter-nationalism is renewing a very "old" tradition of the labour movement, reaching back to the First International of Marx's day. We examine how labour inter-nationalism has developed in the era of globalization as we, supposedly, move beyond the nation state. I suggest that this new internationalism has not always surpassed the traditional conception of transnational collective bargaining. It needs to embrace a more "social movement" type of unionism in order to remain relevant and to represent the emerging global working class.

The national era

It is remarkable how relevant the debates of nineteenth-century internationalism are for us now in the era of globalization. The second half of the nineteenth century also saw a move towards globalization, with world trade increasing sixfold between 1850 and 1890. Van der Linden, writing about the period of Western state formation, could be referring to the present when he writes: "[A]n improved transport and communication network led to a heightened mobility of labour power and capital, and in its wake a weakening of unions organised solely at a local level" (van der Linden 1988: 324). In a very real sense these local unions were forced to become international before they became national. It is as well to remember that in this era, especially after the European revolutionary year of 1848, internationalism was the ideology of the rising liberal bourgeoisie. *The Communist Manifesto* made the ringing declaration of "Workers of the world, unite" in 1848, and from then on internationalism became the banner of the ascendant labour movement too, in a way that transformed the term utterly. In the relatively open borders of Western Europe in the second half of the nineteenth century, craft workers could, and did, travel in search of work across countries quite readily. International contracts between workers happened regularly, and solidarity across frontiers followed inevitably. As Hobsbawm puts it, the class struggle, in its most elementary but also spontaneous forms, was rooted within the trade union struggle, which was internationalist in so far as any division along national, racial or religious or other lines inevitably weakened the collective of workers in dispute with an employer (Hobsbawm 1988: 91). There were common experiences, common problems and a certain community of interests shared by British, French, German and Dutch artisans. Mutual help across borders was a logical extension to mutual help within a particular country. The use of overseas "scab" labour was being used by employers in the 1850s, and this, in particular, needed to be countered by links between workers in different countries. As British workers put it in a famous address to their French counterparts in 1863: 'A fraternity of peoples is highly necessary for the cause of labour ... not to allow our employers to play us off one against the other and so drag us down to the lowest possible condition' (cited in van der Linden 1988: 331).

If internationalism was an active and crucial ingredient of the nascent labour movement, it also had its limits. It was essentially limited to Western Europe and the lands that those countries had colonized, such as North America and Australasia. There was little concern with the inhabitants of the colonies, and this was largely pacifist and humanitarian in tone. There was no specific labour or socialist discourse on the colonial questions that might distinguish the labour movement from bourgeois liberalism. The labour movement shared the notion of "White man's burden" of the time, in relation to the colonies and semi-colonies.

A landmark in the early history of internationalism was, clearly, the foundation of the International Working Men's Association, or First International, in 1864. This first labour international was formed on the crest of a strike wave and in a mood of revolutionary democracy. As Knud Knudsen puts it, "The International represented the future, the emancipation of the labouring poor, the entire liberation of the working class from all forms of social, political and religious oppression" (Knudsen 1988: 307). In the late 1860s a wave of strikes in continental Europe put the First International firmly on the map and reinforced its transnational ethos and practice. By now "proletarian internationalism" was coming into its own, with a distinctive oppositional profile. Employers now began to counter workers with an aggressive nationalism. Workers and the labour movement were becoming firmly identified discursively, and in practice, with internationalism. The First International brought together diverse social categories of labour and different political ideologies. It was not a particularly strong organization and was riven by personal and political conflicts. It had to fight hard just to remain in existence; consequently, it was eventually dissolved acrimoniously, in 1876.

From the 1870s through to the end of the nineteenth century, labour was to become steadily "nationalized", as the European nation states were consolidated, and rudimentary welfare states began to wean workers away from an internationalist perspective. From the Franco-Prussian War of 1870–1 onwards, the labour movements of Europe began to enter a close relationship with their respective nation states. The phrase *la nation des proletaires* ("the nation of proletarians") springs from this era and reflects the growing symbiosis between nation building and the social advance of labour. Internationalism from now on would have a distinctively "national" flavour.

With the formation of the Second International, in 1889, a new labour and socialist ideology, "social democracy", was now being forged. International networking and activity certainly continued in this era from 1890 to 1914. As Jelle Visser puts it, "[A] considerable volume of international exchange, through migration, travel propaganda or money did occur and helped to propagate ideas or set example" (Visser 1998: 180). There was international support for striking workers and "best practice" was generalized across national frontiers. The 1890s also saw the creation of the main international trade secretariats, bringing together national unions in a given sector, organizations that have continued to the present day. The struggle for trade union rights and the eight-hour working day was an international one, although, significantly, the struggle to improve social regulation was reserved for the national sections of the Second International.

Simplifying somewhat, we can say that labour internationalism died in 1914 as the European powers lined up for the First World War, a conflict generated by the scramble for colonies. The collapse of internationalist rhetoric was dramatic, as labour and socialist leaders across Europe scurried to stand behind "their" respective nation states and armies. If the outbreak of war and the subsequent collapse of the Second International was a shock for its leaders, the workers of Europe saw less of a contradiction. As Hobsbawm puts it, "In 1914 class-conscious workers in belligerent countries rushed to the colours in a spontaneous *levée en masse* ... Having won the right to be full members of their nation through their movement, they now behaved as full citizens were supposed to" (Hobsbawm 1988: 11). So, while 1914 brought out the contradiction between the rhetoric and the reality of workers' internationalism, it was more a confirmation of trends towards a "nationalizing" of the working classes than a dramatic bolt out of the blue.

Following the Second World War the development of the international trade union movement was dominated by the Cold War between the West and the "communist" East. Pragmatic and isolationist tendencies now came to the fore, and there was not even the pretence of "labour internationalism" that even the bad patches of the previous period had still seen, on paper. Although, in the earlier period, the labour movements of the West had become largely "nationalized", now the state/union nexus became truly consolidated. After the war the struggle of many in the Western unions focused on the "communist threat" and they continued to work with their national governments to this end. This is when "trade union imperialism" as we know it took shape. The trade unions of the North began to see their external policy as part of that of their respective national governments. Western trade unions, particularly those of the United States, were firm believers and active players in the Cold War. In Western Europe the wartime role of the unions, in terms of production and the national war effort, was extended into the postwar period, when they played a major role in reconstruction.

At the global level the postwar period was dominated by political splits in the trade union movement. In 1945 the formation of the World Federation of Trade Unions, claiming some 65 million members, seemed to signal a fragile unity between communist and non-communist trade unions. No amount of diplomacy could hide the rifts, however, and a split soon emerged over the US Marshall Plan for the reconstruction of Europe, which was opposed by the unions of the East. By 1949 the ICFTU had been formed, led by the now unified US labour movement in the shape of the AFL–CIO, which had overcome its own "communist" problem. From then on the whole history of international trade unionism was dominated by the conflict between the ICFTU and the now explicitly pro-Soviet WFTU. Both set up regional organizations in the various regions of the South, where the Cold War was also played out by proxy. In 1949 the ICFTU claimed 48 million members worldwide, a figure which had increased to 67 million by 1979. Hegemonic in the West, the ICFTU also made serious advances in the South through its undoubted power and influence.

Trade union internationalism could be based on universalist solidaristic principles or on pragmatic self-interest, but in the Cold War era it also became part of the diplomatic dimension of nation state interactions. Internationalism became a rhetorical cover for a politicized trade union foreign policy, on behalf of Western powers and the Soviet Union. As MacShane puts it, "[N]ational traditions, national demands, and national political culture" (MacShane 1992: 294) could hardly be subsumed by the shallow internationalist rhetoric of conferences. So, while the Northern unions were hardly internationalist in the spirit of the First International, their international reach increased dramatically during this period, mirroring, to some extent at least, the development of capitalism internationally.

The transition

The global economy of the "golden era" (see Chapter 2) was dominated by the multinational or transnational corporations. The international trade unions, from the 1960s onwards, made a concerted effort to build "countervailing" labour power against the MNCs on a transnational basis. In essence, the theory was that trade unions could develop structures to mirror the reach of the MNCs, with which they could eventually engage in transnational collective bargaining. The key players were to be the ITSs, which were now beginning to come into their own as transnational labour organizations. The most influential ITSs in terms of international outreach were the International Metalworkers' Federation (IMF), the International Union of Food and Allied Workers and the International Federation of Chemical and General Workers' Union. Charles Levinson, as assistant general secretary of the IMF, began planning for union regulation by industry as far back as the mid-1950s and then took the concept to fruition as head of the ICF in the 1970s. Levinson went on to popularize the notion of trade union countervailing power across the labour movement. In his popular book *International Trade Unionism* (Levinson 1972), he argues, essentially, that, "in terms of international action to develop a new countervailing union response to the multinational companies, the most important thing is that there exist bargaining relations directly with these undertakings" (Levinson 1972: 106). In what was a very early engagement by a labour intellectual with the internationalization of capital, Levinson advanced a three-stage model of union responses, summarised as: (1) company-wide support for a single union in one country in a dispute with a foreign subsidiary; (2) multiple negotiations with a company in several countries at the same time; and (3) integrated negotiations across the multinational around common demands (Levinson, 1972: 110). According to Levinson, there were already plenty of examples of unions showing solidarity with an overseas union in dispute, as per stage 1, and he believed the move towards full transnational collective bargaining would come sooner rather than later.

One of the most significant experiences was that of the IMF world auto councils, set up at the instigation of the US United Automobile Workers, a leading progressive union in that country. The auto councils consisted of representatives from each trade union in a given company, involving both the parent company and its overseas subsidiaries. These were formed in Ford, Volkswagen, Nissan and other auto industry MNCs. Apart from basic but essential exchange of information, they sought to move towards a harmonization of conditions in the various plants. The late 1970s was the period when MNCs were beginning to transfer production to low-wage areas, so this was a particularly acute concern. One of the most detailed studies of world auto councils, by Burton Bendiner, concludes that the type of action engaged in by those IMF bodies "was and still is uphill work and often more unsuccessful than successful" (Bendiner 1977: 71). There were success stories, and examples of labour internationalism that did at least have a significant symbolic effect. In general, however, "very few of the WCCs stood the test of time or achieved the sort of results for which they were intended" (Gumbrell-McCormick 2000: 381). After some early successes the MNCs were able to counter a labour strategy on this terrain. It was almost as if labour leaders knew they were engaging in a game of bluff with the MNCs, aware they did not have the strength to impose anything like transnational collective bargaining. Finally, the divisions in the international trade union movement, between the "free world"-ICFTU and the communist affiliated unions, had a debilitating effect.

In conclusion, trade unions in the 1970s did make a concerted effort to develop structures and strategies to confront transnational capitalism. There was nothing inevitable about this, and labour structures do not just mirror capital's development. In short, we cannot just see labour's "subjective" development catching up with capital's "objective" development, as it were. There is a fundamental asymmetry between capital and labour that needs to be recognized and not just brushed aside. Essentially, the policy of transnational collective bargaining was a syndicalist and economistic one. That is to say, its logic was a trade union one and not necessarily a labour movement, let alone a socialist, one. There are many obstacles to workers organizing generally, let alone taking action across national frontiers.

The global era

Many observers were rather surprised at the Davos 2001 meeting to hear John Sweeney, president of the US AFL–CIO, proclaim that the counter-globalization protest in Seattle 1999 and other actions were not a "backlash" against globalization but, rather, the "birth pangs of a new internationalism" (AFL–CIO 2001).

There had already been a shake-out in the AFL–CIO Foreign Affairs Department and an explicit critique of the old "trade union imperialism" ways. But this was now the top leader of the AFL–CIO, at a major business international forum, calling for a renewal of proletarian internationalism. Sweeney declared: "This movement for a new internationalism is building from the bottom up, not the top down ... Its forum is the public square, not the boardroom" (AFL–CIO 2001). In this "new morning dawning", Sweeney saw "workers, environmentalists, religious leaders and students coming together to call for workers' rights and human rights and consumer and environmental protections in the global economy" (AFL–CIO 2001). While one must never confuse rhetoric and reality – and we must bear in mind that Sweeney was seeking to protect AFL–CIO jobs as much as anything else – this discourse did seem to signal a new awareness of the international dimension in the ranks of the labour movement.

Jay Mazur, chair of the AFL–CIO International Affairs Committee in the influential US policy-makers' journal *Foreign Affairs* (Mazur 2000), sought, on the back of the Seattle debacle for the WTO, to develop a responsive trade union view on globalization. He recalls how, "not so long ago, a major union's international activity could be carried out by a single person who might even have other organizational responsibilities" (Mazur 2000: 86). Since the turn of century many of a union's departments (research, health, legal, safety, corporate affairs, political action, etc.) have had a central international dimension, as a result of the effects of globalization. Given the perceived "race to the bottom" in terms of labour rewards and conditions, unions in the rich countries must, of necessity, concern themselves with the plight of the majority of workers in the South. The transformation of the world economy, and the disruptions caused to the global elite's plans at Seattle, meant, for Mazur, that the time was now ripe for trade unions to demand a "seat at the table" of global capitalism's board of management. This did not deliver the expected results, though, and the global financial crisis of 2007–9 saw both sides retreating to a more confrontational approach.

However remarkable the apparent turnaround of the AFL–CIO might have been, it was of course the ITSs that, in practice, had been steadily pursuing an internationalist path since the 1960s. Thus the ICEM, for example, organized its Second World Congress in 1999 around the issue of "Facing global power: strategies for global unionism". In terms of the new concern with the issue of "global governance", the ICEM posed a stark alternative: the "globalization of greed" or the "globalization of solidarity" (ICEM 1999: 34). Neoliberal globalization was based squarely on the rule of competition, and is inimical to any conception of human solidarity. For the ICEM, some corporations have already acknowledged the integrated nature of their operations and see the advantage of dealing with the ITSs on issues that are intrinsically global, such as the environment. The ICEM was optimistic for the future that "global corporations need global unions"

(ICEM 1999: 42). In practice, however, it gradually returned to a traditional Northern union dialogue and bargaining approach that would simply reproduce the incorporating logic of the corporatist model. It focused on organizing in the parent company where the transnational corporation was based, hoping thus to impact on its global production network. Although it did back the formation of corporate networks in Brazil and in Asia, its main effort was inevitably in Europe.

Our balance sheet of recent moves towards trade union internationalism needs to be a cautious one. On the one hand, the official trade union strategy has moved away from the notion of trade unions as countervailing power to capital, to embrace, again, the supposed benefits of seeking a partnership with corporations. The chosen vehicle, the international framework agreement, has had a limited impact, and there have been fewer than 100 – that is, less than 10 per cent of the number of European works councils. Employers have found ways to hollow them out and divert them. Given that they have not been able to broaden their scope, one careful analysis concludes that the danger of this strategy is that "it may become increasingly corporate-bound, circumscribing union policy choices and turning into a cross-border reproduction of national structural power-related asymmetries" (Fichter & McCallum 2015: S71–S72), both with regard to how the unions operate and in terms of their relations with the corporations. If we do not rethink our strategies then, inevitably, the old and trusted strategies will return to prominence. If they did not work in the golden era, when labour had a place at the table, they certainly will not work now. There has been a recognition in global union structures since 2000 that social movements need to be engaged with, but what that translates into is an invitation to the NGOs or organizations such as SEWA to international conferences. Where they have failed to engage at all on a transnational level is with regard to the informal sector, such that some labour-based NGOs have made an impact but the official trade unions have shown little interest. The conditions have been laid for a new internationalism, and the history of the labour movement shows many precedents; it is now a question of making the political choices that need to be made.

As for the ICFTU, around 2000 it finally began to take a more progressive (as against Cold War) stance towards global capitalism. Having overcome its Cold War divisions, the ICFTU is now better placed to act as general labour interlocutor in the corridors of financial and political power. Much of its philosophy is based on the simple dictum "The global economy needs global rules" (ICFTU 1997: 57), recalling its classic golden era pluralist conception of industrial relations. It was interesting, in this regard, to see the World Bank (1997) report giving the trade unions a much more positive role than had ever been the case for such a body previously. It is hard, though, to envisage how a traditional "social partnership" approach might work at the international level in today's climate. Nor does the rather contradictory "social movement" orientation, advanced at other times by the ICFTU, seem particularly viable politically, at least as it is being articulated by the trade union leaders, who have not forged the necessary alliances to make it possible. The ICFTU should not, in brief, be seen as a "slumbering giant", about to awaken to lead the international proletariat. Its recent "internationalist" turn does, however, create a more favourable environment for labour solidarity actions, but the reform of its own structures and policies is a prerequisite for the emergence of a new internationalism.

The motivation behind the new global outreach of the ITSs and others was perhaps best articulated around the slogan "Global business – global workers' rights". For MacShane, "[g]lobal action is not now the narrow preserve of big governments, rich banks and multinational companies [as] we can all act globally to assert humankind's place in the new world economy" (MacShane 1996: 3). If organizations such as the World Trade Organization exist to safeguard the global rights of capital and intellectual property rights (currently a very contentious area), so should labour seek global representation. Social and environmental rights also require international regulation. The underlying ethos of the global unionism movement, according to this perspective, should be that "the global economy has to meet its social obligations" (MacShane 1996: 3). In brief, the new international social movements are called on to reverse the 1960s' feminist and ecology slogan "Think global, act local", with global action seen as the only way to confront the now firmly globalized capitalist system.

While the global context appears more pressing today than in the heyday of national regulation, we can only really say that global unionism and internationalism constitute a tendency rather than a social reality. They exist mainly because, as the ICFTU argues, "unions at the national level are seeing much of what they have achieved being undermined by global financial and industrial decisions" (ICFTU 1997: 5). A problem that arises here is that there is an inherent tendency for trade unions to simply replicate their national strategy at the international level. Yet we know from the experience of the 1970s that transnational collective bargaining is unlikely, and possibly even non-viable if advanced as a simple scaling up of national structures. Andreas Breitenfellner (of the Austrian Federation of Trade Unions), for example, notes: "The legal basis for transnational industrial action is circumscribed by the different national legislations and labour relations system" (Breitenfellner 1997: 547). He argues that global unionism needs to go beyond congress diplomacy and information exchange: "[T]rade unions should perceive themselves as being part of a global civil society" (Breitenfellner 1997: 552).

There was an emerging sense at the turn of the century that globalization has created opportunities as well as causing severe problems for labour. New and cheaper communications technologies provide the basis for better global links. There is a call for strategies and actions at a global level, drawing on "the tradition of labour internationalism" (Breitenfellner 1997: 552). Yet, when Breitenfellner comes to drawing up the actual mechanisms whereby labour will seek to exercise some social regulation over the global economy, he is disappointingly traditional, arguing that "[t]he ultimate aim of global unionism would be to institutionalise a system of tripartite social partnership" (Breitenfellner 1997: 552) – that is to say, the tried and failed postwar tripartism of capital, labour and nation state. This is simply not viable when capital has moved into an entirely new terrain in which the formation of a global precariat has superseded any quaint notions of partnerships with labour and the state in a cosy three-way arrangement.

In practice, the first thing we note when surveying the world of international solidarity is that it is often women rather than workers (not necessarily contradictory categories, of course) who are the prime movers on the global stage. The 1970s concept of "global sisterhood" (Morgan 1984) may have been severely criticized for eliding differences, but it reflected a very real aspiration. The drive to unify women's struggles for emancipation across the globe reached its peak, perhaps, with the 1995 UN World Conference on Women in Beijing. The women's movement has been global not just in its transnational orientation but also in its holistic approach to the oppression of women. In this way it has, indeed, been exemplary in its practice and its theoretical elaboration of what "global solidarity" might mean. Furthermore, in recent years the international women's movement has had a significant impact on the labour movement, so that even the ICFTU often refers to "sexism" and "oppression", terms once far removed from the traditional trade union lexicon. Universal "sisterhood" may have been a white Northern middle-class construct (see Mohanty 1993), but it did signal a new "moral" internationalism.

Apart from gender and human rights, it is unquestionably around environmental issues that some of the most dynamic transnational activity is to be found today. Organizations such as Greenpeace have successfully made an impact on global politics, not just because the environment is quite clearly (at least, after Chernobyl) a transnational issue but also because they have been adept at matching their campaigning strategies to the nature of the "new" capitalism. The notion of "sustainable development" has entered the mainstream since the 1992 Earth Summit in Rio. Whatever its precise meaning, this concept has acquired considerable legitimacy and can be used by campaigning groups as a yardstick. Clearly, if a global concept of "fair labour standards" was to acquire similar status, it would represent a breakthrough for labour. Of course, as with the notion of "global sisterhood" or "universal" human rights, there are huge differences between the dominant Northern perspective and the "view from the South". Campaigners in the South have argued, against the dominant conception of "sustainability", that poverty itself is an environmental problem and conspires against sustainability.

While gender, human rights and the environment are all aspects of the new labour internationalism (broadly understood), it is the relationship between production and consumption that is the immediate issue. It is a truism to say that capitalism in the North is all about consumerism. Although for a certain strand of Marxism – and the international development movement – this is to be lamented, it nevertheless opens up new possibilities for labour solidarity across the world. In the mid-1990s there were a series of consumer boycotts in the United States aimed at big brands, especially in the apparel industry. Carefully nurtured publicity scandals around Gap, Calvin Klein, Levi-Strauss, Reebok and other high-profile companies were successful in forcing them to implement "codes of conduct" with regard to labour conditions in their overseas plants. In Europe, the "Clean clothes" campaign was also very successful in forcing the retail sector and the consumer to examine the "labour behind the label", exposing oppressive conditions, especially of domestically based female homeworkers in the South. Not only were some retailers moved to accept ILO-set fair labour standards for their subcontractors, but a general renaissance of transnational consciousness and solidarity resulted from this campaign.

The turn-of-the-century sweatshop campaigns in the United States, according to Ross, "provided a successful model for coalitions between labour, environmental, and social justice interests: local and international, government and non-government, organised labor and community groups ... and targeting the weak links in capital's chain" (Ross 1997: 37). In many ways these events were paradigmatic of the new labour internationalism. They cut across the boundaries of national/international, production/consumption, labour/community, and so on. A small campaigning organization, the National Labor Committee, which organized much of this work, exposed a weak link in capital's armoury. It also became a player on the stage of globalization, and effectively changed the terms of the struggle. The "name" of the blue chip company was only as good as consumer confidence made it. The "new" capitalism had found a "new" solidarity movement opposing it, just as adept at trading in images as the companies themselves, but based on a progressive broad front of worker, student, faith-based, human rights and community groups.

There were clear tensions and debates surrounding the issue of the new labour internationalism, however, which can be gauged, for example, in a statement by Lane Kirkland, veteran president of the AFL–CIO at the time of the NAFTA negotiations, who declared that "[y]ou can't be a trade unionist unless you are an internationalist", the reason being that "substandard conditions anywhere" (such as Mexico) were "a threat to good conditions anywhere" (meaning the United States) (cited in French, Cowie & Littleham 1994: 1). This, of course, just shows that internationalism and self-interest are not incompatible. Transnational labour activity can now be seen in slightly more complex terms; it is not just labour "going global" to match capital's globalizing strategy. Nor is it a simple localist strategy to compensate for labour's weakness at the international level. Local and global labour activity cannot be seen as mutually exclusive; nor are they in a hierarchy of importance. The local and the global can be understood only in relational terms. Amin rejects "the territorial idea of sequestered globalization and labour spatial logics – local, national, continental and global – pitted against each other" (Amin 1997: 133). These are not separate "places" but, rather, intermixed social relations. Thus, labour cannot really pursue a progressive strategy of transformation based on territorial units; instead, it needs to take account of the hybrid and intertwined social logics of globalization/regionalization/localization.

There are problems with any simple understanding of labour solidarity becoming global to match capital. Indeed, it may actually be demoralizing to propose a strategy that cannot be achieved. Perhaps linked-up local struggles could be another way to "go global". Herod mentions in this regard the successful 1998 General Motors dispute in the United States, in which two plants in one community successfully brought the giant auto company to a standstill (Herod 2001). Herod is undoubtedly correct to conclude that, "in an increasingly interconnected planetary economy, a locally focused campaign against a TNC may sometimes prove highly effective, particularly if such local disputes target crucial parts of that corporation's global operation" (Herod 2001: 412). This would be a truly global strategy, in so far as it would be well attuned to the nature of globalization, but applied locally.

Another example of this is the 1998 Liverpool dockers' strike, for which there was considerable international solidarity activity. Undoubtedly, this occurred to some extent because the local and national levels for labour advancement were hostile, if not closed down. Nevertheless, some commentators constantly sought to return the struggle to its local context, to pursue "class action" as in the 1970s dockers' disputes. Here we detect a localism that, in its blind denial of the complexity of globalization (seeing it only as a unified bloc), constricts labour's options. Put more generally, the local cannot be seen as a stable island in the stormy seas of globalization. There is even a certain reactionary tinge to this localism, which can all too easily lead to protectionist demands and chauvinist sentiments. As Hardt and Negri put it, "[T]his 'localist' position is misleading in so far as it rests on a false dichotomy between the global and the local, assuming that the global entails homogenisation and undifferentiated identity whereas the local preserves heterogeneity and difference" (Hardt and Negri 2000: 44). Local differences are not "natural", and can in fact be seen to be "produced" by globalization. An abstract labour "global solidarity" strategy may actually be disempowering, as we saw above. Nor can localization – empowering the local – be an adequate response to globalization.

Trade unions need to develop a strategy attuned to the particularities of their locality. They also require a broad social movement orientation, bringing in the whole community when possible, if they are not to be limited to syndicalism.

Globalization will probably not be threatened by a sum of many little local actions. Macro-level responses are clearly necessary to articulate a labour-based global alternative to free market globalization. Bridging the apparent gulf between local and global strategies can be achieved, I believe, through what Jeremy Brecher, Tim Costello and Brendan Smith call "linking the nooks and crannies" (Brecher, Costello & Smith 2000: 23), whereby labour activity takes place across the world, thus coordinating and "developing a common vision and program" (Brecher, Costello & Smith 2000: 25) to contest neoliberal globalization effectively.

If neoliberal globalization provided the main incentive for the (re-)emergence of the new trade union internationalism, it has been the communications/information revolution that provided the tools to deliver it. It is not a form of technological determinism to argue that the internet is a crucial facilitator and enabler of labour internationalism. Although he is a sober realist compared to some internet enthusiasts, Eric Lee has rightly proclaimed that, "[t]hanks to the Internet, a century-long decline in internationalism has already been reversed. For thousands of trade unionists who log on every day, the International has already been reborn" (Lee 1997: 186). It is, indeed, tempting to draw analogies between the brave new world opened up by international labour communications, based on the internet, and the perspective Marx had as the First International started up. What is particularly interesting is that the present wave of communication-based internationalism really began with Levinson, who developed the notion of "countervailing power" in the 1970s but who also promoted the use of computers and computer communications through his leading role in the international trade secretariats.

The early proponents of internet-based internationalism were quite optimistic about the changes that online connectivity would bring. There were a number of early pioneers, such as Lee (1997), who took this perspective forward in a practical way. It seemed in the 1980s and 1990s that the internet would usher in a new era for labour communications, and permit a more fluid exchange of ideas and building of solidarity action. There were many examples at national and international levels, starting with Lee's own Labour Start site (www.labourstart.org). A 1981 strike by teachers in Canada saw online mobilizations promoted as the great new mobilizing tool. Union leader Harry Kuehn commented:

> [W]e seemed unafraid of the future and what it would bring. That's one
> of the messages a union broadcasts to the members – and others – when

it adopts a new technology, live computer networking. It's a way of saying: we're changing because we intend to survive.

(cited in Burgmann 2016: 61)

The labour/internet synergy really took off after that.

By the early 2000s the internet had become normalized as a means of communication and organization for unions worldwide, but had it delivered on its promises? There were online guides and manuals produced that showed how labour could be empowered by ICT. To information and organization, we could add the vital progressive task of building solidarity. In 2008, however, Eric Lee, who had been such an early proponent of online activism, posted a piece entitled "How the Internet Makes Union Organizing Harder" (www.ericlee.info/2008/02/how_the_internet_makes_union_o.html). What had happened? Sometimes cyberspace solidarity did not translate into real-time action. Neither are the new social media exactly an alternative to the mainstream any more. And governments, employers and conservatives are just as adept at using the internet as labour and progressives are. At a more mundane level, unions need to consider the question of the resources and time that need to be allocated to online activities, when many other pressing tasks of organization and representation loom large. Labour is at the forefront of Web 2.0 technology, but it still needs to consider the dilemma posed by Burgmann: "[A] literally virtual union or union movement, existing only in cyberspace, and with minimal membership fees, offers a labourist equivalent to Facebook" (Burgmann 2016: 73), but what would be lost if the old-style unionism was simply replaced by Facebook-style unionism?

In conclusion, I would argue that there is no hard and fast divide between the "old" and the "new" labour internationalism, in the same way that the world was global long before "globalization" became a buzzword. But there is a paradigmatic shift operating at a meta-level we need to bear in mind. This is expressed most clearly by Boa de Sousa Santos, who contrasts the old anti-capitalist internationalism of the twentieth century with the new twenty-first century internationalism embodied by the World Social Forum. The first was based on "a privileged social actor (workers or workers and peasants); a privileged type of organisation/trade unions and working-class parties along with their federations and Internationals; a centrally defined strategy (the Internationals' resolutions); [and] a politics originating in the North" (de Sousa Santos 2014: 38). It assumed social and political homogeneity among those it sought to organize internationally. The new internationalism – as embodied by the World Social Forum, for example – is, in contrast, not based on homogeneity but, rather, on social, cultural and political diversity.

The crux of the new internationalism, according to de Sousa Santos, is that "[t]he WSF assumes that it is possible to develop strong ties, coalitions, networks among non-homogeneous groups and organizations and, moreover, that the cultural and political differences are enabling rather than paralysing as sources of political innovation" (de Sousa Santos 2014: 38). This is, indeed, part of the philosophical underpinning of the new social movements and the global justice movements. This is not the place to carry out a balance sheet of these movements, but we must note that since 2000 the WSF and the broader social justice movement have simply not been able to articulate a viable alternative to globalization. We are most probably living through a transitional period, still, when the old is dying and the new cannot yet be born. It would be wrong, in my view, to write off the workers of the world and the labour movement as players in the new struggle for survival and socialism, or, at least, for a society beyond blind market subservience.

CONCLUSION: POSSIBLE FUTURES

Workers, as we have seen, are central to capitalism's development and are always an antagonistic element at its heart. This is important for the workers of the world, of course, but also for the wider society, in so far as they – and their organizations – may play a role in the creation of a progressive, sustainable global development strategy.

I begin this conclusion with an analysis that seeks to take us beyond the impasse that I detect in most current research in labour and globalization. The field is dominated by debilitating binary oppositions, such as that between old and new social movements, or between a mobilizing strategy based on recognition versus one oriented towards redistribution. There is a need, I argue, for a more dialectical understanding of the dilemmas and choices faced by workers and others in the contemporary era. This analysis understands capitalism as always being subject to and shaped by workers' struggles, while of course itself setting the context for these.

I then move on to develop a complexity framework that is, I would argue, necessary for understanding the role of labour both as a driver of capitalist development and as a possible agent for its undoing. Complexity allows us to move beyond binary oppositions and is also cognizant of contradictions and the dialectical nature of development. It is also, at least in the way in which I deploy it here, compatible with thinking about possible futures that are not simply utopian but based on real alternatives before us in many parts of the world, and that often prefigure a future that might be ours.

Finally, returning to the world of labour today, I consider whether another world might be possible, which is a slogan popularized by the World Social Forum that is in need of some concrete action if it is to be more than wishful thinking. I examine what might be termed reformist labour futures, such as the "Decent work" campaign of the ILO and others. I also assess the more radical social movement unionism, which has sought to take labour beyond the reformist economic and political unionism of the past. I posit a range of options for social transformation and for an open-ended future for labour, which surpasses the old reform-versus-revolution binary opposition, which is badly in need of deconstruction.

Beyond the impasse

Current debates on the way forward for labour tend to be rather one-sided. The majority of analysts, both conservative and radical, believe that labour, as a relevant social actor, is an anachronistic idea and that labour unions constitute an archaic organizational model, irrelevant to our postmodern globalized world. It is understandable that pro-market fundamentalists will emphasize any way in which unions, as collective organizations, may no longer be relevant. The neoliberal theoretical revolution of the 1990s was based precisely on the virtues of the market and the evils of collectivism. There is also a radical approach to "the crisis of world labour" exemplified by Marcel van der Linden, who argues that "both old-style trade unionism and old-style worker's parties can no longer cope with the challenges offered by the contemporary world" (van der Linden 2015). This is correct, but he then goes on to argue that the global union density of 7 per cent worldwide, as well as the decline of the global capital/labour ratio, makes the task of confronting the new global order extremely difficult, if not impossible. This analysis is one-sided, in that it focuses only on some very broad – and inevitably partial – aspects of how labour organizes globally.

Contemporary critical thinking is still strongly influenced by binary oppositions, in which two theoretical concepts are defined strictly in opposition to one another. "Old" and the "new" social movements are a case in point: labour, being the paradigmatic example of "old", is deemed bureaucratic and stale, whereas the "new" movements are regarded as democratic and vibrant. A whole set of related binaries could be mentioned: state versus civil society, North versus South, top-down versus bottom-up and, of course, local versus global. All these binary oppositions are characterized by a presence–absence, a dominance–resistance dichotomy. The political critique of binary oppositions – as practised throughout this book – is not simply the reversal of the opposition but its deconstruction. The problem of logocentrism – using words as a fundamental expression of an external reality – which lies behind these binary oppositions is often ethnocentric and as much an issue on the Left of politics (as in local = good) as on the Right.

Just one (quite technical) term we could deconstruct is that of "trade union density" across time and space. Most often this apparently simple indicator is used to show that unions are in terminal decline, at least in the advanced industrial societies since the onset of neoliberal policies in the 1980s. Yet union density is not the only factor affecting the bargaining power of a union. Employer/state negotiations are equally important, not to mention the political power of the unions. John Kelly goes further in decoupling union density from the prospects for union revitalization, arguing on the basis of complex data that, "despite the problems they have faced in recent years and their denigration as a merely sectional interest group, unions remain a powerful force both for egalitarianism and for democracy" (Kelly 2003: 21). In shaping their role in society, unions may reshape their identity and goals, fundamentally altering their economic, political and social roles and influencing society as a consequence.

So, moving beyond the impasse, we can see, for example, that it is not a question of counterposing a pessimistic analysis with an optimistic one; that would be a poor critical response. But a longer-term analysis of the making and remaking of the global working class and its organizations over time, from a broadly Polanyian double movement perspective, would provide an alternative framework. As against the fairly static negative view outlined above, the emphasis here is placed on the dynamic and dialectical nature of the capital/ wage labour relation. Silver and Karataşli stress how "one of the key driving forces behind [capitalism's] tendency towards 'ceaseless change' is labour–capital conflict" (Silver & Karataşli 2015: 49). If capitalism, as we know it today, in its informationalized and globalized form, is in part due to historic labour resistance then capitalism has not leapt beyond its dependent relationship with labour, established during the Industrial Revolution. Each time workers' bargaining power is weakened by technological advances or relocation to low-wage regions, this contradiction comes to the fore once again.

The Polanyian frame made sense around 2000, not because it was optimistic but because it allowed us to capture the significance of seemingly disconnected signs that the one true model of market-driven globalization was being contested. It seems wrong to see this as an example of the "Pollyanna principle" (a subconscious bias towards the positive), as Michael Burawoy argues, somewhat less than constructively (Burawoy 2010). Burawoy's attack on "the false optimism of global labour studies" argues that the adoption of the Polanyian "double movement" hypothesis leads inevitably to an unfounded optimism around the prospects for labour successfully responding to neoliberal globalization. Apart from an unnecessary attack on the practitioners of the new global labour studies and a disabling pessimism that sees all resistance as futile, Burawoy does make a rational point. Burawoy argues that we first need to decide "where one sits in relation to [whether] exploitation [Marx] or commodification [Polanyi] [will] dictate the strategy one deploys in moving forward" (Burawoy 2010: 307). He argues that we can either promote transnational labour alliances or local alliances embracing all impacted by market-driven commodification. In reality, this binary opposition presents no such stark choice, workers make alliances across national borders and, often at the same time, broad social and community layers nationally are in pursuit of social movement unionism, as we have seen in the previous chapters.

There is, nonetheless, the somewhat inflated nature of the optimism/pessimism binary and a real problem with the way in which the new global labour studies (this author not excepted) builds general pictures of labour and globalization based on somewhat scarce empirical material. As Marissa Brookes and Jamie McCallum note in a review of the field, "[T]he labour as countermovement strand [of the new global labour studies] suffers from a tendency to assume that several individual instances of transnational action comprise a single global movement" (Brookes & McCallum 2017: 202). Many instances of cross-national organizing and international bargaining have actually ended in failure, something not usually noted in triumphalist accounts. There has been since 2000 a veritable explosion in concrete studies of transnational labour action, and they need to be integrated into the bigger picture of the Polanyian counter-movement thesis, to prove or disprove its assumptions. In short, a facile optimism is an inadequate answer to the debilitating pessimism of Burawoy.

Looking back at the 30 years or so since globalization made its entry into the social sciences as well as global politics, we can see how it has created as many opportunities for labour as it has caused problems or closed off traditional avenues for contestation. Peter Evans, among others, has stressed how

> globalization, both as generic shrinking of geographic and social space, and in the form of specific structures of the contemporary neoliberal capitalist political economy, stimulates and facilitates the mobilization of labour solidarity at the transnational level, as well as the construction of labour movement organizations and networks.   (Evans 2014: 356)

If capital can reinvent and revitalize itself, so can labour and its organizations, which should never be seen as static.

As to where we stand today, Antonio Gramsci – a labour activist and leader before he was a theorist – wrote in relation to the "modern crisis" of the 1930s that "the crisis consists precisely in the fact that the old is dying and the new cannot be born" (Gramsci 1971b: 276). The old ruling class had lost its consensus and was no longer leading nor hegemonic. Yet the new class – the workers – and their organizations were not ready to take power, even though "the great masses have become detached from their traditional ideologies, and they no longer believe what they used to believe previously" (Gramsci 1971b: 276). We can, I think, adapt his model to the situation since the 2007–9 crisis. Neoliberal capitalism is no longer hegemonic and does not convince or create consensus among the "great masses". As traditional labour ideologies, such as social democracy, are not convincing either, however, we do not as yet see a credible and sustainable option for transformation. As Gramsci said for the 1930s, this inevitably leads to an interregnum period, in which many irrational phenomena emerge (such as the election of Donald Trump and the Brexit referendum result).

We could simply say that the new globalized information-based capitalism will eventually create a new working class, and a new form of unionism will logically emerge. In practice, things are not so simple, and, while capitalism is one system, its replacement will not be born fully formed and its advance will be uneven across time and space. A networked society tends to produce a networked trade unionism. More democratic and participatory forms of work-place organization have emerged. Yet there are many national, sectoral and ideological differences still to be overcome. Nor do the "old" labour movement problems of routinization and bureaucratization simply disappear because cap-italism has changed in its forms of production. We need only think of the World Social Forum, which began with great promise as the new social movement response to globalization, but gradually became subsumed in the old politics and ways of doing politics. Many of the old problems that beset unions in the past – such as "organizing the unorganized" – are still there, despite the advent of the new model capitalism. To understand the prospects for a new unionism we need to take a long-term view.

To move beyond the impasse, we need to foreground a dialectical view of the capital/wage labour relation. The Italian *operaista* (poorly translated as "workerist") current of the late 1960s provided the most explicit articulation of this view, which brought into the modern era the Gramsci of the 1920s council movement (before he became the iconic Gramsci of the *Prison Notebooks*). Mario Tronti, whose *Operai e capitale* (Tronti 1966) had a huge influence in generating the autonomist discourse, argued that a

> new era in the class struggle is beginning. The workers have imposed it on the capitalists, through the violent reality of their organised strength in the factories. Capital's power appears to be stable and solid ... [T]he balance of forces appears to be weighed against the workers ... and yet precisely at the points where capital's power appears most dominant, we see how deeply it is penetrated by this menace, this threat of the working class. (Tronti 1966: 45)

That is to say, capital does not advance according to a self-referential pattern. Capital and capitalist development are constantly and profoundly shaped by workers' struggles. Thus, Marx showed how the advent of industrial machinery in Britain followed the workers' demand for a shorter working day.

Labour is for capital always a problematic "other" "that must constantly be controlled and subordinated and that, as persistently, circumvents or challenges this command" (Dyer-Witheford 1999: 65). Workers are not a passive result of capitalist development but exist at its very core, shaping its form and development. The working class is defined by its struggle against capital, but the reverse is also true. The inexorable logic of capital does not unfold according to its own ineluctable law, but in response to the reluctance of workers to allow full incorporation and subordination. We need to conceive of the capital/wage labour relation as the real engine of capitalist development. Capitalisms have always responded to strong labour movements through technological innovation, or through the shift of production to other locations. As capital always strives to reduce labour costs to enhance competitiveness and increase its level of control over the workplace, labour was, and still is, the "ghost in the machine". Silver (2013), in a broad analysis of the capital/wage labour relation through the ages, has referred to the above processes of automation and relocation as a "technological fix" and a "spatial fix" to its inherent contradictions.

Traditionally, the literature on industrial relations and labour history has tended to see technology as weakening labour. Yet deskilling (Braverman 1974) was never a linear process. The introduction of the assembly line actually led to an increase in workplace bargaining power. Current debates on new technology can also be cast in both a negative and a more positive light. Likewise, the "spatial fix" for capital – that is, outsourcing or moving to cheaper labour locations – is not always a simple win for capital. In fact, when capital relocates branches of production – for example, automobile production – in the Global South, it most often leads to an intensification of labour struggles by the "new" working classes brought *into* the capitalist system. Taking this analysis forward to the more concrete analysis that follows, I would emphasize "the recurrent making and *remaking* of working classes *across time and space* with the evolution of historical capitalism" (Silver 2013: 47).

The other strand of analysis we need to consider in order to break beyond the current impasse is a long-term view of labour's relation with *democracy*. For Gerald Friedman, "the labour movement began as a popular struggle for democracy" (Friedman 2008: 15), and, if it is to have any meaning today, it needs to renew that commitment. Labour – as a social category and as a social movement – basically advances a project for social, economic and political democracy. What the ideas of the French Revolution – *liberté, égalité, fraternité* – meant for the original labour movement, perhaps today the five principles of the global justice movement – monetary, social, economic, environmental and peace aspects of justice – could provide similar inspiration for labour. The success of the trade union and labour movement in the past was based on organization and solidarity to create a genuine community of interest. Turning away from spontaneity and grass-roots democracy led only to bureaucratization, demoralization and, ultimately, decline – because this is hardly a social movement that will attract new members. But if labour is a social movement (and that is, of course, debatable) then it has the capacity to renew and reinvent itself so as to meet the new challenges of the era.

What is often ignored, or at least downplayed, by North-centric accounts of labour is that the democratic mission of labour in the Global South often took the form of support for national liberation movements. Nationalism as a common denominator for all subaltern classes under conditions of colonialism or dependent capitalism is not something Northern socialists are comfortable with, understandably so after the First World War destroyed labour solidarity in Europe. But it is vital to recognize the role of labour in national liberation struggles and their ongoing interaction – sometimes symbiotic, sometimes more conflictual – with the national question and global inequality. In the struggles for independence in Asia, Africa and Latin America, labour movements have played an uneven, but always important, role. If national independence is seen as a democratic question – as in current-day Palestine – then the role of labour cannot be an indifferent one. And, of course, there are massive contradictions between a labour movement and a national liberation movement – as witnessed in post-apartheid South Africa, as the coalition that took the ANC to power was in many ways a loser in the era that followed – but the point is that they are socially and politically intertwined, not existing in separate silos.

So what might be the democratic tasks of the labour movement today? If we go back to the formative stage of the labour movement, we note a strong engagement with broader political issues of the day, centred on democratization. The workplace and the community were not seen as separate domains, and nor were economics and politics, distinct though they later became. Workers' organizations did not separate the employed from the unemployed or the native from the immigrant workers. As against the later tradition of craft unionism, the early labour organizers did not recognize divisions based on skill or race (gender was another matter, of course). This tradition of labour organizing, known variously as community unionism, social movement unionism and "deep organizing", has revived at various conjunctures, such as in the 1930s in the North, in the 1970s in the South and more recently across the board. What it points to, I would argue, is that the future of democracy is inextricably linked to the struggles of workers worldwide for a better life, which cannot be reduced to a narrow sectoral or corporatist interest group politics, if labour practises the unionism that it began with in its formative stage.

Workers struggling for democratization of the economic, political and social spheres are often accused by those claiming to represent the new social movements of focusing on redistribution rather than recognition. As Nancy Fraser has put it: "[T]he 'struggle for recognition' is fast becoming the paradigmatic form of political conflict in the late twentieth century" (Fraser 1995: 68). Gender, race and other forms of identity politics seem to trump a seemingly old-fashioned preoccupation with class. Certainly, orthodox Marxism was often blind to non-class forms of identity and was, more generally, culture-blind (see Munck 2015). Like other binary oppositions, however, this one can only weaken progressive alternatives by pitting one against the other. Clearly, struggles for recognition are set in a context of increasing social and economic inequality at a global level (see Therborn 2013). An alternative politics to that of the dominant order needs to articulate a range of interests and struggles from a critical cultural political economy approach that does not falsely counterpose cultural identity and material needs.

At this point it is worth making a methodological point that might also help us move beyond impasse thinking. What is somewhat noticeable in much left-wing thinking, in particular, is what we might call "necessitarianism" – basically, that things are how they are because they must be so. Brazilian political philosopher Roberto Unger has promoted an anti-necessitarian social theory to understand current social and political arrangements, without building indivisible categories and creating law-like explanations. Marxism has not been immune to this type of "false necessitarianism" despite the liberatory, more open stance of some of its strands. The leftist analysis of globalization and of neoliberalism also seems to suffer from this negative tendency towards seeing people as the object of a law-given fate (albeit not always, of course). While there are, certainly, structural constraints on people's actions – as Marx used to say, people "make their own history but under circumstances existing already" – we do need to bring to the fore human self-affirmation and, in particular, the ability of the working class to create its own future.

A positive proposal to move beyond this type of negative thinking comes from J. K. Gibson-Graham, in two landmark books (Gibson-Graham 1996; 2006), in which they seek to build a viable post-capitalist politics. Contrary to the view of capitalism as necessarily and naturally hegemonic, they foreground a space of economic difference in which a non-capitalist politics of the economy thrives. Where others see constraints, Gibson-Graham see possibilities, not least in relation to globalization, which, as argued above, opens as many doors as it closes for social transformation. The creation of a new political imaginary for labour and social transformation is not, of course, an easy task, but we can see signs of a politics of possibility in the here and now if we focus close enough with Gibson-Graham on:

- the role of place as a site for a global politics of local transformations;
- the uneven spatiality and negotiability of power through ethical practices of freedom; and

- the everyday temporality of change as continual struggle to transform the conditions of life despite difficulty and uncertainty (Gibson-Graham 2006: xxvii).

These are all issues that come into play in the day-to-day forging of alternative labour futures. Since the global crisis of 2007–9 many analysts – conservative and radical alike – have been asking whether we are now living in a post-neoliberal world. The answer probably depends on how we define neoliberalism. If we believe in a monolithic integrated and stable social-economic system called neoliberalism then it clearly is in crisis, in so far as it does not have total hegemony. If we adopt a dynamic conception of a process of neoliberalization, however, as Jamie Peck, Nik Theodore and Neil Brenner do, "then it follows that crises and contradictions will often impinge on particular social spaces, regulatory networks, sectoral fields, local formations, and so on, rather than necessarily reverberate through the unevenly developed complex as a whole" (Peck, Theodore & Brenner 2010: 101). Given that neoliberalism (or neoliberalization) is a process and not an end-state condition, it cannot fail in a big bang manner. But it is fraying at the edges and beginning to unravel, and its contradictions are coming to the surface.

To conclude this discussion of getting beyond the impasse, I want to revisit Karl Polanyi's intuition that history moves in a series of double movements, which clearly have an overwhelming impact on the capital/wage labour relation. In the first phase, the unregulated market expands, colonizes and commodifies the social world. In the second counter-movement, society, or groups within it, react to seize back some control and re-embed the market in society. What 2007–9 marked, if not the end of neoliberalism, was the end of the "easy" phase of the unregulated global market. For now it is Keynesianism and developmentalism that are back on the agenda, as the pendulum swings back to regulation. We see nationalizations (albeit emergency measures) having taken place, and even industrial policies are back in vogue. The labour movement, and other social groups within society, have begun to use this new space that has opened up to organize and seek to regain social control over market forces whenever and wherever possible.

A complexity frame

Complexity is a way of thinking beyond the certainties of modernism and Eurocentrism. In a world that is always "on the edge of chaos", it is the complexity frame that allows us to both understand the world and how it might be transformed. Essentially, as John Urry puts it, "complexity … repudiated the dichotomies of determinism and chance, as well as nature and society, being and becoming, stasis and change" (Urry 2003: 22). In the same way that physical systems are not characterized by unchanging structural stability, so the social system is always open to transformation.

Globalization emerged in the 1990s as a grand narrative. It was a vision as all-embracing as capitalism, colonialism or socialism. It proclaimed a new moment in history, a transition to a brave new world. For the liberal globalizers, the essence of the phenomenon in question was the free movement of goods, services, capital and labour "so that, economically speaking, there are no foreigners" (Wolf 2004: 14). They believed in "the magic of the market", which was not only the source of all material wealth but also the "absolute basis of freedom and democracy" (Wolf 2004: 57). For the opponents of globalization, it was an equally powerful and novel phenomenon, except that all its effects were seen as negative. It was an all-powerful, all-seeing machine, created in the corridors of power to promote a turbo-charged capitalism that would deny democracy to nations, peoples and communities. Globalization permeated all areas of life and seemed to cut off all possibilities for progressive social transformation.

If we are to pose a new problematic of "labour and globalization" we must consider what Urry refers to as "the limitations of many globalization analyses that deal insufficiently with the *complex* character of emergent global relations" (Urry 2003: 39, emphasis in original). Certainly, the globalization paradigm was correct in positing the new ways in which events in one part of the world impacted on other places that were remote in time and space. As Marx, Polanyi and others had foreseen, the world was bound to become more integrated as capitalism spread and brought all the workers of the world under its sway. These new global properties could not, however, explain totally what changes were occurring, except in a complexity science setting. Too often globalization was conceived in a linear fashion, part of the inevitable march of history, and was highly reductionist and simplifying in the way the "global" was seen as an all-powerful determinant of history and a block on progressive social transformation.

Complexity as a general frame and complex adaptive systems as a methodology for analysis have become widely accepted approaches in the analysis of development under late globalization. Complexity allows us to avoid the limitations of economic reductionism and those of structuralism in sociology. Complexity theory emphasizes the interaction between different elements of a social phenomenon. It places stress on the feedback loops that constantly change systems. My own analysis above of labour and globalization has consistently shown how interaction between capital and labour fed the development of capitalism. It has also shown the feedback loops that were generated when capital credited new sites of accumulation, which, in turn, created a new proletariat to confront it. Not only are structures complex and interaction dynamic but, also, we must bear in mind how organizations – be they the corporation or the trade union – adapt to their environments and cope with the permanent uncertainty of life under globalization.

At one level what I am proposing is hardly controversial. Few analysts would contest that "in the social world, and in much of reality including biological reality, causation is complex" (Byrne 1998: 20). Likewise, in many areas of policy implementation, there is an acceptance of the notion of "complex adaptive systems" (McEvoy, Brady & Munck 2016). We understand that trade unions – not to mention industrial relations systems – are characterized not by linearity and predictability but, rather, by interdependence, emergence (larger entities emerging through interaction) and an open "space of possibilities". What this approach has meant for new management theory has been a turn towards flatter, more flexible organizations and, at least in terms of rhetoric, a move beyond the command-and-control style of management. What a complexity (and complex adaptive systems) approach might mean for trade unions might also entail a move beyond top-down and bureaucratic forms of organization and a turn towards organizing as the *sine qua non* of progressive trade union practice (see McAlevey 2016).

A key element for a complexity lens to be applied to globalization and labour would be the new "politics of scale", which shows that the world is not, indeed, flat, as some of the early globalization gurus proclaimed. An understanding of how social life is constructed through social relations leads us to the concept of a "socio-spatial dialectic" (Soja 1980), in which both aspects are mutually constitutive of each other. Labour studies, labour history and industrial relations theory have all operated in a more or less a-spatial world in the past. Globalization accentuated this tendency, with its triumphalist proclamation of the "death of distance" because of time–space compression. In this new "borderless world" it seemed that geography was now irrelevant, and capital and labour were in quite different spheres: the first was hypermobile and fluid, the second was fixed firmly (at least on the whole) in places and was also "sticky" – that is, embedded in traditional social relations. In practice, the mobility of one (footloose and fancy-free capital) and the immobility of the other (this was the "era of migration", after all) were exaggerated, but the conceptual problem was a deeper one.

The spatial pattern of human activity is, of course, complex and cannot be reduced to a local-versus-global binary. There are national, subregional, supraregional and transnational levels in which both capital and labour operate. And it is not only the case that capital is global but also that labour has made links transnationally. These new social-spatial dynamics have created new forms of interconnections across scales of human activity and new geographies of social relations. Social relations have somehow been "stretched" by workers in different places making these connections. Capital, for its part, is not a completely free actor in this process, as we might believe from much of the literature on outsourcing. Scaling up the autonomist approach, which focuses on the capital/wage labour relation as the source of the dynamism in capitalist society, we might see how the relocation of production overseas often responds to the struggles of workers at home. We now have a complex landscape of different social and spatial scales that set the context for labour activity in the present world order.

By focusing on the spatial as well as the social complexity of capital/wage labour relations and contestation, we move beyond the paradigm of globalization as subject. The debates around the "political economy of scale" (Taylor 1982) and the underlying notion that "space is a social construct" (Lefebvre 1991 [1974]) have directed our attention towards the neglected spatial domain of labour formation and action. Social relations simply cannot be conceived adequately without understanding how they are grounded in particular places. Contending political projects all have a particular spatial vision, how they conceive the world and how they propose to impact on it. As we have seen, the forces of capital have deployed a range of "spatial fixes" to overcome their contradictions, from classical colonialism to modern outsourcing. Labour likewise has – or, at least, needs – its own, often quite different, spatial vision and its own politics of place. As Neil Smith once put it, somewhat cryptically, "[T]he scale of struggles and the struggle over scale are two sides of the same coin" (Smith 1990: 101).

While they may be in principle two sides of the same coin, in practice the social and the spatial readings of labour struggles are most often separate. In common usage it tended to be reduced to a global–local binary opposition. As Andrew Herod puts it, "[T]he global and the local each derive meaning from what they are not" (Herod 2011: 228). There is often an assumption that the global is all-powerful, only reinforced perhaps by contesting narratives around the need for local primacy in terms of production, consumption and politics. There is often a quite untenable counter-position between an abstract space and a concrete place. Although the "politics of scale" debates have added a new dimension to critical labour analysis, they have often assumed that these scales are out there, ready to be skipped (local to global, for example) and not socially constructed. In the years to come labour organizations may well become more conscious of how complex geographic scale is and how it relates to their forms of organization, be they vertical or more horizontal.

So, labour is both subject to complex pulls and pushes and operates on distinctive geographical or spatial scales. What does this mean for a diagnosis of labour's future? We could argue that there is now a need to bring together and synthesize the Polanyi and the spatial turns in order to shape a new transnational, trans-scalar labour studies discipline. In this regard, if we were to construct a basic social-spatial matrix to set our own narrative of labour's varied and multidimensional responses to globalization in context, it would look something like that shown in Figure 10.1. In this diamond diagram, the horizontal element sets up a basic Polanyian tension between labour organizations, which primarily represent workers in the labour market defending the price for their labour power (the left-hand side), and those labour organizations that are more socially embedded (the right-hand side) and take workers to be part of a broader society and community. Trade union strategies might thus be categorized in terms of whether they lean more towards market discipline or take social need as a priority. They are also pulled in different spatial ways, however, from the global (at the top) to the local (at the bottom), reflecting the different scales of human activity. Neither the Polanyian horizontal tension nor the scalar or vertical element can be seen as self-sufficient; rather, they act in a combined, if uneven, manner.

Certainly, the spatial dimension has always been with us, but it is probably fair to say that it has been insufficiently theorized. Anyone who has been involved in labour activities in the South and East must be conscious of geography, to put things at their most basic. Indeed, our own engagement with globalization at global regional, national and local levels has heightened this awareness. Nevertheless, we now need to bring to the fore, much more explicitly, the fact that labour relations and labour movements are always spatially specific. Our social place in society is also a geographical space. We must understand, however, that the vertical element in our diamond is not a ladder but a fluid network, or spider's web. This is significant, for, as Susan McGrath-Champ, Andrew Herod and Al Rainnie put it, in using the metaphor of a network or a spider's web rather than, say, that of a ladder to describe the relationship between the local and the global, "it is still possible to recognise that different scales exist ... but it is much more difficult to determine exactly where one scale ends and another begins" (McGrath-Champ, Herod & Rainnie 2010: 12).

Our rather basic diamond, then, might be taken as a set of force fields pulling labour organizations in various directions. These organizations are pulled in different spatial ways, from the global (at the top) to the local (at the bottom), reflecting the different scales of human activity. A holistic labour studies and labour strategy must, perforce, be fully cognizant of the complex combinations of the horizontal and vertical force fields. Hence, just as capital has always operated on the basis of "spatial fixes" (Harvey 2003) to deal with crises of profitability through geographical relocation, so does labour also need its own spatial strategy based on a strategic analysis of the politics of scale in the era of globalization.

Although it is purely illustrative, Figure 10.1 does allow us to operate some fairly basic distinctions. Starting at the bottom left quadrant, we can see how traditional US "business unionism" operates at a national level and orients almost exclusively to the market, where labour power is sold like any other commodity.

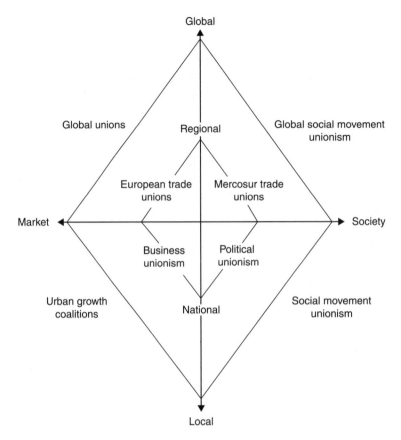

Figure C.1 Socio-spatial representation of labour's responses to globalization

In Latin America, on the other hand, in the bottom right quadrant, there has been a prevalence in the past of a "political unionism", also operating at nation state level but much more cognizant of labour as a political or state-oriented actor. Locally, unions can engage in the boosterism of urban growth coalitions or take on a more social movement unionism character, as we see in the inner quadrants of the diamond. At the global level, in the top left quadrant, the new global unions represent categories of workers as defined by their role in the production process, as prescribed by capital, and thus can be seen as market-oriented, as against the new global social movement unionism emerging in the South in particular (top right quadrant). Finally, there is the somewhat neglected in-between space of the regional, where we have rather staid organizations such as the ETUC (see Wills 2001), but also somewhat more socially oriented labour organizations, such as those contesting the Mercosur in the southern cone of Latin America. This heuristic device is not meant to reflect the real world of labour worldwide in any meaningful way but, rather, is designed as a tool to think through labour futures strategically, based on a complex mind map that has a strong social and spatial component.

This rough diamond diagram can assist us only if it is considered dynamically, with all its elements interacting. Thus, in terms of the politics of scale, workers and their organizations think and operate at local, national, regional and global scales concurrently. Trade unions may also make alliances – tactical or strategic – with community organizations and, even with employers' organizations when their interests align. Global unions may have a strong alliance with official organizations such as the ILO and the European Commission while also, at the same time, forging alliances with grass-roots coalitions in the Global South. Clearly, trade unions – like any other body – do not simply choose between a market and a society orientation; rather, they interact with a range of hybrid forms, which are pulled one way or the other at different times and in different places. This is a non-linear diamond, with organizations constantly adapting to changing situations. Just by way of example, I can mention, via Peter Evans, that "[a]ssessing the connections among national labour movements and the new global organizational infrastructure that has emerged under neoliberalism is a necessary foundation for building theories of labour's evolving contestation with global capital" (Evans 2014: 281). I would add only that the local and regional dimensions are equally important to this emerging complex scenario.

Furthermore, the diamond is far from static historically, and my locating of different union practices would need constant revision. Although here a US-style "business unionism" is an exemplar of a national-level pro-market labour strategy, that is not necessarily where we would place US unions today. When social movement studies were at their peak in the 1970s, the US labour movement was, indeed, a conservative and limiting organizational form. Since the mid-1990s trade unions in the United States have begun to share many of the characteristics of the social movements (Mann 2014). "Trade unions in the US continue to be locked into a bargaining situation that severely limits their freedom of action. Nevertheless they are always in motion," as Rick Fantasia and Judith Stepan-Norris (2004) note. Likewise, the regional associations of trade unions in Europe, South America (Mercosur) and elsewhere may change in composition and orientation over time. Their positioning *vis-à-vis* the market and society will evolve, not least if forced to do so by employer pressure and the impact of pro-market economic policies.

The notions of complexity and distinct spatial scales drive us inevitably, I would argue, to a focus on the future. Of course, social science is not a futurology and Marxism is not crystal ball gazing, but we do need to think about the future if we are ever to build a better world than the one we live in. Globalization, and all its attendant physical, economic, financial, social and cultural features, seeks to lock us securely into a pre-given distant future. Yet problems emerge that are not always amenable to simple or unproblematic solutions; consider the 2007–9 global crisis, for example. Urry makes a powerful call to democratize the future, which may be a "murky world", as he puts it, but "it is one that we have to enter, interrogate and hopefully reshape" (Urry 2016: 192). We need to reclaim a labour-oriented future with a social transformation mission distinct from the technological futures being put into place by vested interests as we speak.

To be future-oriented is also to be constantly examining the making and remaking of the working classes. If class is fluid then we cannot work with a static analysis. Labour history is replete with myths about this or that group of workers, this or that militant union, but the fact is that the world of workers is constantly shifting, being remade and reimagined. Michael Hardt and Antonio Negri, in *Commonwealth* (2009), carry out an interesting analysis of the Bolivian labour movement and the replacement of the once hegemonic miners by other factions of the working classes. In 1952 there was a national revolution in Bolivia, led by the miners and the peasants, that created a myth (in the Sorelian sense) of working-class power. In 2001 Bolivia once again witnessed a formidable insurgency, the so-called Water Wars, when the indigenous communities of Cochabamba successfully resisted the privatization of water. This time, though, there was no phalanx of marching miners in tin hats carrying sticks of dynamite, as had been the case in 1952. Any mythical connection between 1952 and 2001 was denied by the dramatic deconstruction of the Bolivia working class under neoliberalism in the 1980s and 1990s.

Bolivia, like the rest of Latin America, was, and is, a country where temporalities are mixed – the past is the present is the future – and society takes on a motley or variegated character (in local terms, it is a *sociedad abigarrada*). In the 1980s and early 1990s many of the mines – in what was an economy based on mining – closed and the Bolivian miners lost their central role in national politics. Miners became coca cultivators or small-scale producers or were simply cast into a world of migration and joblessness. As with other working classes, the Bolivian working class became more flexible and mobile as it lost its centre. Miners could no longer – like autoworkers or steelworkers elsewhere – represent hegemonically the broader working class through vertical structures. But, crucially, as Hardt and Negri stress, "this shift … signals no farewell to the working class or even a decline in worker struggles, but rather an increasing multiplicity of the proletariat and a new physiognomy of struggle" (Hardt & Negri 2009: 110). In this new, more multitudinous array of working classes no single sector can provide hegemony, and horizontal, as against vertical, forms of organization emerge, which are more fitted to the networked society of the global era.

Finally, I think a complexity lens helps us steer clear of universal truths – regarding labour's decline as a social movement, for example. It is common to hear that union density worldwide today is below 10 per cent, so therefore organized labour is unlikely to have a future as an effective counter to the new capitalism. We can build a whole edifice of labour co-option through consumerism, labour division through precarization and union incorporation through bureaucratization. But, first, in a world characterized by uneven development, we cannot take a so-called global trend (such as union density) as one that determines the future of a very complex movement across all regions. Nor can we ever confuse trends with an overall situation; there are always counter-trends, new factors enter into the equation, and uneven development, as always, means that complexity prevails. We might also add that academic disciplines are slow to change and tend to maintain paradigms for quite some time after the world around them has moved on.

Is another world possible?

To pose this question is really to ask whether there is a credible alternative to the dominance of neoliberalism, globalization and the subordination of labour. In the preceding chapters, I have detailed how labour's relationship to capitalism has evolved and responded at different times and in different places, and that there are as many varieties of labour as there are capitalisms. The emergence of a global working class presents an opportunity for a renewal of labour as a social movement. So, one answer to this question is to say that the future is already with us.

Google and Facebook are the harbingers of a post-neoliberal future that is already being born in the midst of capitalism, at least in the advanced industrial societies, and that transition is already under way to a different kind of system of production. Paul Mason argues that "capitalism is a complex, adaptive system which has reached the limits of its capacity to adapt" (Mason 2015: xiii). The problem lies in the second half of this sentence: has capitalism really reached the limits of its capacity to reinvent itself? Technology has created, for Mason, the possibility that capitalism can supersede itself, creating a more dynamic system from within the old system. Karl Marx himself (in the *Grundrisse*) once presented such a scenario, in which the use of machines and knowledge begins to liberate humans from work and create the possibility for social development on a massive scale (see Pitts 2017). This would seem to be just an example of wishful thinking, not reflected in any real tendencies observable in global capitalism and its relation to the workers of the world. It simply forgets another lesson of Marx, namely that capital is an antagonistic social relationship that it cannot simply slip out of.

I do not think that utopian visions around the future of work can (or should) be countered by dystopian visions of mass unemployment and the exponential increase of the precariat. The impact of automation in specific industries and jobs is well understood but does not adequately counter the utopian vision of post-capitalism. As Ursula Huws notes in relation to the future of work, "Both forecasts tend to be based on a somewhat blinkered vision, in which the known landscape of labour is assumed to be constant, with changes taking place only within its currently visible borders" (Huws 2017). Not least, they both assume that the current gendered division of labour and the household economy will remain static. The zero-sum logic in relation to jobs – and the analysis of North–South relations – shows little cognizance of the complex and integrated nature of the world today. Again, for an emancipatory project to be (re)invented or (re)imagined we would need to have a more open engagement with alternative social futures and their prefiguration in today's world.

Another possible answer to the question of whether another world is possible is to say "Yes" if the forces of reform triumph over the forces of reaction. At the core of the reform strategy of the international labour movement in its official guise is the "Decent work" campaign sponsored by all the major international economic, political and social bodies. No one working with labour organizers in the majority world (or anywhere, for that matter) would wish to prevent mean-ingful reform of work practices and would support any campaign for the right to organize. The issue would be twofold. (1) Is the campaign for decent work well structured, adequately resourced and likely to deliver tangible benefits for workers on the ground? (2) Is this the most productive use of labour movements resources (both in terms of personnel and funding) compared, for example, to a dynamic campaign to organize the unorganized? While I am sceptical on both counts I would really welcome an open debate on these questions.

To be clear, I am not saying the "Decent work" campaign is wrong because it is 'reformist'. There are good reasons why market regulation and human devel-opment have gathered widespread support in the field of international develop-ment, for example. Reforms that are winnable create a dynamic for social and political transformation that can be very positive. To articulate Keynesian or redistributive policies rather than the "abolition" of capitalism is entirely positive (and sensible) from a labour perspective. The problem arises, as I see it, when a reformist strategy refuses any broader horizons of possibilities. Then we see that, in practice, even reformist objectives are not feasible. If we never question the fundamental tenets of capitalism as an economic and political order, we will never be able to envisage even the possibility of a post-capitalist scenario. Without a unifying vision of what that might entail – we can call it a utopia, per-haps – it will be hard to mobilize and incentivize people to seek a better future.

The appeal (or strength) of reformism is clear, according to Ash Amin and Nigel Thrift, namely the difficulty of finding an alternative on account of "the all-encompassing nature of modern capitalism, which means it is very difficult to locate an outside to the system from which it is possible to build a standpoint" (Amin & Thrift 2013: 831). I would argue that this all-encompassing nature of capitalism is something of an illusion and that this analysis suffers from the false necessitarianism shared by much of the Left today. The monolithic and homogeneous nature of capitalism and the restricted political options it allows for are, to some extent, a myth of the Left. With J. K. Gibson-Graham, we might begin to see this "capitalism not as our 'reality' but as a fantasy of wholeness, one that operates to obscure diversity and disunity in the economy and society alike" (Gibson-Graham 1996: 260). A new emancipatory project for labour as a social movement would need to leave behind all "totalitarian" and unified illusion about capitalism.

Since 2000 there has been a growing sense that "another world is possible", after the gloomy 1990s slogan "There is no alternative", which was not just a neoliberal slogan but a real reflection of the zeitgeist of the era. It was not only the anti-capitalist movements congregated at the World Social Forum that (predictably) articulated this feeling but wider layers of the political spectrum, especially following the global crisis of 2007–9. There was a widespread feeling that "business as usual" was no longer a viable option for global capitalism. Paradigms do not disappear after one or two knocks, however. For example, the Washington Consensus of the 1980s seamlessly transitioned into the post-Washington Consensus of the 1990s. But the continued crisis of the 2000s finally broke the hold of messianic or fundamentalist neoliberalism. Not surprisingly, in this partial ideological vacuum, we saw the re-emergence of Keynes and Marx; in addition, though, the (once seen as wild) ideas of the counter- and alter-globalization movements entered the mainstream – or, at least, were taken seriously.

In considering the debates around globalization and its contestation since the protests in Seattle in 1999, we might start by questioning a hierarchy of strategies that assigns some special quality to action from below. Globalization itself would appear to be multifaceted and complex, even to some extent dissolving traditional conceptions of levels in society and political processes. So, why would labour, for example, prioritize actions from below? An intervention from above, say, in relation to the WTO, can sit easily with a grass-roots labour-environmentalist campaign, for example, against the Rio Tinto Zinc Corporation. In between, the national level would continue to be important in terms of dictating the level of the social wage, for example. Nor can we neglect the city as a framework for much labour activity, and there are also vital regional and subregional repertoires of labour activity. These facets of labour action may combine in different ways, and their interrelationship may not always be harmonious. But to assert a debilitating binary opposition – globalization "from below" versus globalization "from above" – does not seem to be a credible basis for a transformative labour politics in the twenty-first century.

An underlying, not always explicit, assumption in the globalization-from-below arguments is that the key actors will be the new social movements around environmental, gender and peace issues (see, for example, Brecher, Costello & Smith 2000), and that they are open in their belief that "[g]lobalization in all its facets presents new problems that the old [social] movements failed to address. That is part of why they declined so rapidly" (Brecher, Costello & Smith 2000: 17). The new social movements are seen to represent a qualitatively different form of transformative politics and, in embryo, a new societal paradigm. They stress their autonomy from party politics and prioritize civil society over the state. Power itself is redefined, not as something to be seized but as a diffused and plural element woven into the very fabric of society. We should not draw too stark a counter-position, however, between bad/old social movements and good/new ones. While a certain type of trade union and labour politics may well be defunct, the workers' movement has been at the forefront of many new movements for change. Nor have the new social movements, such as the environmental campaign, escaped the problems of routinization and bureaucratization, which have bedevilled the labour movements at certain points.

For me, the basic dispute underlying the post-Seattle globalization debates is, in fact, the very "old" one between reform and revolution as strategies for social transformation. The revolutionary strategy suffers from necessitarianism and is usually based on a deep structure social theory that "treats the formative institutional and imaginative frameworks of social life as indivisible units, each of which stands or falls as a piece" (Unger 1998: 83). The political approach, taken by a positivist social theory, will, instead, advocate incremental social reform. What Unger advocates from a radical anti-necessitarian theoretical perspective is a strategy of radical reform as a type of transformative politics, in which "[r]eform is radical when it addresses and changes the basic arrangements of a society: its formative structure of institutions and enacted beliefs" (Unger 1998: 18–19). A radical reform perspective might allow us to reimagine the presuppositions that are made about globalization and the possible role people may play in constructing a different, more democratic future. Better than an all-or-nothing perspective – reflected in the "Fix it or nix it" slogan from Seattle 1999 – the revolutionary reform political outlook refuses binary oppositions and opens up exciting vistas of social transformation.

The stability of global governance is now contested in a whole series of different ways. International organizations – and the World Bank is a particular case in point – are not the monoliths they were once thought to be, or, at least, that they were portrayed as being by radical critics. Over the past 20 years international organizations of capitalism have increasingly engaged with global social movements and shown a certain permeability. Governance is moving away from an exclusively state-based mode of operation to embrace elements of civil society. The study by Richard O'Brien, Anne Goetz, Jan Scholte and Marc Williams of multilateral economic institutions and global social movements goes so far as to argue that we are witnessing a "transformation in the nature of governance" (O'Brien *et al.* 2000: 206) at a global level because of the encounter. This complex multilateralism that they identify should not be confused with some naïve unilinear move towards the democratization of global governance. Indeed, much of the dialogue with civil society on the part of these international organizations is motivated by a desire to neutralize or co-opt social and democratic opposition to their hegemonic aspirations. It is just as well to recognize that contradictions are opening up and not just assume that globalism has already won the day, especially after the deep shock to the system caused by the 2007–9 global financial crisis.

A few years ago even referring to post-capitalism would have seemed somewhat eccentric or deem one a reality denier. Yet, since the 2007–9 crisis, a wide layer of commentators refer to the system we live under as capitalism (beforehand it was not named, so obvious was its normality), and think about alternatives. Thus, for Wolfgang Streeck, a German political economist, the "end of capitalism" is now "already under way", even though an alternative cannot yet be discerned on the horizon (Streeck 2014: 47). The decline in secular growth rates in the North, the steady increases in government debt and the steady rise in wealth and income inequality all add up to a terminal crisis for the system, in the sense that there is no technological or spatial "fix" that can take it to a new level. For his part, Paul Mason offers a clear diagnosis of our crisis-prone future from a Northern perspective that argues that we are already living in a post-capitalist era. These, and other, analysts take us back to Marx and Engels, who wrote: "Communism is for us not a *state of affairs* which is to be established, an *ideal* to which reality will have to adjust itself [but] a *real* movement which abolishes the present state of things" (Marx & Engels 1976 [1848]: 49).

What we might note, in the post-capitalist discourse, is a placement of the debate within the most advanced capitalist countries. The model they are opposing is the classical Marxist scenario of the working class gathering force and, either through the ballot box or the barricades, using the levers of the state to replace the market by a more rational social mode of allocating resources. A new dynamic is now seen to be taking shape, much as capitalism once began to sprout roots and gradually grew within the old feudal mode of production. For Mason, there are three ways in which the new technology has impacted upon society in the last quarter of a century, signalling the emergence of a new *post-capitalist mode of production*: (1) ICTs have blurred the relationship between work and free time; (2) the goods produced by ICTs corrode the ability of the market to set prices and lead to unstable monopolies (e.g. Google); and (3) we see the rise of collaborative production outside the remit of the market and managerial control (e.g. Wikipedia) (Mason 2015: xv). Almost unnoticed, we are moving into a post-capitalist order – or are we?

The problem, of course, is that most workers worldwide are not living under conditions of advanced information-based networked capitalism. They are, rather, barely carving out a living, on the fringes of the system. A genuine "politics of possibility" for the present era would have to take cognizance of all those who have been cast aside by the system and deemed marginal and who do not even have a role as consumers keeping the system ticking over. In these parts of the world, it is not Karl Marx who has resonance but, rather, Karl Polanyi. From a Polanyian perspective, we need to look backwards to see what the future might hold. The self-sufficient, pre-capitalist peasant household was not regulated by the market but, rather, by a moral order. Economic relations, then and since, have always been submerged within social relations that are at the core of human existence. Even today, at the height of globalization, as a free market capitalist order, this development matrix coexists with many spheres of social life, such as the household, that are not subordinated to the logic of the market. Post-capitalism will emerge only when it comes to grips with pre-capitalism, we might say.

To get a more localized or complex understanding of how the intertwined futures of capitalism and anti-capitalism could play out, we might examine the 2000s, the "decade of the Left" in Latin America, from a labour perspective. The labour movement had played a major role – alongside other social movements such as the human rights and women's movements – in creating the conditions for the return of democracy. In strike actions, support for human rights organizations, go-slows and general social resistance the labour movement played a significant part in preventing the consolidation of authoritarian rule, as happened in Franco's Spain in the 1930s. If the military dictatorships had been able to dismantle trade union organization – as against just decapitating its leadership – then the outcome for democracy might have been very different. Although the neoliberal period – under both military and, later, civilian rule – decimated the working class, it was able to recompose itself and began to play a role – alongside peasant and indigenous movements in particular – in bringing to power left-wing governments after 2000 across most of the continent, with the exception of Mexico and Colombia.

The trade union movement also played a major transnational role during this period as the impact of globalization worked itself out in Latin America, as the continent became part of the broader alter-globalization movement, following the Zapatista rebellion of 1994. The Hemispheric Social Alliance (HSA) brought together trade union and civil society organizations across the Americas and had considerable success. It was formed, in the first instance, to share information, but then broadened out to develop joint strategies and transnational actions. The HSA was a conspicuous success in terms of blocking the Free Trade Area of the

Americas imperial project and went on to promote alternative democratic and labour-based models for hemispheric integration. The trade unions also played a significant – if uneven – role in the World Social Forum, which originated in Porto Alegre. While at first there was a considerable distance between the alter-globalization activists – often from the environmental or women's movement – over time the trade unions (both Latin American and global) became an integral part of the broad social and political alliance that the WSF became.

I must also stress the role of the labour movement in relation to the issue of informal work, bearing in mind that, in the 1990s, nine out of ten jobs in Latin America were in the informal sector. Across Latin America there are many examples of the left turn impacting on the tendency towards informalization and precarization. To "organize the unorganized" has always been a challenge for the trade union movement, as these workers are less accessible, and they do not fit into standard industrial relations bargaining structures. It is not always clear who the bargaining counterpart is when neither the state nor the capitalist employer is present. Yet the unions recognize that they need to reach beyond the standard workplace if the working classes are to exercise their full potential power. Thus, in 1992, the powerful Central Única dos Trabalhadores in Brazil sponsored the formation of the Sindicato dos Trabalhadores da Economía Informal (SINTEIN), which took up issues around microcredit and entrepreneur support with the Ministry of Labour Solidarity Economy Board. It also promoted the formation of co-operatives, which would strengthen the sector in bargaining with wholesale dealers. A wide range of organizations – some more durable than others – have been formed by informal workers and street traders in Brazil and elsewhere.

So, where does this leave us in terms of answering the question of whether "another world is possible" from a transformative labour perspective? The first point to make is that globalization has fundamentally altered the terrain of labour struggles. The organizational forms, political thinking and even cultural references of the 1950s are simply inadequate for the present situation, not least because they all assume the nation state to be a self-sufficient framework for action. The workers of the world today exist in a global context, not just an international one. Capitalism reformed itself as globalization precisely to meet the challenges posed by labour in the 1970s and 1980s. What is most noticeable today is how discrete labour struggles so rapidly become global. As Hardt and Negri argue in *Empire*, "Each struggle, though firmly rooted in local conditions, *leaps immediately to the global level* and attacks the imperial constitution in its generality" (Hardt & Negri 2000: 56, emphasis added). These new struggles, which are always already global, can be economic, political, social or cultural, and they articulate a new conception of life beyond commodification and show, in practice, that another world is possible.

In political terms, there is a pressing need to move "beyond the fragments" – a term previously deployed by feminists seeking to create a new political methodology in the 1970s (Rowbotham, Segal & Wainwright 1979). Against the political sectarianism of that era, it created a vision of citizens forming horizontal connections across civil society, across politics and across economics. Since then the "old" politics of class and the "new" politics of identity have become more polarized. For the latter, the whole language of class is an anachronism. For the proponents of class, such as David Harvey, only the working class can create the dynamic for social transformation to a new order based on socialism. We could also argue, with people such as Hardt and Negri, that the new social movements are but different aspects of the struggle against capitalism, still part of labour's DNA, whether it wants it or not. The new struggles and the new subjectivities are thus not to be seen as somehow antagonistic to, or a negation of, working-class struggles. In fact, what globalization has created is a huge blossoming of new contradictions and struggles, all pointing towards the need for a society not based on exploitation and oppression.

Finally, in terms of strategy, the outcome will depend on the ongoing debates across the labour movement and its others. We can put forward, however, the provisional framework of a new "global social movement unionism", defined by Kim Moody 20 years ago as "a perspective that can maximise working-class power by drawing together the different sectors within the class ... a perspective that embraces the diversity of the working class in order to overcome its fragmentation" (Moody 1997: 290). A simple model would posit economic unionism as one focused on labour in the market, a political unionism centred on labour and the state, and a social unionism that conceived of labour as offering a social alternative to the global order. The social movement unionism of the 1970s and the "community unionism" of the 2000s were distinguishable by their complex understanding of workers as not being restricted to the workplace but part of communities, both social and spatial. This tendency within global unionism is unevenly developed at present and it is subject to setbacks, as much when it wins (leading to co-option) as when it loses. But it does not only take us "beyond the fragments"; it also takes us back to the era when labour took shape as a social movement, which may well be the future ahead of us.

For a global labour movement to develop and to represent the emerging global working class it would have to do two things: first, it would need to forge more egalitarian alliances and articulate its programme with other social movements, such as those around global justice, sustainable development and gender equity; second, its international strategy would need to break with traditional corporatist trade union strategies and seek more imaginative and creative ways of working. The old way of doing business is now clearly not sufficient even to maintain the gains of the past, let alone to move things onto another plane. There is an opportunity provided by the worldwide extension of capitalism and levelling of conditions of workers everywhere. There is an extreme concentration of wealth in the top 1 per cent to a degree that even Marx would not have envisaged. The history of labour is rich with examples of struggle and innovation. We have seen advances in terms of social movement unionism since the turn of the century, albeit geographically limited and with considerable defeats and retreats. Now is the time for a major leap forward, not least in the imaginary of labour, to promote democracy in the workplace and across society. This is necessary not only for the workers of the world but for everybody, living as we are in a highly unstable, unequal and clearly unsustainable world.

REFERENCES

Adams, R. 2008. "From Statutory Right to Human Right: The Evolution and Current Status of Collective Bargaining". *Just Labour: A Canadian Journal of Work and Society* 12: 48–67.

AFL–CIO 2001. "Remarks by AFL–CIO President John J. Sweeney, World Economic Forum, Davos, Switzerland", 28 January.

Aglietta, M. 1979. *A Theory of Capitalist Regulation: The US Experience*. London: Verso Books.

Aglietta, M. 1998. "Capitalism at the Turn of the Century: Regulation Theory and the Challenge of Social Change". *New Left Review* 232: 41–90.

Agnew, J. & S. Corbridge 1995. *Mastering Space: Hegemony, Territory and International Political Economy*. London: Routledge.

Althusser, L. 1971. "Ideology and Ideological State Apparatuses (Notes towards an Investigation)". In *Lenin and Philosophy and Other Essays*, L. Althusser, 85–126. London: Verso Books.

Altvater, E. 1992. "Fordist and Post-Fordist International Division of Labor and Monetary Regimes". In *Pathways to Industrialization and Regional Development*, M. Storper & A. Scott (eds), 19–41. London: Routledge.

Alvarez, S., E. Dagnino & A. Escobar (eds) 1998. *Cultures of Politics/Politics of Cultures: Re-visioning Latin American Social Movements*. Boulder, CO: Westview Press.

Amin, A. 1997. "Placing Globalization". *Theory, Culture and Society* 14 (2): 123–37.

Amin, A. & N. Thrift 2013. *Arts of the Political: New Openings on the Left*. Durham, NC: Duke University Press

Anderson, L. & B. Trentin 1996. *Trabajo, derechos y sindicato en el mundo*. Caracas: Nueva Sociedad.

Anner, M. 2011. *Solidarity Transformed: Labor Responses to Globalization and Crisis in Latin America*. Ithaca, NY: Cornell University Press.

Antunes, R. (ed.) 1980. *Por un novo sindicalismo*. São Paulo: Brasiliense.

Armstrong, P., A. Glyn & J. Harrison 1984. *Capitalism since 1945*. London: Methuen.

Arrighi, G. 1990. "Marxist Century, American Century: The Making and Remaking of the World Labour Movements". *New Left Review* 179: 29–63.

Arrighi, G. 1996. "Workers of the World at Century's End". *Review* 19 (3): 335–51.

Arrighi, G., N. Aschoff & B. Scully 2010. "Accumulation by Dispossession and Its Limits: The Southern African Paradigm Revisited". *Studies in Comparative International Development* 45 (4): 410–38.

Bales, K. 2005. *Disposable People: New Slavery in the Global Economy*. Los Angeles, CA: University of California Press.

Barbier, J.-C. 2002. "A Survey of the Use of the Term Précarité in French Economics and Sociology", Working Paper 19. Paris: Centre d'études de l'emploi.

Barchiesi, F. 2012. "Precarity as Capture: An Exercise in Conceptual Genealogy". Mimeo, Johannesburg.

Barratt Brown, M. 1974. *The Economics of Imperialism*. London: Penguin Books.

Bauder, H. 2006. *Labor Movement: How Migration Regulates Labor Markets*. New York: Oxford University Press.

Beandet, P. 2016. "The World Social Forum at the Crossroads". Systemic Alternatives, 8 June. https://systemicalternatives.org/2016/06/08/the-world-social-forum-at-the-crossroads/ (accessed 26 March 2018).

Bendiner, B. 1977. "World Automotive Councils: A Union Response to Transnational Bargaining". In *Multinationals, Unions and Labor Relations in Industrialized Countries*, R. Banks & J. Stieber (eds), 186–91. Ithaca, NY: Cornell University Press.

Berger, S. & R. Dore (eds) 1996. *National Diversity and Global Capitalism*. Ithaca, NY: Cornell University Press.

Bienefeld, M. 1993. "Capitalism and the Nation State in the Dog Days of the Twentieth Century". In *Between Globalism and Nationalism: Socialist Register 1994*, R. Miliband & L. Panitch (eds), 94–129. London: Merlin Press.

Blackburn, R. 2011. "Crisis 2.0". *New Left Review* 72: 33–62.

Blecher, M. 2010. "Globalization, Structural Reform, and Labour Politics in China". *Global Labour Journal* 1 (1): 92–111.

Blyton, P., M. Lucio, J. McGurk & P. Turnbull 1998. *Contesting Globalisation: Airline Restructuring, Labour Flexibility and Trade Union Strategies*. London: International Transport Workers' Federation.

Bourdieu, P. 2003 [1998]. *Against the Tyranny of the Market*, vol. 2: *Firing Back*. London: Verso Books.

Boyer, R. 1988. "Defensive or Offensive Flexibility?". In *The Search for Labour Market Flexibility*, R. Boyer (ed.), 222–51. Oxford: Clarendon Press.

Boyer, R. 1995. "Capital–Labour Relations in OECD Countries: From the Fordist Golden Age to Contrasted National Trajectories". In *Capital, the State and Labour: A Global Perspective*, J. Schor & J.-I. You (eds), 18–69. Cheltenham: Edward Elgar.

Boyer, R. 2000. "Is a Finance Growth Regime a Viable Alternative to Fordism?". *Economy and Society* 29 (1): 111–45.

Boyer, R. & J. R. Hollingsworth 1996. "From National Embeddedness to Spatial and Institutional Nestedness". In *Contemporary Capitalism: The Embeddedness of Institutions*, J. Hollingsworth & R. Boyer (eds), 449–52. Cambridge: Cambridge University Press.

Braverman, H. 1974. *Labor and Monopoly Capital: The Degradation of Work in the Twentieth Century*. New York: Monthly Review Press.

Brecher, J., T. Costello & B. Smith 2000. *Globalization from Below: The Power of Solidarity*. Cambridge, MA: South End Press.

Breitenfellner, A. 1997. "Global Unionism: A Potential Player". *International Labour Review* 136 (4): 531–54.

Breman, J. 2009. "Myth of the Global Safety Net". *New Left Review* 59: 29–36.

Breman, J. 2013. "The Precariat: A Bogus Concept". *New Left Review* 84: 130–8.

Brenner, R. 1998. "The Economics of Global Turbulence". *New Left Review* 229: 1–264.

Brookes, M. & J. McCallum 2017. "The New Global Labour Studies: A Critical Review". *Global Labour Journal* 8 (3): 201–18.

Bruce, I. 2004. *The Porto Alegre Alternative: Direct Democracy in Action*. London: Pluto Press.

Bryant, C. 1994. "Economic Utopianism and Sociological Realism: Strategies for Transformation in East-Central Europe". In *The New Great Transformation? Change and Continuity in East-Central Europe*, C. Bryant & E. Mokrzycki (eds), 58–77. London: Routledge.

Buketov, K. 1999. "The Russian Trade Unions: From Chaos to a New Paradigm". In *Labour Worldwide in the Era of Globalization*, R. Munck & P. Waterman (eds), 97–106. London: Macmillan.

Burawoy, M. 2010. "From Polanyi to Pollyanna: The False Optimism of Global Labor Studies". *Global Labour Journal* 1 (2): 301–13.

Burawoy, M. & J. Lukács 1992. *The Radiant Past: Ideology and Reality in Hungary's Road to Capitalism*. Chicago, IL: University of Chicago Press.

Burgmann, V. 2016. *Globalization and Labour in the Twenty-First Century*. Abingdon: Routledge.

Byrne, D. 1998. *Complexity Theory and the Social Sciences: An Introduction*. London: Routledge.

Cardoso, F. H. 1971. "Comentarios sobre os conceitos de superpopulação relativa e marginalidade". *Estudos CEBRAP* 1: 99–130.

Caruso, G. 2005. "Report on the World Social Forum at Mumbai". Sign of Our Times. www.signofourtimes. org/UK/WSF/html (accessed 8 February 2005).

Cassen, B. 2003. "On the Attack". *New Left Review* 19: 41–60.

Castel, R. 1995. *Les métamorphoses de la question sociale: une chronique du salariat*. Paris: Fayard.

Castells, M. 1996. *The Information Age*, vol. 1: *The Rise of the Network Society*. Oxford: Blackwell.

Castells, M. 1997. *The Information Age*, vol. 2: *The Power of Identity*. Oxford: Blackwell.

Castells, M. 1998. *The Information Age*, vol. 3: *End of Millennium*. Oxford: Blackwell.

Castells, M. & A. Portes 1989. "World Underneath: The Origins, Dynamics and Effects of the Informal Economy". In *The Informal Economy: Studies in Advanced and Less Developed Countries*, A. Portes, M. Castells & L. Benton (eds), 11–37. Baltimore, MA: Johns Hopkins University Press.

Castles, S. 2000. "International Migration at the Beginning of the Twenty-First Century: Global Trends and Issues". *International Social Science Journal* 52 (3): 269–81.

Castles, S. & G. Kosack 1973. *Immigrant Workers and Class Structure in Western Europe*. Oxford: Oxford University Press.

Chan, C. K. C., P. Ngai & J. Chan 2010. "The Role of the State, Labour Policy and Workers' Struggles in Globalized China". *Global Labour Journal* 1 (1): 132–51.

Chesnais, F. 1997. *La mondialisation du capital*. Paris: Syros.

Chhachhi, A. & R. Pittin 1996. "Introduction". In *Confronting State, Capital and Patriarchy: Women Organizing in the Process of Industrialization*, A. Chhachhi & R. Pittin (eds), 1–32. London: Macmillan.

Clarke, S. 1992. "Privatization and the Development of Capitalism in Russia". *New Left Review* 196: 3–28.

CLASS 2018. *Labour Market Realities 2018: Workers on the Brink*. London: Centre for Labour and Social Studies. http://classonline.org.uk/docs/Labour_Market_Realities_Workers_on_the_Brink_final_3.pdf (accessed 30 May 2018).

Clawson, D. 2003. *The Next Upsurge: Labor and the New Social Movements*. Ithaca, NY: ILR Press.

Coates, D. 2000. *Models of Capitalism: Growth and Stagnation in the Modern Era*. Cambridge: Polity Press.

Cohen, R. 1991. *Contested Domains: Debates in International Labour Studies*. London: Zed Books.

Coriat, B. 1992. "The Revitalization of Mass Production in the Computer Age". In *Pathways to Industrialization and Regional Development*, M. Storper & A. Scott (eds), 121–39. London: Routledge.

Cotton, E. 2013. "The Catastrophe of Precarious Work: Elizabeth Cotton Challenges Guy Standing". Public World: Democracy at Work, 21 February. www.publicworld.org/blog/the_catastrophe_of_precarious_work_elizabeth_cotton_challenges_guy_standing (accessed 29 February 2016).

Cox, R. 1996. *Approaches to World Order*. Cambridge: Cambridge University Press.

Crouch, C. & W. Streeck (eds) 1997. *Political Economy of Modern Capitalism: Mapping Convergence and Diversity*. London: Sage.

Croucher, R. & E. Cotton 2009. *Global Unions, Global Business: Global Union Federations and International Business*. London: Middlesex University Press.

Cusumano, M. 1992. "Japanese Technology Management: Innovations, Transferability, and the Limitations of 'Lean' Production", Working Paper 3477–92. Cambridge, MA: Sloan School of Management, Massachusetts Institute of Technology.

David, N. 2002. "Migrants Get Unions Back to Basics". *Labour Education* 129: 71–5.

Davis, M. 2006. *Planet of Slums*. London: Verso Books.

Davis, M. 2011. "Spring Confronts Winter". *New Left Review* 72: 5–15.

De Haas, H. 2007. "Turning the Tide? Why Development Will Not Stop Migration". *Development and Change* 38 (5): 819–41.

De la Rocha, M., E. Jelin, J. Perlman, B. Roberts, H. Safa & P. Ward 2004. "From the Marginality of the 1960s to the 'New Poverty' of Today". *Latin American Research Review* 39 (1): 183–203.

De Oliveira, F. 1972. "A econômia Brasileira: crítica a razão dualista". *Estudos CEBRAP* 2: 4–70.

De Soto, H. 1986. *El otro sendero: la revolución informal*. Lima: El Barranco.

De Sousa Santos, B. 2014. *Epistemologies of the South: Justice against Epistemicide*. London: Paradigm.

Delgado Wise, R. & H. Covarrubias 2009. "Understanding the Relationship between Migration and Development: Toward a New Theoretical Approach". *Social Analysis* 53 (3): 85–105.

DeMartino, G. 1991. "Trade-Union Isolation and the Catechism of the Left". *Rethinking Marxism* 4 (3): 29–51.

Drache, D. 1999. "Globalization: Is There Anything to Fear?", Working Paper 23. Warwick: Centre for the Study of Globalisation and Regionalisation, University of Warwick.

Dyer-Witheford, N. 1999. *Cyber-Marx: Cycles and Circuits of Struggle in High-Technology Capitalism*. Champaign, IL: University of Illinois Press.

The Economist 2018. "Rulers of the World: Read Karl Marx!" 5 May.

Elger, T. & C. Smith 1994. "Global Japanization? Convergence and Competition in the Organization of the Labour Process". In *Global Japanization? The Transnational Transformation of the Labour Process*, T. Elger & C. Smith (eds), 31–59. London: Routledge.

Elson, D. 1996. "Appraising Recent Developments in the World Market for Nimble Fingers". In *Confronting State, Capital and Patriarchy: Women Organizing in the Process of Industrialization*, A. Chhachhi & R. Pittin (eds), 35–55. London: Macmillan.

Elson, D. & R. Pearson 1981. "The Subordination of Women and the Internationalisation of Production". In *Of Marriage in the Market: Women's Subordination in International Perspective*, K. Young, C. Wolkowitz & R. McCullagh (eds), 18–40. London: CSE Books.

Emmanuel, A. 1972. *Unequal Exchange: A Study of the Imperialism of Trade*. London: Verso Books.

EPSU 2015. "Liberalisation of Public Services in Trade Agreements a Danger for Our Social Model", 15 January. www.epsu.org/article/liberalisation-public-services-trade-agreements-danger-our-social-model (accessed 31 May 2018).

Escobar, A. 1995. *Encountering Development: The Making and Unmaking of the Third World*. Princeton, NJ: Princeton University Press.

Evans, P. 2014. "National Labor Movements and Transnational Connections: Global Labor's Evolving Architecture under Neoliberalism". *Global Labour Journal* 5 (3): 258–82.

Evers, T. 1985. "Identity: The Hidden Side of New Social Movements in Latin America". In *Social Movements and the State in Latin America*, D. Slater (ed.), 43–72. Amsterdam: CEDLA.

Fairbrother, P. 1989. *Workplace Unionism in the 1980s: A Process of Renewal?* London: Workers' Educational Association.

Fairbrother, P. 1999. "The Changing State and Implications for Trade Unions". Cardiff: School of Social Sciences, Cardiff University.

Fairbrother, P. & N. Hammer 2005. "Global Unions: Past Efforts and Current Prospects". *Industrial Relations* 60 (3): 405–31.

Falk, R. 1999. *Predatory Globalization: A Critique*. Cambridge: Polity Press.

Fantasia, R. & J. Stepan-Norris 2004. "The Labour Movement in Motion". In *The Blackwell Companion to Social Movements*, D. Shaw, S. Some & H. Kriesi (eds), 555–71. Oxford: Blackwell.

Farnhill, T. 2016. "A Small-N Cross-Sectional Study of British Unions' Environmental Attitudes and Activism – and the Prospect of a Green-Led Renewal". *Cogent Social Sciences* 2: 1–21.

Ferguson, J. 2007. "Formalities of Poverty: Thinking about Social Assistance in South Africa". *African Studies Review* 50 (1): 71–86.

Fichter, M. & J. McCallum 2015. "Implementing Global Framework Agreements: The Limits of Social Partnership". *Global Networks* 15 (S1): S65–S85.

Fine, J. 1999. "Moving Innovation from the Margins to the Center". In *A New Labor Movement for the New Century*, G. Mantsios (ed.), 119–46. New York: Monthly Review Press.

Fine, J. 2006. *Worker Centers: Organizing Communities at the Edge of the Dream*. Ithaca, NY: ILR Press.

FNV 2009. *Guide to the Construction of Union Networks within Multinational Enterprises: Systematizing CUT's Experience*. The Hague: Federatie Nederlandse Vakbeweging. www.fnv.nl/site/over-de-fnv/internationaal/mondiaal-fnv/documenten/english/publications/Guide_to_construction_union_networks_within_multinational_enterprises.pdf (accessed 31 May 2018).

Fraser, N. 1995. "From Redistribution to Recognition? Dilemmas of Justice in a Post-Socialist Age". *New Left Review* 212: 68–93.

Freeman, R. 1994. "Comments". In *Labor Markets and Integrating National Economies*, R. Ehrenberg (ed.), 107–10. Washington, DC: Brookings Institution Press.

Freeman, R. 2008. "The New Global Labor Market". *Focus* 26 (1): 1–6.

Frege, C. & J. Kelly (eds) 2004. *Varieties of Unionism: Strategies for Union Revitalization in a Globalizing Economy*. Oxford: Oxford University Press.

French, J., J. Cowie & S. Littleham 1994. *Labor and NAFTA: A Briefing Book*. Durham, NC: Duke University Press.

Friedman, G. 2008. *Reigniting the Labor Movement: Restoring Means to Ends in a Democratic Labor Movement*. Abingdon: Routledge.

Fröbel, F., J. Heinrichs & U. Kreye 1980. *The New International Division of Labour: Structural Unemployment in Industrialised Countries and Industrialisation in Developing Countries*. Cambridge: Cambridge University Press.

Fukuyama, F. 1989. "The End of History?". *National Interest* 16: 3–18.

Gallin, D. 1999. "Organized Labor as a Global Social Force", paper presented to the 40th annual convention of the International Studies Association, Washington, DC, 20 February.

Gambino, F. & D. Sacchetto 2014. "The Shifting Maelstrom: From Plantations to Assembly-Lines". In *Beyond Marx: Theorising the Global Labour Relations of the Twenty-First Century*, M. van der Linden & K. Roth (eds), 89–119. Chicago, IL: Haymarket Books.

Gamble, A. 2009. *The Spectre at the Feast: Capitalist Crisis and the Politics of Recession*. Basingstoke: Palgrave Macmillan.

GCIM 2005. *Migration in an Interconnected World: New Directions for Action*. Geneva: Global Commission on International Migration.

Germani, G. 1964. *La sociología en la América Latina: problemas y perspectivas*. Buenos Aires: Eudeba.

Gibson-Graham, J. K. 1996. *The End of Capitalism (as We Knew It): A Feminist Critique of Political Economy*. Oxford: Blackwell.

Gibson-Graham, J. K. 2006. *A Postcapitalist Politics*. Minneapolis, MN: University of Minnesota Press.

Gill, S. 1995. "Theorising the Interregnum: The Double Movement and Global Politics in the 1990s". In *International Political Economy: Understanding Global Disorder*, B. Hettne (ed.), 45–99. London: Zed Books.

Gills, B. 2000. "Introduction: Globalization and the Politics of Resistance". In *Globalization and the Politics of Resistance*, B. Gills (ed.), 3–11. London: Macmillan.

Glasman, M. 1994 "The Great Deformation: Polanyi, Poland and the Errors of Planned Spontaneity". In *The New Great Transformation? Change and Continuity in East-Central Europe*, C. Bryant & E. Mokrzycki (eds), 191–217. London: Routledge.

Glyn, A. 1999. "Internal and External Constraints on Egalitarian Policies". In *Globalization and Progressive Economic Policy*, D. Baker, G. Epstein & R. Pollin (eds), 391–411. Cambridge: Cambridge University Press.

Gough, I. 1979. *The Political Economy of the Welfare State*. London: Macmillan.

Gould, K., T. Lewis & T. Roberts 2004. "Blue-Green Coalitions: Constraints and Possibilities in the Post 9-11 Political Environment". *Journal of World-Systems Research* 10 (1): 91–116.

Gramsci, A. 1971a. "Some Theoretical and Practical Aspects of Economism". In *Selections from the Prison Notebooks of Antonio Gramsci*, Q. Hoare & G. Nowell Smith (eds), 158–69. London: Lawrence & Wishart.

Gramsci, A. 1971b. "Americanism and Fordism". In *Selections from the Prison Notebooks of Antonio Gramsci*, Q. Hoare & G. Nowell Smith (eds), 277–318. London: Lawrence & Wishart.

Gray, B. 2008. "Putting Emotion and Reflexivity to Work in Researching Migration". *Sociology* 42 (4): 916–36.

Gumbrell-McCormick, R. 2000. "Facing New Challenges: The International Confederation of Free Trade Unions (1971–1990s)". In *The International Confederation of Free Trade Unions*, M. van der Linden (ed.), 341–518. Berne: Peter Lang.

Hale, A. (ed.) 1999. *Trade Myths and Gender Realities*. Uppsala: Global Publications Foundation.

Hardt, M. & A. Negri 2000. *Empire*. Cambridge, MA: Harvard University Press.

Hardt, M. & A. Negri 2009. *Commonwealth*. Cambridge, MA: Harvard University Press.

Harrison, A., T. Britton & A. Swanson 2004. "Working Abroad: The Benefits Flowing from Nationals Working in Other Economies". Paris: Organisation for Economic Co-operation and Development.

Harriss-White, B. & N. Gooptu 2000. "Mapping India's World of Unorganised Labour". In *Working Classes, Global Realities: Socialist Register 2001*, L. Panitch & C. Leys (eds), 89–118. London: Merlin Press.

Hart, K. 1973. "Informal Income Opportunities and Urban Employment in Ghana". *Journal of Modern African Studies* 11 (1): 6–84.

Harvey, D. 2003. *The New Imperialism*. Oxford: Oxford University Press.

Harvey, D. 2006. *Spaces of Global Capitalism: Towards a Theory of Uneven Geographical Development*. London: Verso Books.

Held, D., A. McGrew, D. Goldblatt & J. Perraton 1999. *Global Transformations: Politics, Economics and Culture*. Cambridge: Polity Press.

Henderson, J. & R. Cohen 1982. "On the Reproduction of the Relations of Production". In *Urban Political Economy and Social Theory*, R. Forrest, J. Henderson & P. Williams (eds), 112–43. Aldershot: Gower.

Herod, A. (ed.) 1998. *Organizing the Landscape: Geographical Perspectives on Labor Unionism*. Minneapolis, MN: University of Minnesota Press.

Herod, A. 2001. "Labor Internationalism and the Contradiction of Globalization: Or, Why the Local Is Sometimes Still Important in a Global Economy". *Antipode* 33 (3): 407–26.

Herod, A. 2011. *Scale*. Abingdon: Routledge.

Hirst, P. & G. Thompson 1996. *Globalization in Question*. Cambridge: Polity Press.

Hirst, P. & J. Zeitlin (eds) 1989. *Reversing Industrial Decline? Industrial Structure and Policy in Britain and Her Competitors*. London: Berg.

Hobsbawm, E. 1951. "The Tramping Artisan". *Economic History Review* 3 (3): 299–320.

Hobsbawm, E. 1988. "Working Class Internationalism". In *Internationalism in the Labour Movement 1830–1940*, F. van Holthoon & M. van der Linden (eds), 3–16. Leiden: Brill.

Hobsbawm, E. 1994. *Age of Extremes: The Short Twentieth Century 1914–1991*. London: Michael Joseph.

Holgate, J. 2009. "Contested Terrain: London's Living Wage Campaign and the Tension between Community and Union Organising". In *The Complexity of Community Unionism: A*

Comparative Analysis of Concepts and Contexts, J. McBride & I. Greenwood (eds), 49–74. Basingstoke: Palgrave Macmillan.

Hollingsworth, J. R. & R. Boyer 1996. "Coordination of Economic Actors and Social Systems of Production". In *Contemporary Capitalism: The Embeddedness of Institutions*, J. R. Hollingsworth & R. Boyer (eds), 1–47. Cambridge: Cambridge University Press.

Hölmstrom, M. 1984. *Industry and Inequality: The Social Anthropology of Indian Labour*. Cambridge: Cambridge University Press.

Huws, B. 2000. "The Making of a Cybertariat? Virtual Work in a Real World". In *Working Classes, Global Realities: Socialist Register 2001*, L. Panitch & C. Leys (eds), 1–24. London: Merlin Press.

Huws, U. 2017. "The Future of Work: Neither Utopias nor Dystopias but New Fields of Accumulation and Struggle". Transform!, 21 February. www.transform-network.net/en/publications/yearbook/overview/article/yearbook-2017/the-future-of-work-neither-utopias-nor-dystopias-but-new-fields-of-accumulation-and-struggle.

Hyman, R. 2004. "The Future of Trade Unions". In *Unions in the Twenty-First Century: An International Perspective*, A. Verma & T. Kochan (eds), 17–29. Basingstoke: Palgrave Macmillan.

ICEM 1996. *Power and Counterpower: The Union Responses to Global Capital*. London: Pluto Press.

ICEM 1999. *Facing Global Power: Strategies for Global Unionism*. Geneva: International Federation of Chemical, Energy, Mine and General Workers' Unions.

ICFTU 1990. *On Organising Workers in the Informal Sector*. Brussels: International Confederation of Free Trade Unions.

ICFTU 1997. *The Global Market: Trade Unionism's Greatest Challenge*. Brussels: International Confederation of Free Trade Unions.

ILO 1972. *Employment, Incomes and Inequality: A Strategy for Increasing Productive Employment in Kenya*. Geneva: International Labour Organization.

ILO 1995. *World Employment 1995*. Geneva: International Labour Organization.

ILO 1997. *Industrial Relations, Democracy and Stability: World Labour Report 1997–98*. Geneva: International Labour Organization.

ILO 1999. "Conference on Organised Labour in the 21st Century", 20 October.

ILO 2001. *Stopping Forced Labour*. Geneva: International Labour Organization.

ILO 2004. *The World Commission on the Social Dimension of Globalization*. Geneva: International Labour Organization.

ILO 2008. *Forced Labour and Human Trafficking*. Geneva: International Labour Organization.

ILO 2011. "ACTRAV Symposium on Precarious Work (4–7 October, 2011)". www.ilo.org/actrav/what/events/WCMS_153972/lang--en/index.htm (accessed 16 February 2016).

ILO 2012. "Decent Work". www.ilo.org/global/topics/decent-work/lang--en/index.htm (accessed 16 February 2016).

ILO 2017. "ILO Labour Force Estimates and Projections (LFEP) 2017: Key Trends". Geneva: International Labour Organization. www.ilo.org/ilostat-files/Documents/LFEPbrief.pdf (accessed 31 May 2018).

Independent Commission on International Development Issues 1980. *North–South: A Programme for Survival*. London: Pan Books.

IOM 2005. *Costs and Benefits of Migration: World Migration Report 2005*. Geneva: International Organization for Migration.

Jameson, F. 1998. "Notes on Globalization as a Philosophical Issue". In *The Cultures of Globalization*, F. Jameson & M. Miyoshi (eds), 54–77. Durham, NC: Duke University Press.

Jhabvala, R. 1994. "Self-Employed Women's Association: Organising Women by Struggle and Development". In *Dignity and Daily Bread: New Forms of Economic Organising among Poor Women in the Third World and the First*, S. Rowbotham & S. Mitter (eds), 114–38. London: Routledge.

Johnston, W. 1991. "Global Work Force 2000: The New World Labor Market". *Harvard Business Review* 69 (2): 115–27.

Jordan, B. 2000. "Remarks by Bill Jordan, ICFTU General Secretary, at the Reception of the International Conference 'The Past and Future of International Trade Unionism'", Gent, 18 May.

Kabeer, N., R. Sudarshan & K. Milward (eds) 2013. *Organizing Women Workers in the Informal Economy: Beyond the Weapons of the Weak.* London: Zed Books.

Kahmann, M. 2002. "Trade Unions and Migrant Workers: Examples from the United States, South Africa and Spain", Discussion and Working Paper 2002.02.03. Brussels: European Trade Union Institute.

Kalecki, M. 1971 [1943]. "Political Aspects of Full Employment". In *Selected Essays on the Dynamics of the Capitalist Economy*, M. Kalecki, 138–45. Cambridge: Cambridge University Press.

Kay, C. 1989. *Latin American Theories of Development and Underdevelopment.* London: Routledge.

Kelly, J. 2003. "Labour Movement Revitalization? A Comparative Perspective". Countess Markievicz Memorial lecture, Dublin, 7 April. www.ul.ie/iair/sites/default/files/2003%20 Lecture%20by%20John%20Kelly.pdf.

Keynes, J. M. 1936. *The General Theory of Employment, Interest, and Money.* London: Macmillan.

Kloosterboer, D. 2007. *Innovative Trade Union Strategies.* Utrecht: Federatie Nederlandse Vakbeweging.

Knowles, C. 2003. *Race and Social Analysis.* London: Sage.

Köllö, J. 1995. "After a Dark Golden Age in Eastern Europe". In *Capital, the State and Labour: A Global Perspective*, J. Schor & J.-I. You (eds), 282–318. Cheltenham: Edward Elgar.

Knudsen, K. 1988. "The Strike History of the First International". In *Internationalism in the Labour Movement 1830–1940*, F. van Holthoon & M. van der Linden (eds), 304–22. Leiden: Brill.

Krings, T. 2007. "'Equal Rights for All Workers': Irish Trade Unions and the Challenge of Labour Migration". *Irish Journal of Sociology* 17 (1): 43–61.

Lawrence, A. 2014. *Employer and Worker Collective Action: A Comparative Study of Germany, South Africa, and the United States.* New York: Columbia University Press.

Lee, E. 1997. *The Labour Movement and the Internet: The New Internationalism.* London: Pluto Books.

Lefebvre, H. 1991 [1974]. *The Production of Space.* Oxford: Blackwell.

Levi, M. & D. Olson 2000. "The Battles in Seattle". *Politics and Society* 28 (3): 309–29.

Levinson, C. 1972. *International Trade Unionism.* London: Allen & Unwin.

Li, T. 2010. "To Make Live or Let Die? Rural Dispossession and the Production of Surplus Populations". In *The Point Is to Change It: Geographies of Hope and Survival in an Age of Crisis*, N. Castree, P. Chatterton, N. Heynen, W. Larner & M. Wright (eds), 66–93. Oxford: Wiley-Blackwell.

Lipietz, A. 1987. *Mirages and Miracles: The Crises of Global Fordism.* London: Verso Books.

Lipietz, A. 1995. "Capital–Labour Relations at the Dawn of the Twenty-First Century". In *Capital, the State and Labour: A Global Perspective*, J. Schor & J.-I. You (eds), 345–72. Cheltenham: Edward Elgar.

Luxemburg, R. 1951 [1913]. *The Accumulation of Capital.* London: Routledge.

McAlevey, J. 2016. *No Shortcuts: Organizing for Power in the New Gilded Age.* New York: Oxford University Press.

McEvoy, P., M. Brady & R. Munck 2016. "Capacity Development through International Projects: A Complex Adaptive Systems Perspective". *International Journal of Managing Projects in Business* 9 (3): 528–45.

McGovern, P. 2007. "Immigration, Labour Markets and Employment Relations: Problems and Prospects". *British Journal of Industrial Relations* 45 (2): 217–35.

McGrath-Champ, S., A. Herod & A. Rainnie (eds) 2010. *Handbook of Employment and Society: Working Space*. Cheltenham: Edward Elgar.

McMichael, P. 2000. *Development and Social Change: A Global Perspective*. Thousand Oaks, CA: Pine Forge Press.

MacShane, D. 1992. *International Labour and the Origins of the Cold War*. Oxford: Clarendon Press.

MacShane, D. 1996. "Global Business: Global Rights", Pamphlet 575. London: Fabian Society.

MacShane, D., M. Plaut & D. Ward 1984. *Power! Black Workers, Their Unions and the Struggle for Freedom in South Africa*. Nottingham: Spokesman Books.

Mann, K. 2014. "Social Movement Literature and US Labour: A Reassessment". *Studies in Social Justice* 8 (2): 165–79.

Mantsios, G. 1998a. "Introduction". In *A New Labor Movement for the New Century*, G. Mantsios (ed.), xi–xviii. New York: Monthly Review Press.

Mantsios, G. 1998b. "What Does Labor Stand For?". In *A New Labor Movement for the New Century*, G. Mantsios (ed.), 51–74. New York: Monthly Review Press.

Manzo, K. 1991. "Modernist Discourse and the Crisis of Development Theory". *Studies on Comparative International Development* 26 (2): 3–36.

Marfleet, P. 2006. *Refugees in a Global Era*. Basingstoke: Palgrave Macmillan.

Marglin, S. 1990. "Lessons of the Golden Age: An Overview". In *The Golden Age of Capitalism: Reinterpreting the Postwar Experience*, S. Marglin & J. Schor (eds), 1–38. Oxford: Clarendon Press.

Marino, S., R. Penninx & J. Roosblad 2015. "Trade Unions, Immigration and Immigrants in Europe Revisited: Unions' Attitudes and Actions under New Conditions". *Comparative Migration Studies* 3 (1): 1–16.

Marx, K. 1976 [1867]. *Capital*, vol. 1. London: Penguin Books.

Marx, K. & F. Engels 1976 [1848]. "The Communist Manifesto". In *The Revolutions of 1848: Political Writings*, vol. 1, D. Fernbach (ed.), 62–98. London: Penguin Books.

Mason, P. 2015. *Postcapitalism: A Guide to Our Future*. London: Penguin Books.

Mazur, J. 2000. "Labor's New Internationalism". *Foreign Affairs* 79 (1): 79–93.

Meiksins, P. 1997. "Same as It Ever Was? Structure of the Working Class". *Monthly Review* 49 (3): 31–45.

Melucci, A. 1988. "Getting Involved: Identity and Mobilization in Social Movements". In *International Social Movement Research*, vol. 1: *From Structure to Action: Comparing Social Movement Research across Cultures*, B. Klandermans, H. Kriesi & S. Tarrow (eds), 329–48. Greenwich, CT: JAI Press.

Mezzadra, S. 2012. "How Many Histories of Labor? Towards a Theory of Postcolonial Capitalism". *Transversal* 1. http://eipcp.net/transversal/0112/mezzadra/en (accessed 16 February 2016).

Mezzadri, A. 2016. "Class, Gender and the Sweatshop: On the Nexus between Labour Commodification and Exploitation". *Third World Quarterly* 37 (10): 1877–900.

Michels, R. 1962 [1911]. *Political Parties: A Sociological Study of the Oligarchical Tendencies of Modern Democracy*. New York: Crowell-Collier.

Mies, M. 1986. *Patriarchy and Accumulation on a World Scale: Women in the International Division of Labour*. London: Zed Books.

Milanovich, B. 2011. "Global Inequality: From Class to Location, from Proletarians to Migrants", Policy Research Working Paper 5820. Washington, DC: World Bank.

Miles, R. 1987. *Capitalism and Unfree Labour: Anomaly or Necessity?* London: Tavistock.

Milkman, R. 2006. *L. A. Story: Immigrant Workers and the Future of the US Labor Movement*. New York: Russell Sage.

Milne, S. 2000. "Unions Aim to Swallow Amazon". *Guardian*, 7 December, 7.

Mintz, S. 1974. *Caribbean Transformations*. Chicago, IL: Aldine.

Mitter, S. 1994. "On Organising Women in Casualised Work: A Global Overview". In *Dignity and Daily Bread: New Forms of Economic Organising among Poor Women in the Third World and the First*, S. Rowbotham & S. Mitter (eds), 14–52. London: Routledge.

Moghadam, V. 1995. "Gender Aspects of Employment and Unemployment in a Global Perspective". In *Global Employment: An International Investigation into the Future of Work*, vol. 1, M. Simai (ed.), 111–39. London: Zed Books.

Mohanty, C. 1993. "Under Western Eyes: Feminist Scholarship and Colonial Discourse". In *Colonial Discourse and Post-Colonial Theory*, P. Williams & L. Chrisman (eds), 196–218. Hemel Hempstead: Harvester Wheatsheaf.

Moody, K. 1997. *Workers in a Lean World: Unions in the International Economy*. London: Verso Books.

Morgan, O. 2000. "An Open Shop in the New Economy". *Observer*, 10 September, 5. www.theguardian.com/business/2000/sep/10/theobserver.observerbusiness9.

Morgan, R. (ed.) 1984. *Sisterhood Is Global: The International Women's Movement Anthology*. London: Penguin Books.

Moser, C. 1994. "The Informal Sector Debate, Part 1: 1970–1983". In *Contrapunto: The Informal Sector Debate in Latin America*, C. Rakowski (ed.), 11–29. Albany, NY: State University of New York Press.

Munck, R. 2005. *Globalization and Social Exclusion: A Transformationalist Perspective*. Bloomfield, CT: Kumarian Press.

Munck, R. 2015. *Marx 2020: After the Crisis*. London: Zed Books.

Munck, R., R. Falcon & B. Galitelli 1987. *From Anarchism to Peronism: Workers, Unions and Politics in Argentina 1855–1985*. London: Zed Books.

Murphy, G. 2004. "The Seattle WTO Protests: Building a Global Movement". In *Creating a Better World: Interpreting Civil Society*, R. Taylor (ed.), 27–42. Bloomfield, CT: Kumarian Press.

Ness, I. 2005. *Immigrants, Unions, and the New US Labor Market*. Philadelphia, PA: Temple University Press.

Nun, J. 1969. "Superpoblación relativa, ejército industrial de reserva y masa marginal". *Revista Latinoamericana de Sociología* 5 (2): 180–225.

Nun, J. 1999. "El future de empleo y la tesis de la masa marginal". *Desarrollo Económico* 38 (152): 985–1004.

O'Brien, R., A. Goetz, J. Scholte & M. Williams 2000. *Contesting Global Governance: Multinational Economic Institutions and Global Social Movement*. Cambridge: Cambridge University Press.

O'Grady, F. 2004. "Globalisation Makes Unions and Social Movements Natural Allies". *Guardian*, 16 October.

OECD 1996. *Trade, Employment and Labour Standards: A Study of Core Workers' Rights and International Trade*. Paris: Organisation for Economic Co-operation and Development.

Ohmae, K. 1990. *The Borderless World: Power and Strategy in the Interlinked Economy*. London: Collins.

ONS 2018. "Understanding the Gender Pay Gap in the UK", 17 January. www.ons.gov.uk/employmentandlabourmarket/peopleinwork/earningsandworkinghours/articles/understandingthegenderpaygapintheuk/2018-01-17 (accessed 31 May 2018).

Palmer, B. 2013. "Reconsiderations of Class: Precariousness as Proletarianization". In *Registering Class: Socialist Register 2014*, L. Panitch, G. Albo & V. Chibber (eds), 40–62. London: Merlin Press.

Peck, J. 1996. *Work-Place: The Social Regulation of Labor Markets*. New York: Guilford Press.

Peck, J., N. Theodore & N. Brenner 2010. "Postneoliberalism and Its Malcontents". *Antipode* 41 (1): 94–116.

Penninx, R. & J. Roosblad (eds) 2000. *Trade Unions, Immigration, and Immigrants in Europe, 1960–1993: A Comparative Study of the Attitudes and Actions of Trade Unions in Seven West European Countries*. Oxford: Berghahn.

Peterson, S. 2003. *A Critical Rewriting of Global Political Economy: Integrating Reproductive, Productive and Virtual Economies*. Abingdon: Routledge.

Piore, M. & C. Sabel 1984. *The Second Industrial Divide: Possibilities for Prosperity*. New York: Basic Books.

Pitts, F. 2017. "Beyond the Fragment: Postoperaismo, Postcapitalism, and Marx's 'Notes on Machines', 45 Years on". *Economy and Society* 46 (3/4): 324–45.

Piven, F. & R. Cloward 1977. *Poor People's Movements: Why They Succeed, How They Fail*. New York: Vintage Books.

Polanyi, K. 2001 [1944]. *The Great Transformation: The Political and Economic Origins of Our Time*. Boston, MA: Beacon Press.

Portes, A. 1985. "Latin American Class Structures: Their Composition and Change during the Last Decade". *Latin American Research Review* 20 (3): 7–39.

Portes, A., M. Castells & L. Benton (eds) 1989. *The Informal Economy: Studies in Advanced and Less Developed Countries*. Baltimore, MD: Johns Hopkins University Press.

Portes, A. & K. Hoffman 2003. "Latin American Class Structures". *Latin American Research Review* 38 (1): 41–82.

Quijano, A. 1966. "El proceso de urbanización en Latinoamérica". Mimeo, Santiago.

Quijano, A. 2006. "Alternative Production Systems". In *Another Production Is Possible: Beyond the Capitalist Canon*, B. de Sousa Santos (ed.), 417–45. London: Verso Books.

Rakowski, C. 1994. "Introduction: What Debate?". In *Contrapunto: The Informal Sector Debate in Latin America*, C. Rakowski (ed.), 3–10. Albany, NY: State University of New York Press.

Ramsay, H. 1999. "In Search of International Union Theory". In *Globalization and Patterns of Labour Resistance*, J. Waddington (ed.), 192–219. London: Mansell.

Räthzel, N. & D. Uzzell 2012. "Mending the Breach between Labour and Nature: Environmental Engagements of Trade Unions and the North–South Divide". *Interface* 4 (2): 81–100.

Räthzel, N. & D. Uzzell 2013. *Trade Unions in the Green Economy: Working for the Environment*. Abingdon: Routledge.

Rediker, M. 2003. "'The Red Atlantic'; or, 'A Terrible Blast Swept over the Heaving Seas'". In *Sea Changes: Historicizing the Ocean*, B. Klein & G. Mackenthum (eds), 111–30. New York: Routledge.

Roberts, B. 2004. "From Marginality to Social Exclusion: From Laissez Faire to Pervasive Engagement". *Latin American Research Review* 39 (1): 195–7.

Roldan, M. 1996. "Women Organising in the Process of Deindustrialisation". In *Confronting State, Capital and Patriarchy*, A. Chhachhi & R. Pittin (eds), 56–92. London: Macmillan.

Rosa, K. 1994. "The Conditions and Organisational Activities of Women in Free Trade Zones: Malaysia, Philippines and Sri Lanka, 1970–1990". In *Dignity and Daily Bread: New Forms of Economic Organising among Poor Women in the Third World and the First*, S. Rowbotham & S. Mitter (eds), 73–100. London: Routledge.

Ross, A. 1997. "Introduction". In *No Sweat: Fashion, Free Trade, and the Rights of Garment Workers*, A. Ross (ed.), 9–38. London: Verso Books.

Rowbotham, S., L. Segal & H. Wainwright 1979. *Beyond the Fragments: Feminism and the Making of Socialism*. London: Merlin Press.

Roxborough, I. 1984. *Unions and Politics in Mexico: The Case of the Automobile Industry*. Cambridge: Cambridge University Press.

Rubery, J. & C. Fagan 1994. "Does Feminisation Mean a Flexible Labour Force?". In *New Frontiers in European Industrial Relations*, R. Hyman & A. Ferner (eds), 140–66. Oxford: Blackwell.

Sahlström, E. 2008. "Migration: A Lever for Union Renewal?". Eurozine, 22 July. www.eurozine. com/migration-a-lever-for-union-renewal (accessed 29 June 2018).

Sassen, S. 1994. "The Informal Economy: Between New Developments and Old Regulations". *Yale Law Journal* 103 (8): 2289–304.

Sassen, S. 1999. *Guests and Aliens*. New York: New Press.

Savage, L. 2008. "Labour Rights as Human Rights? A Response to Roy Adams". *Just Labour: A Canadian Journal of Work and Society* 12: 68–75.

Schor, J. & J.-I. You (eds) 1995. *Capital, the State and Labour: A Global Perspective.* Cheltenham: Edward Elgar.

Schumpeter, J. 1994 [1942]. *Capitalism, Socialism and Democracy.* London: Routledge.

Scott, A. 1994. *Divisions and Solidarities: Gender, Class and Employment in Latin America.* London: Routledge.

Scott, J. 1985. *Weapons of the Weak: Everyday Forms of Peasant Resistance.* New Haven, CT: Yale University Press.

Seidman, G. 1994. *Manufacturing Militance: Workers' Movements in Brazil and South Africa, 1970–1985.* Berkeley, CA: University of California Press.

Sen, A. 2000. "Work and Rights", *International Labour Review* 139 (2): 119–28.

Sen, J. 2004. "A Tale of Two Charters". In *World Social Forum: Challenging Empires*, J. Sen, A. Arnaud, A. Escobar & P. Waterman (eds), 72–5. New Delhi: Viveka Foundation.

Shailor, B. & G. Kourpias 1998. "Developing and Enforcing International Labor Standards". In *A New Labor Movement for the New Century*, G. Mantsios (ed.), 319–28. New York: Monthly Review Press.

Shiva, V. 1996. "Social and Environmental Clauses: A Political Diversion". In *Labour, Environmentalism and Globalization*, J. John & A. Chenoy (eds), 101–12. New Delhi: Centre for Education and Communication.

SID 1997. "A New Global Agenda: Visions and Strategies for the 21st Century". Specialarbejderförbundet i Danmark.

Silver, B. 2003. *Forces of Labour: Workers' Movements and Globalization since 1870.* Cambridge: Cambridge University Press.

Silver, B. 2013. "Theorising the Working Class in Twenty-First-Century Global Capitalism". In *Workers and Labour in a Globalised Capitalism: Contemporary Themes and Theoretical Issues*, M. Atzeni (ed.), 46–69. Basingstoke: Palgrave Macmillan.

Silver, B. & Ş. Karataşli 2015. "Historical Dynamics of Capitalism and Labor Movements". In *Oxford Handbook of Social Movements*, D. della Porta & M. Diani (eds), 133–45. Oxford: Oxford University Press.

Simai, M. 1995. "The Politics and Economics of Global Employment". In *Global Employment: An International Investigation into the Future of Work*, vol. 1, M. Simai (ed.), 3–29. London: Zed Books.

Simms, M., J. Holgate & E. Heery 2012. *Union Voices: Tactics and Tensions in UK Organizing.* Ithaca, NY: ILR Press.

Singer, P. 1973. "Urbanização dependência e marginalidade na América Latina". In *Economia política da urbanização*, 63–90. São Paulo: Brasiliense.

Singh, A. 1994. "Global Economic Change, Skills and International Competitiveness". *International Labour Review* 133 (2): 135–48.

Smith, J. 2001. "Globalizing Resistance: The Battle of Seattle and the Future of Social Movements". *Mobilization: An International Quarterly* 6 (1): 1–19.

Smith, J. 2016. *Imperialism in the Twenty-First Century: The Globalization of Production, Super-Exploitation, and the Crisis of Capitalism.* New York: Monthly Review Press.

Smith, N. 1990. *Uneven Development: Nature, Capital, and the Production of Space*, 2nd edn. Atlanta, GA: University of Georgia Press.

Soja, E. 1980. "The Socio-Spatial Dialectic". *Annals of the Association of American Geographers* 70 (2): 207–25.

Standing, G. 1989. "Global Feminization through Flexible Labor". *World Development* 17 (7): 1077–95.

Standing, G. 1999. *Global Labour Flexibility: Seeking Distributive Justice.* Basingstoke: Palgrave Macmillan.

Standing, G. 2001. *The Precariat: The New Dangerous Class.* London: Bloomsbury Academic.

Stevis, D. & T. Boswell 2001. "International Labor Organizing, 1864–2000", paper presented to the 42nd annual convention of the International Studies Association, Chicago, 23 February.

Streeck, W. 2014. "How Will Capitalism End?". *New Left Review* 87: 35–64.

Tabb, W. 1999. "Labor and the Imperialism of Finance". *Monthly Review* 51 (5) 1–13.

Tait, V. 2005. *Poor Workers' Unions: Rebuilding Labor from Below*. Cambridge, MA: South End Press.

Taylor, P. 1982. "A Materialist Framework for Political Geography". *Transactions of the Institute of British Geographers* 7 (1): 15–34.

Taylor, R. 1999. "Trade Unions and Transnational Industrial Relations", Discussion Paper 99/1999. Geneva: International Institute for Labour Studies.

Thelen, K. & I. Kume 1999. "The Effect of Globalization on Labor Revisited: Lessons from Germany and Japan". *Politics and Society* 27 (4): 477–505.

Therborn, G. 2013. *The Killing Fields of Inequality*. Cambridge: Polity Press.

Tickell, A. & J. Peck 1995. "Social Regulation *after* Fordism: Regulation Theory, Neoliberalism and the Global–Local Nexus". *Economy and Society* 24 (3): 357–86.

Tilly, C. & C. Tilly 1998. *Work under Capitalism*. Boulder, CO: Westview Press.

Tronti, M. 1966. *Operai e capitale*. Turin: Einaudi.

Turner, L. 2004. "Globalization, Participation, and the Renewal of the Labor Movement". In *The Future of Labor Unions: Organized Labor in the 21st Century*, R. Marshall & J. Getman (eds), 111–25. Austin, TX: Lyndon B. Johnson School of Public Affairs, University of Texas.

UNEP 2007. *Labour and the Environment: A Natural Synergy*. Nairobi: United Nations Environment Programme.

Unger, R. 1998. *Democracy Realised: The Progressive Alternative*. London: Verso Books.

Urry, J. 2003. *Global Complexity*. Cambridge: Polity Press.

Urry, J. 2016. *What Is the Future?* Cambridge: Polity Press.

Van der Linden, M. 1988. "The Rise and Fall of the First International: An Interpretation". In *Internationalism in the Labour Movement 1830–1940*, F. van Holthoon & M. van der Linden (eds), 323–35. Leiden: Brill.

Van der Linden, M. 2008. *Workers of the World: Essays toward a Global Labor History*. Amsterdam: Brill.

Van der Linden, M. 2015. "The Crisis of World Labor". *Against the Current* 176, https://solidarity-us.org/atc/176/p4424 (accessed 29 June 2018).

Van der Walt, L. 2007. "The First Globalisation and Transnational Labour Activism in Southern Africa: White Labourism, the IWW, and the ICU, 1904–1934". *African Studies* 66 (2/3): 223–51.

Van Dijk, M. 1995. "The Internationalisation of the Labour Market". In *Global Employment: An International Investigation into the Future of Work*, vol. 1, M. Simai (ed.), 110–32. London: Zed Books.

Visser, J. 1998. "Learning to Play: The Europeanisation of Trade Unions". In *Working-Class Internationalism and the Appeal of National Identity: Historical Debates and Current Perspectives*, P. Pasture & J. Verberckmoes (eds), 231–56. Oxford: Berg.

Wacquant, L. 1994. "The New Urban Color Line: The State and Fate of the Ghetto in PostFordist America". In *Social Theory and the Politics of Identity*, C. Calhoun (ed.), 231–76. Oxford: Blackwell.

Waddington, J. (ed.) 1999. *Globalization and Patterns of Labour Resistance*. London: Mansell.

Wahl, A. 2016. "The Role of Labour in the Fight against Climate Change". TransformDanmark. www.transformdanmark.dk/?page_id=1112 (accessed 31 May 2018).

Wainwright, H. 2005. "Why Participatory Democracy Matters – and Movements Matter to Participatory Democracy". Transnational Institute, 1 June. www.tni.org/en/article/why-participatory-democracy-matters-and-movements-matter-to-participatory-democracy (accessed 5 April 2018).

Wallerstein, I. 1983. *Historical Capitalism*. London: Verso Books.

Warren, B. 1980. *Imperialism: Pioneer of Capitalism*. London: Verso Books.

Waterman, P. 2003. "Place, Space and the Reinvention of Social Emancipation on a Global Scale: Second Thoughts on the Third World Social Forum", Working Paper 19138. The Hague: International Institute of Social Studies, Erasmus University Rotterdam.

Waters, M. 2001. *Globalization*. London: Routledge.

Webber, M. & D. Rigby 1996. *The Golden Era Illusion: Rethinking Postwar Capitalism*. New York: Guilford Press.

Weiss, L. 1997. "Globalization and the Myth of the Powerless State". *New Left Review* 225: 3–27.

Weiss, L. 1999. "Managed Openness: Beyond Neoliberal Globalism". *New Left Review* 238: 126–40.

Williams, E. 1944. *Capitalism and Slavery*. Chapel Hill, NC: University of North Carolina Press.

Williams, K., C. Haslam, J. Williams, T. Cutler, A. Adcroft & S. Johal 1992. "Against Lean Production". *Economy and Society* 6 (4): 517–55.

Wills, J. 2001. "Uneven Geographies of Capital and Labour: The Lessons of the European Works Councils". *Antipode* 33 (3): 484–509.

Wolf, E. 1982. *Europe and the People without History*. Los Angeles, CA: University of California Press.

Wolf, M. 2004. *Why Globalization Works*. New Haven, CT: Yale University Press.

Womack, J., D. Jones & D. Roos 1990. *The Machine that Changed the World: How Lean Production Revolutionized the Global Car Wars*. New York: Rawson Associates.

Wood, A. 1994. *North–South Trade, Employment and Inequality: Changing Fortunes in a Skill-Driven World*. Oxford: Clarendon Press.

World Bank 1995. *Workers in an Integrating World: World Development Report 1995*. Oxford: Oxford University Press.

World Bank 1996. *From Plan to Market: World Development Report 1996*. Oxford: Oxford University Press.

World Bank 1997. *The State in a Changing World: World Development Report 1997*. Washington, DC: World Bank.

World Bank 2008. *Agriculture for Development: World Development Report 2008*. Washington, DC: World Bank.

World Bank 2018. *The Changing Nature of Work: World Development Report 2019*, working draft. Washington, DC: World Bank. http://pubdocs.worldbank.org/en/816281518818814423/2019-WDR-Draft-Report.pdf (accessed 31 May 2018).

Wrench, J. 2004. "Trade Union Responses to Immigrants and Ethnic Inequality in Denmark and the UK: The Context of Consensus and Conflict". *European Journal of Industrial Relations* 7 (2): 7–30.

Wright, E. 1985. *Classes*. London: Verso Books.

Wright, E. 2015. "Is the Precariat a Class?". *Global Labour Journal* 10 (1): 123–35.

Yeates, N. 2009. *Globalizing Care Economies and Migrant Workers: Explorations in Global Care Chains*. Basingstoke: Palgrave Macmillan.

You, J.-I. 1995. "Changing Capital–Labour Relations in South Korea". In *Capital, the State and Labour: A Global Perspective*, J. Schor & J.-I. You (eds), 111–51. Cheltenham: Edward Elgar.

Young, B. 2000. "The 'Mistress' and the 'Maid' in the Globalised Economy". In *Working Classes, Global Realities: Socialist Register 2001*, L. Panitch & C. Leys (eds), 315–28. London: Merlin Press.

INDEX